Joy to the World

Joy to the World

Two Thousand Years of Christmas

Edited by
Francis G. James & Miriam G. Hill

with illustrations by
Hilary Langhorst

FOUR COURTS PRESS

Set in 10.5 on 12 point Bembo for
FOUR COURTS PRESS LTD
Fumbally Lane, Dublin 8, Ireland
e-mail: info@four-courts-press.ie
and in North America
FOUR COURTS PRESS
c/o ISBS, 5804 N.E. Hassalo Street, Portland, OR 97213.

A catalogue record for this title
is available from the British Library.

ISBN 1-85182-474-x

Printed in Great Britain
by MPG Books, Bodmin, Cornwall

Contents

Acknowledgments

We are grateful to all who assisted with the anthology. We wish especially to thank Kenneth Harl, Ruth Jolly, Peggy Langenstein, Brian Murphy, Bríd Goggin and Bridgette Johnson for reading sections of the manuscript and R.M. Frazer for translating Latin quotations. We also wish to thank the following for suggesting ideas or selections we have incorporated in the anthology: William Brinner, Herman Freudenberger, Jessie Poesch, Sara Knight, Yvonne Riley and Francis James Jr. A special 'thank you' to Kathryn Page for introducing us to one another.

Finally, thanks to Barbara and Ger for their encouragement and enthusiasm and for sharing Christmas with us twelve months of the year.

Francis G. James & Miriam G. Hill

Introduction

Carousels and well-laden tables ... The impulse to spend seizes everyone, he who the whole year through has taken pleasure in saving ... becomes suddenly extravagant ... People are not only generous towards themselves, but towards their fellow men. A stream of presents pours out on all sides.[1]

The Christmas season is a special time of the year in western society when, even in the modern urban world, the traditions of previous generations are observed. At Christmastime we like to recreate for our children the essential elements, both religious and secular, of the Christmases of our childhood and in this way pass down the tradition. But how many have stopped to wonder where these traditions come from and how far back the elements of the Christmas we celebrate today reach? The above quotation, for example, could as well describe a modern Christmas as it does the ancient Roman festival of Kalends.

Although Christians observed Good Friday, Easter and Pentecost within a few years of Jesus' crucifixion, they did not celebrate his birth until two or three hundred years later. The gospels of Luke and Matthew (both written before AD 100) state where Jesus was born, and who was then Roman emperor and local governor, but there is no specific information in the gospels, the epistles or other early sources as to what time of the year the Nativity took place. In the fourth century church authorities selected December 25, *Dies Natalis Invicti* – the birthday of the unconquerable [sun] – as the date on which to commemorate the feast of the Nativity. The Romans had long celebrated the *Saturnalia* (December 17-21) at the time of the winter solstice and Kalends on New Year's day. The selection of December 25 seems to owe its origin to the influence of the followers of Mithraism, who also observed a festival of light at the winter solstice.

Others besides the Romans and the Persians regarded the winter solstice as sacred. In Europe December is a gloomy month: Rome lies as far north as Chicago or Boston. Further north in Germany, France and Britain daylight begins at eight or after, and the sun, which never climbs high, sinks below the south-western horizon by four in the afternoon. In the words of John Donne, it is the 'midnight of the year':

> The Sunne is spent, and now his flashes
> Send forth light squibs, no constant rayes.
> The world's whole sap is sunke.

No wonder the ancient inhabitants greeted the birth of the solar year with joy. In the pre-historic passage tomb at Newgrange in Ireland, the rays of the sun penetrate its inner sanctuary only at the winter solstice. The leaders of the early church often encouraged the assimilation of pagan customs that did not conflict with basic Christian beliefs. What more appropriate time to solemnise the birth of the Messiah than on the birthday of the invincible sun?

The Italian, Spanish and French names for Christmas are all derived from the Latin natus (birth). The English word *Christmas* (Christ's mass or communion service) is of later date. The earliest known use of the term *Christes Masse* appears in the Anglo-Saxon Chronicle for 1101, which states that King Henry I kept Christmas that year at Westminster.

It is almost impossible for us, living in the age of electricity, to appreciate how dark the long winter nights were before the introduction of gas and kerosene in the nineteenth century, even for affluent city-dwellers. In December 1783, Horace Walpole wrote from London to a friend, remarking that for the past two days he had needed to light a candle at noon to be able to read a book. The giant bonfires with which medieval inhabitants of Scandinavia and elsewhere greeted the winter solstice, and which are still lighted on the levees above New Orleans on Christmas eve, take on a new meaning when we recall the enveloping darkness that winter nights once brought to our forebears.

In the northern hemisphere the shortest afternoon of the year comes on December 6; the 21st or the 22nd marks the shortest day from sunrise to sunset. January 6 is the day on which the sun rises latest. Most ceremonies celebrating the winter solstice come during this month of darkness between December 6 and January 6. In the Christian calendar St Nicholas' day falls on December 6 and the twelve days of Christmas end on the eve of Epiphany (January 6). A few festivities associated with the solstice and with the Christmas season occur earlier or later – starting as soon as Halloween (the eve of All Saints' day) and lasting until Candlemas (February 2) or even to Shrove Tuesday (Mardi Gras).

Not all cultures mark the winter (or summer) solstice. The Mohammedans follow a lunar calendar of 354 days, so that their sacred ninth month of Ramadan moves through all four seasons every 32½ solar years. The Jewish calendar also has twelve lunar months, but adjusts to the solar calendar by repeating the sixth month seven times every nineteen years. The primary Jewish holy days (Passover, Rosh Hashanah, Yom Kippur) are tied to the vernal and the autumnal equinox, rather than to either solstice. However, Chanuka (the eight-day festival commemorating the rededication of the Temple) begins around the time of the winter solstice and has become a feast of light. It is also worth noting that, although the Celtic inhabitants of Ireland do not appear to have marked the winter solstice, their most sacred day, *Samain*, fell on November 1, and February 2 was another sacred day.

From the beginning, celebrations marking Christmas have included revelry as well as religious rituals, pagan as well as Christian customs. This apparent contradiction brought condemnation from strict religious groups such as the Puritans in both old and New England in the seventeenth century. A few years ago, in protest against the influence of modern American commercialism, an effigy of Santa Claus was hanged in front of a French cathedral. Every year, sermons deploring the secularisation of Christmas are delivered from hundreds of pulpits. Stephen Nissenbaum in his new history of American Christmas traditions, *The Battle for Christmas*,[2] sees the conflict primarily in terms of a contest between middle-class respectability and popular rowdiness, rather than between religious and secular influences.

For the most part, church leaders have condoned the secular customs of the season, often incorporating them into the body of religious festivities and decorations associated with the season. Such tolerance often disturbs the devout, and sometimes offends free thinkers as hypocritical. Most of us accept the season's combination of pagan and Christian customs, and of material and spiritual values, as a reflection of our heritage, the synthesis of diverse traditions, creating a magic festival of rebirth and hope – whether human or divine. Scholarly research can trace the diverse strands which have been woven together to form our modern Christmas. Yet it is impossible to understand the historical significance of the holiday simply by identifying its component parts. One must survey the total tapestry. To begin with, it is essential to understand Christmas' religious meaning.

Many people today believe that religion simply represents an attempt to find a meaning for what science and experience have not yet explained – that God is a human invention. For such people the gospel accounts of Jesus are fictitious, and the celebration of Christmas, as Scrooge so aptly put it, pure 'humbug'. At the opposite extreme are millions of Christians who accept the biblical narratives literally. Still others do not share the conviction of either group. For a number of professing Christians, and others seeking a spiritual interpretation of life, the Bible provides a record of man's discovery of God – parts of it to be taken literally, much of it to be understood poetically or metaphorically. For the sceptic, similarities between the beliefs and practices of different religions, such as between the Roman Saturnalia and modern Christmas, suggests the unreliability of religion. For others, like Joseph Campbell (author of *The Hero with a Thousand Faces*), such similarities point to the validity of religion.

The early accounts of the Nativity found in Chapter I, whatever their historical value, are at the centre of the Christmas tradition. From the very beginning they have been interpreted symbolically. The key components of the story have been given a multitude of different meanings, yet have remained essentially the same. The principal motifs are:

- The incarnation, Jesus both divine and human.
- The virgin birth, explaining the incarnation: Jesus the son of Mary and the Holy Spirit.
- Jesus also the Word of God incarnate, that is, he represents the Hebrew tradition of moral righteousness, of the law and the prophets.
- Jesus is identified with light and salvation, as opposed to darkness and death.
- The humble circumstances of Jesus' birth: no room at the inn, born in a stable or cave, visited by shepherds.
- Bethlehem, David's city, his place of birth.
- Acclaimed by the wise men; then forced to flee from Herod.

These motifs, in one form or another, appear and reappear in Christmas literature, and along with them two central themes: first, a joyful message of *renewal*; second, the *inversion* of the normal order of things.

Renewal and inversion were themes long associated with the Roman feasts of Saturnalia and Kalends, which predate the first celebration of Christmas. Thanksgiving and gift-giving at Kalends were of long standing. As for inversion, a favourite Roman custom at the Saturnalia was the making of a slave 'master for the day', a day with a carnival atmosphere of a world turned upside down. While Christians invented neither theme, they gave both a new meaning. Renewal came to stand for the hope of eternal salvation; inversion for a divine contradiction of worldly order: God made man; right over might; light over darkness; birth without sex; the highest of kings born in a stable; the first shall be last and the last shall be first. As Richard Crashaw in his *Holy Nativity* (1648) expressed it:

> Welcome, all wonders in one sight,
> Eternity shut in a span.
> Summer in winter, day in night
> Heaven in earth, God in man!
> Great little one! whose all-embracing birth
> Lifts earth to heaven, stoops heaven to earth.

The inversion theme carries a further implication – putting yourself in another person's place, or as the Torah expressed it: 'love thy neighbour as thyself' (Leviticus 19:18). Changing places with one's slave or servant was usually just a kind of joke, a silly game; yet it had a symbolic meaning. It served as a reminder of the spiritual equality of all people in the sight of God.

A recent volume, entitled *Unwrapping Christmas*,[3] offers a series of essays by anthropologists analysing the origins and character of the season's traditions. Although it includes explanatory commentary, *Joy to the World* seeks to 'unwrap' Christmas in a different way. It is a collection of original writings about the nativity of Jesus and its celebration from the first century to the twentieth. These enable the reader to explore the development of Christmas traditions through contemporary sources – stories, legends, poems, hymns, prayers, sermons, letters, and diaries. Perusing the selections, the individual reader can discover how people observed and interpreted Christmas for two thousand years.

There have been other historical Christmas anthologies; but, aside from the biblical accounts of the Nativity, they include few selections written before the nineteenth century. Over two-thirds of the selections in *Joy to the World* date from before 1800. The first three chapters contain materials (largely religious) from the first century to the close of the Middle Ages. Chapter IV deals with secular celebrations of Christmas from the late Middle Ages to the end of the eighteenth century; Chapter V offers religious writings from the same period. Chapter VI, composed of excerpts from diaries and letters written between 1550 and 1850, offers a series of vignettes suggesting how ordinary people spent Christmas before the Victorian/Modern era. The last two chapters, focused geographically – one on Ireland, one on the American South – illustrate how local regions develop and retain their own peculiar Christmas customs, even in the homogenised modern world.

CHAPTER I

The Story of the Nativity in the Bible, the Apocrypha and the Koran

In principio erat Verbum, et Verbum erat apud Deum et Deus erat Verbum ... Et Verbum caro factum est, et habitavit in nobis.

In the beginning was the Word, and the Word was with God and the Word was God ... And the Word was made flesh, and dwelt among us.

St John's Gospel 1:1-14 (in the Vulgate Latin and Douai English)

In the generation after Jesus' ministry, when his followers came to write down their recollections of him, their primary purpose was to preserve his religious message – his teachings, parables, miracles. Aside from the events leading up to his trial and execution, they had little interest in the biography of his earthly life. Some thirty years after Jesus' crucifixion, Mark, a disciple of Peter's, completed his gospel, based primarily on Peter's recollections and anecdotes. Mark presents the earliest known chronological story of Jesus' life. The gospels according to Matthew and Luke, written a few years later, also provide accounts of Jesus' life. Mark begins with Jesus' baptism by John, not with his birth; as does the later gospel of St John, quoted above. Although both Matthew and Luke drew heavily on Mark, they made use of other early accounts of Jesus' life, based probably upon oral tradition. Matthew agrees with Luke in attributing the Virgin Mary's pregnancy to the Holy Spirit, and locating Jesus' birth in Bethlehem, but says little else about the event, except for the story of the three wise men, which is found only in Matthew. Our traditional image of the Nativity comes largely from Luke.

According to Matthew, when Joseph discovered that Mary was with child, 'being a just man and not willing to make her a public example', he decided to break the engage-

15

ment privately. Then the angel of the Lord came to Joseph and told him that 'which is conceived in her is of the Holy Ghost'. The angel instructed him to marry Mary and to name her son Jesus (Matthew 1:18-20). Luke's account has quite a different emphasis.

Biblical scholars suggest that Matthew and Luke added their Nativity accounts to show that Jesus' divinity dated from his conception and birth, not from the time of his baptism by John – a popular interpretation in the late first century. That seems likely, but does not necessarily mean that their accounts were totally unfounded. Even if parts of Matthew's and Luke's accounts are imaginary, the essentials of the story may be based on fact. If that is true, the oral tradition from which they are derived must have come down from Joseph or Mary or some other member of Jesus' family.

THE ANNUNCIATION

Luke begins with the conception and the birth of John the Baptist to the aged couple, Zacharias and Elizabeth, a kinswoman of Jesus' mother Mary. The story includes details about Elizabeth and Mary that suggest a feminine source. In contrast to Matthew, the angel Gabriel comes to Mary (not Joseph), and after greeting her, tells Mary that she has found favour with God, that she will conceive by the Holy Spirit and give birth to a son, whom she shall call Jesus. The angel explains that with God nothing is impossible, and tells Mary of Elizabeth's pregnancy despite her old age. After the angel departs, Mary decides to visit her cousin, Elizabeth. Elizabeth greets Mary with a salutation and Mary responds with a kind of a hymn, praising God. This hymn later became one of the great canticles of the church, the Magnificat. The following selections are from King James translation of 1611 (Luke 1:42-44, 46-55).

Elizabeth: Blessed art thou amongst women, and blessed is the fruit of thy womb. And whence is this to me, that the mother of my lord should come to me?

For, lo, as soon as the voice of thy salutation sounded in mine ears, the babe leaped in my womb for joy ...

Mary: My soul doth magnify the lord and my spirit hath rejoiced in God, my Saviour. For he hath regarded the low estate of his handmaiden; for, behold, from henceforth all generations shall call me blessed. For he that is mighty hath done to me great things; and holy is his name. And his mercy is on them that fear him from generation to generation. He hath showed strength with his arm; he hath scattered the proud in the imagination of their hearts. He hath put down the mighty from their seats, and exalted them of low degree. He hath filled the hungry with good things; the rich he hath sent empty away. He hath helped his servant Israel, in remembrance of his mercy; as he spoke to our fathers, to Abraham and to his seed forever.

THE NATIVITY

From John's gospel and the Acts of the Apostles, we know that Mary was alive after the crucifixion and in contact with Jesus' disciples. Her recollections must have been known to many. Mary herself seems the most likely original source for the material found in Luke's gospel. Several times Luke remarks that Mary pondered these things in her heart.

And it came to pass in those days, that there went out a decree from Caesar Augustus, that all the world should be taxed. And this taxing was first made when Cyrenis was governor of Syria. And all went to be taxed, every one into his own city. And Joseph also went up from Galilee, out of the city of Nazareth, into Judea, unto the city of David, which was called Bethlehem, because he was of the house and the lineage of David, to be taxed with Mary his espoused wife, being great with child. And so it was, that while they were there, the days were accomplished that she should be delivered. And she brought forth her first-born son, and wrapped him in swaddling clothes, and laid him in a manger, because there was no room for them in the inn.

And there were in the same country shepherds abiding in the field, keeping watch over their flock by night. And the angel of the Lord came upon them, and the glory of God shone round them; and they were sore afraid. The angel said unto them:

Fear not: for behold I bring you good tidings of great joy, which shall be to all people.

For unto you is born this day in the city of David, a Saviour, which is Christ the Lord.

And this shall be sign unto you; ye shall find the babe wrapped in swaddling clothes, lying in a manger.

And suddenly there was with the angels a multitude of heavenly host praising God, and saying:

Glory to God in the highest and on earth peace, goodwill toward men.

And it came to pass, as the angels were gone away from them into heaven, the shepherds said to one another,

Let us go now even unto Bethlehem and see this thing which has come to pass, which the Lord hath made known unto us.

And they came with haste, and found Mary and Joseph, and the babe lying in manger. And when they had seen it they made known abroad the saying which had told them concerning the child. And all they that heard it wondered at those things which were told them by the shepherds. But Mary kept all these things and pondered them in her heart. And the shepherds returned glorifying and praising God for all the things that they had heard and seen, as it was told them.

THE WISE MEN

Luke says nothing of the coming of the wise men, of Herod's concern at Jesus' birth, his subsequent massacre of the innocents, or the holy family's flight to Egypt – all part of the Christmas tradition. Their source is Matthew 2:1-13.

Now when Jesus was born in Bethlehem of Judea in the days of Herod, the king, behold, there came wise men from the east to Jerusalem saying:

Where is he that is born King of the Jews? For we have seen his star in the east and come to worship him.

When Herod, the king, had heard these things, he was troubled, and all Jerusalem with him. And when they had gathered all the chief priests and scribes of the people together, he demanded of them where the Christ should be born, and they said unto him:

In Bethlehem of Judea, for it is written by the prophet.

'Thou Bethlehem, in the land of Juda, art not the least among the princes of Juda; for out of thee shall come the Governor, that shall rule thy people Israel.'

Then Herod, when he had privately called the wise men, inquired of them diligently what time the star appeared. And he sent them to Bethlehem, and said:

Go and search diligently for the young child: and when ye have found him, bring word to me again, that I may come and worship him also.

When they had heard the king, they departed: and lo, the star, which they saw in the east, went before them, till it came and stood over where the young child was. When they saw the star, they rejoiced with exceeding great joy.

And when they came into the house, they saw the young child with Mary his mother, and fell down, and worshipped him: and when they had opened their treasures, they presented unto him gifts: gold, frankincense and myrrh. And being warned in a dream that they should not return to Herod, they departed, behold, the angel of the Lord appeared to Joseph in a dream, saying:

Arise, and take the young child and his mother, flee into the land of Egypt, and be thou there until I bring thee word: for Herod will seek the young child to destroy him.

SIMEON

Luke does not mention the wise men, Herod's slaughter of the innocents, nor the flight to Egypt. He concludes the Nativity narrative with the naming of Jesus and the visit of the holy family to the temple for purification and sacrifice. There Jesus is greeted by two older worshippers, Simeon and Anna. Simeon's greeting became a canticle still used in Christian liturgies:

> Lord, now lettest thy servant depart in peace, according to thy word,
> For mine eyes have seen thy salvation,
> Which thou hast prepared before the face of all people:
> A light to light the Gentiles, and the glory of thy people Israel.
>
> Luke 2:29-32.

Luke's gospel is also the source for the story of Jesus' visit to the temple when he was twelve (Luke 2:42-50).

The earliest non-biblical accounts of the Nativity are found in the New Testament Apochrypha, which contains gospels, epistles and other materials appearing a century or more after Jesus' time which were not considered sufficiently authentic to be incorporated in the official Bible. Because of their later date, exaggerated language, and often obvious bias, the Apocryphal gospels are considered unreliable. Nevertheless, they may possibly include traces of historical events. More important, they were widely known during the medieval period and thus helped to shape the popular image of the Nativity story.

Among the earliest books in the Apocrypha is a gospel called the Protevangelium, supposedly written by the apostle James the Less. Scholars believe it was first composed some time between 150 and 200. It begins with an account of the birth of the Virgin Mary, the only daughter of Joachim and Anna. Anna, like the mother of John the Baptist, had long been unable to conceive, but the Lord answers her and her husband's prayers for a child. When she gives birth to a daughter they dedicate the child, like Samuel, to the service of the temple, where Mary remains until she joins Joseph.

THE PROTEVANGELIUM ACCOUNT OF NATIVITY[1]

Now there went out a decree from the king Augustus that all those in Bethlehem in Judea should be enrolled. And Joseph said, 'I shall enrol my sons, but what shall I do with this child? How shall I enrol her? As my wife? I am ashamed to do that. Or as my daughter? But the children of Israel know she is not my daughter. On this day of the Lord the Lord will do as he wills.' And he saddled his she-ass and set her on it, his son led the way, and Joseph followed. And they drew near the third milestone. And Joseph turned round and saw her sad and said within himself, 'Perhaps the child within her is paining her.' Another time Joseph turned around and saw her laughing and said to her, 'Mary, why is it that I see your face one moment laughing and at another sad?' And Mary said to Joseph, 'I see with my eyes two people, one weeping and lamenting and the other rejoicing and exulting.' And having come half-way, Mary said to him, 'Joseph, take me down from the she-ass for the child within me presses to come forth.' And he took her down from the she-ass and said to her, 'Where shall I take you and hide your shame? For the place is desert.'

And he found a cave there and brought her into it, and left her in the care of his sons and went out to seek for a Hebrew midwife in the region of Bethlehem …

[Joseph speaks] 'And behold a woman came down from the hill-country and said to me, "Man, where are you going?" And I said, "I seek a Hebrew midwife." And she answered me, "Are you from Israel?" And I said to her, "Yes." And she said to me, "And is she who brings forth in the cave?" And I said, "My betrothed." And she said to me, "Is she not your wife?"

'And I said to her, "She is Mary, who was brought to the temple of the Lord, and I received her by lot as my wife, and she is not my wife, but she conceived by the Holy Spirit."'

And the midwife said to him, 'Is this true?' And Joseph said to her, 'Come and see.' And she went with him. And they stopped at the entrance of the cave, and behold, a bright cloud overshadowed the cave. And the midwife said, 'My soul is magnified today, for my eyes have seen wonderful things; for salvation is born to Israel.' And immediately the cloud disappeared from the cave and a great light appeared so that our eyes could not bear it. A short time afterwards that light withdrew until the baby appeared, and it came and took the breast of its mother Mary. And the midwife cried, 'This day is great for me because I have seen a new sight.'

The midwife then departs. Outside the cave she meets another midwife to whom she says:

'Salome, Salome. I have a new sight to tell you, a virgin has brought forth a thing which her condition does not allow.'

Salome refuses to believe until she examines Mary. Convinced, she asks God's pardon for her disbelief, which an angel grants her. Shortly after Jesus' birth, Joseph takes Mary and her child to Bethlehem. The Protevangelium concludes with an account of the wise men and Herod's massacre of the innocents.

LETTER TO DIOGNETUS

The following is a part of a letter written about AD 150-200 addressed to a Roman official. At the time the government was persecuting Christians as enemies of the state. The writer asserts that Jesus' mission was peaceful and not subversive.[2]

Since I perceive, most excellent Diognetus, that you are exceedingly zealous to learn the religion of the Christians and are asking very clear and careful questions concerning them, both who is the God in whom they believe, and how they worship him ... I ask from God who bestows on us the power both of speaking and of hearing, that it may be granted to me to speak that you may benefit as much as possible by your learning ...

Come then, clear yourself of all the prejudice which occupies your mind, and throw aside the custom which deceives you, and become as it were a new man who is about to listen to a new story.

The author next points out the weakness of pagan beliefs and the narrowness of Jewish teachings, using arguments typical of Christian apologetics. When he comes to explain what the incarnation means to Christians he is more original.

For it is not an earthly discovery which was given to them ... But in truth the Almighty and all-creating and invisible God himself founded among men the truth from heaven, and the holy and incomprehensible word, not as one might suppose, by sending some minister to men, or an angel, or a ruler, or one of those who direct earthly things, but the very artificer and Creator of the universe himself, by whom he made the heavens, by whom he enclosed the sea in its own bounds, whose mysteries all the elements guard faithfully; from whom the sun received the measure of the courses of the day, by whose command the moon is obedient to give light by night, whom the stars obey, ... by whom all things were ordered – him he sent to them. Yes, but did he send him, as a man might suppose, in sovereignty and fear and terror? Not so, but in gentleness and meekness, as a king sending his son, he sent him as King, he sent him as God, he sent him as Man to men, he was saving and persuading when he sent him, not compelling, for compulsion is not an attribute of God. When he sent him he was calling, not pursuing; when he sent him he was loving not judging.

CELSUS AND ORIGEN: A HOSTILE ACCOUNT OF JESUS' BIRTH, AND A CHRISTIAN REPLY

As Christianity spread and gained converts it came increasingly under attack. Among its critics was a Greek writer named Celsus, who offered a very different version of Jesus' origins. No copy of Celsus' manuscript has survived, but we do have an attack on his account by the Christian scholar, Origen of Alexandria (185-254 AD) entitled *Contra Celsum*. According to Origen, Celsus introduces an 'imaginary character', who has a conversation with Jesus in which he accuses Jesus of fabricating the story of his birth:[3]

First, because Jesus 'came from a Jewish village and from a poor country woman who earned her living by spinning'. He says that 'after she had been driven out by her husband, who was a carpenter by trade, as she was convicted of adultery'. Then he says that 'after she had been driven out by her husband and while she was wandering about in a disgraceful way she secretly gave birth to Jesus,' And he says that 'because he [Jesus] was poor he hired himself out as a workman in Egypt, and there tried his hand at certain magical powers on which the Egyptians pride themselves; he returned full of conceit because of these powers, and on account of them gave himself the title of God.'

Origen rejects Celsus' allegations, and goes on to argue that Jesus' humble birth, rather than casting doubt on his divinity, supports its credibility.

In my judgment ... all these things are in harmony with the fact that Jesus was worthy of the proclamation that he is the son of God.

Among men noble birth, honourable and distinguished parents who are able to spend money on the education of their son, and a great and famous native country, are things which help to make a man famous and distinguished and get his name well known. But when a man whose circumstances are entirely contrary to this is able to rise above the hindrances to him and to become well known, and to impress those who hear him so that he becomes eminent and famous throughout the whole world ... should we not admire at once such a nature as noble, for tackling great difficulties, and for possessing remarkable boldness?

If one were also to inquire further into the circumstances of such a man, how could one help trying to find out how a man, brought up in meanness and poverty, who had no general education and had learned no arguments and doctrines by which he could become a persuasive speaker to crowds and a popular leader and have won over many hearers, could devote himself to teaching new doctrines and introduce to mankind a doctrine which did away with the customs of the Jews while reverencing their prophets, and which abolished the laws of the Greeks particularly in respect to the worship of God? How could such a man, brought up in this way, who had received no serious instruction from men (as even those who speak evil of him admit), say such noble utterances about the judgment of God, about punishments for wickedness, and rewards for goodness?

Early Christians were convinced that Jesus was the 'son of God', but they differed in their interpretation of the incarnation. Some did not believe that Jesus could be both the son of God and a human being. The Arians held that Jesus, though divinely chosen and inspired, was not himself divine. At the other extreme, the Docetists believed that Christ had never been a mortal, but a spirit in human form. Around 200, when the latter view was popular, several prominent church fathers, and Tertullian, questioned the virgin birth in their efforts to prove Jesus' humanity. A century later, when the Arian heresy was at its height, most church authorities accepted the virgin birth, although it did not become official doctrine until the council of Ephesus in 431.

In *Unwrapping Christmas*, Daniel Miller notes that the introduction of the feast of the Nativity in the fourth century coincided with a shift of emphasis in Roman society, from the extended to the nuclear family. During this period, Christians became increasingly interested in Jesus' early years and family life. Aside from Luke's account of his visit to the temple at age twelve, there is nothing in the canonical gospels about Jesus' childhood or youth. Furthermore, except for scattered references, there is little about his family beyond what is given in the Nativity stories. A number of apocryphal writings attempted to fill this void, The Protevangelium account states that Joseph was a widower with children when he espoused Mary, thus explaining the canonial gospels' references to Jesus' brothers. Other apocryphal accounts include incidents from Jesus' early life – such as the holy family's sojourn in Egypt and Joseph's efforts to find a teacher for his remarkable son. Most of these narratives contain stories of Jesus' boyhood miracles. The miracle anecdotes are primarily concerned with demonstrating Jesus' power over life, death and nature. In some he is portrayed as impulsive, arrogant – quite unlike the adult Jesus who, in the wilderness, rejected the devil's three temptations to abuse his divine power.

Although these childhood anecdotes are pure fiction, and are often inconsistent with Jesus' later life and teaching, they are part of Christian folklore. They became widely known in the early Middle Ages; they helped to shape popular beliefs about the infant Jesus and his family. Almost all of the apocryphal narratives depict both Mary and Joseph as loving parents. While the following selections have no direct connection with Jesus' birth, they contribute to our understanding of the traditional image of the holy family.

LEGENDS OF JESUS' CHILDHOOD

The apocryphal *Gospel of Pseudo Matthew* was one of the widest known manuscripts during the medieval period. Like the original gospel of St Matthew, it reflects the midrash tradition; that is it attempts to explain Jesus' life and teachings by reference to Hebrew scripture and tradition. The Nativity account in Pseudo Matthew follows that found in the Protevangelium, including an account of Jesus' birth in a cave, but concludes with a different episode.

JESUS IN A MANGER[4]

On the third day after the birth of our Lord Jesus Christ, holy Mary went out from the cave, and went into a stable and put her child in a manger, and an ox and an ass worshipped him. Then was fulfilled that which was said through them prophet Isaiah: 'The ox knows his owner and the ass his master's crib.' Thus the beasts, ox and ass, with him between them, unceasingly worshipped him. Then was fulfilled that which was said through the prophet Habakkuk: 'Between two beasts are you known.' And Joseph remained in the same place with Mary for three days.

After that come a series of stories about Mary, Joseph and the child Jesus, one of which follows (*Pseudo Matthew*, chapters 20-21):

THE HOLY FAMILY IN EGYPT[5]

Now on the third day of their journey, as they went on, it happened that blessed Mary was wearied by the too great heat of the sun in the desert, and seeing a palm tree, she said to Joseph: 'I should like to rest a little in the shade of this tree.' And Joseph led her quickly to the palm and let her dismount from her animal. And when blessed Mary had sat down, she looked up at the top of the palm-tree and saw that it was full of fruits, and said to Joseph: 'I wish someone could fetch some of the fruits of the palm-tree.' And Joseph said to her: 'I wonder that you say this; for you see how high this palm-tree is, and (I wonder) that you even think about eating the fruits of the palm. I think rather of the lack of water, which already fails us in the skins, and we have nothing with which we can refresh ourselves and our animals.'

And the child Jesus, who was sitting with a happy countenance in his mother's lap, said to the palm: 'Bend down your branches, O tree, and refresh my mother with your fruit.' And immediately at this command the palm bent its head down to the feet of blessed Mary, and they gathered all its fruits, it remained bent down and waited to raise itself again at the command of him at whose command it had bent down. Then Jesus said to it: 'Raise yourself, O palm, and be strong, and join my trees which are in the paradise of my Father. And open beneath your roots a vein of water which is hidden in the earth, and let the waters flow so that we may quench our thirst from it.' And immediately it raised itself, and there began to gush out by its roots a fountain of water very clear, fresh and completely bright ...

On the next day, when they went out from there, and at the hour when they set out, Jesus turned to the palm and said to it: 'O palm, I give you this privilege, that one of your branches be carried by my angels and be planted in the paradise of my Father. This blessing I confer on you, that to all who shall be victorious in a contest it shall be said: 'You have won the palm of victory.' When he said this, behold, an *angel of the Lord* appeared, standing above the palm-tree, and took one of its branches and flew to heaven with the branch in its hand.

THE CHILD JESUS AND HIS PLAYMATES

Another anecdote of Jesus' stay in Egypt comes from an Arabic infancy gospel; the same anecdote is also found in a Syriac *History of the Virgin*.[6]

One day the Lord Jesus went into the street and saw children who had come together to play. He followed them, but the children hid themselves from him. Now when the Lord Jesus came to the door of the house and saw women standing there, he asked them where those children had gone. They replied that no one was there; and the Lord Jesus said: 'Who are those whom you see by the furnace?' 'They are three-year-old goats', they answered. And the Lord Jesus said: 'Come out to your shepherd, you goats.' Then the children in the form of goats came out and began to skip around him. When those women saw this, they were seized with wonder and fear, and speedily fell down before the Lord Jesus and implored him, saying, 'O Lord Jesus, son of Mary, truly you are the *good shepherd* of Israel, have mercy on your handmaids who stand before you and have never doubted: for you have come, our Lord, to heal and not to destroy.' The Lord Jesus answered and said: 'The children of Israel are like the Ethiopians among peoples.' And the women said: 'You, Lord, know everything, and nothing is hidden from you; but now we beg and implore you of your mercy to restore their former state to these children, your servants.' So Lord Jesus said: 'Come children, let us go and play.' And immediately in the presence of these women the goats were changed into children.

JESUS AND THE CLAY BIRDS

Our third Nativity legend about the child Jesus is from the *Infancy Gospel of St Thomas*, probably of North African origin, from the third or fourth century.[7]

When the boy Jesus was five years old he was playing at the ford of a brook, and gathered together into pools the water that flowed by, and made it at once clean, and commanded it by his word alone. He made soft clay and fashioned from it twelve sparrows. And it was the sabbath when he did this. And there were also many other children playing with him. Now when a certain Jew saw what Jesus was doing in his play on the sabbath, he at once went and told his father Joseph: 'See, your child is at the brook, and he has taken clay and fashioned twelve birds and has profaned the sabbath.' And when Joseph came to the place and saw, he cried out to Jesus, saying: 'Why do you do on the sabbath what ought not to be done?' But Jesus clapped his hands and cried to the sparrows: 'Off with you!' And the sparrows took flight and went away chirping …

THE BOY JESUS AND THE LIONS OF JERICHO

The final selection from the infancy narratives comes, like the first one, from *Pseudo Matthew*. Here, as in several other stories, Jesus is portrayed as unharmed amidst wild beasts who worship him. C.S. Lewis could have had this passage in mind when he created Aslan.[8]

There is a road going out of Jericho and leading to the river Jordan, to the place where the children of Israel crossed; and there the ark of the covenant is said to have rested. And Jesus was eight years old, and he went out of Jericho and went towards the Jordan. And there was beside the road, near the bank of the Jordan, a cave where a lioness was nursing her whelps; and no one was safe to walk that way. Jesus, coming from Jericho, and knowing that in the cave the lioness had brought forth her young, went into it in the sight of all. And when the lions saw Jesus, they ran to meet him and worshipped him. And Jesus was sitting in the cavern and the lion's whelps ran round his feet, fawning and playing with him. And the older lions, with their heads bowed, stood at a distance and fawned upon him with their tails. The people who were standing far off and did not see Jesus, said, 'Unless he or his parents have committed grievous sins, he would not of his own accord expose himself to the lions.' And when the people were reflecting within themselves and were overcome with great sorrow, behold suddenly, in the sight of the people Jesus came out of the cave and the lions went before him, and the lion's whelps played with each other before his feet. And the parents of Jesus stood afar off with their heads bowed and they watched, likewise the people stood at a distance on account of the lions, for they did not dare to come close to them. Then Jesus began to say to the people, 'How much better are the beasts than you, seeing that they recognize their Lord and glorify him, while you men, who have been made in the image of God, do not know him! Beasts know me and are tame; men see me but do not acknowledge me.'

After these things Jesus crossed the Jordan in the sight of them all with the lions, and the water of the Jordan was divided on the right hand and on the left. There he said to the lions so that all could hear, 'Go in peace

and hurt no one: neither let any man injure you, until your return to the place where you have come from.' And they, bidding him farewell, not only with their voices but their gestures, went to their own place. But Jesus returned to his mother.

Toward the close of the second century church authorities agreed on the contents of the New Testament as we know it. During the next two centuries copies of the canonical New Testament, in several different languages, spread throughout the Roman Empire and into adjoining regions. Early in the fifth century St Jerome's (d. 420) Latin translation of both the Old and New Testaments became the official Bible of western Christendom. The apocryphal writings of the Old and New Testaments, however, continued to be widely known among both western and eastern Christians.

By the fifth century Christianity had become the dominant religion in the Roman Empire – from Britain to North Africa, from Spain to Asia Minor. By then there were also Christians in many adjacent regions, such as Arabia, the home of Mohammed (570-632). Mohammed grew up strongly influenced by Judaism and Christianity. A man of deep faith, he became convinced that God had chosen him as the ultimate prophet, who could explain the true meaning of these different traditions. The Koran, the sacred book of Islam, is a compilation of God's revelations to Mohammed, who dictated them to his followers over a number of years.

Mohammed recognised the chief patriarchs and prophets of the Old Testament as authentic. He likewise believed that John the Baptist and Jesus were prophets, and he accepted the virgin birth, but not the divinity of Christ. Mohammed believed that if God could create Adam, he could certainly create Jesus; what God decides to do is done!

The following selections from the Koran come from a translation published in 1737 by an English lawyer, George Sale, who became a noted Arabic scholar. His was the first English version translated directly from Arabic. Although its language is somewhat archaic, it is vivid and resembles that of the King James version of the Bible, used else-where in this chapter. A few words have been changed where a modern translation seems necessary. The material in parentheses is that of commentators from early versions of the Koran.

The stories of the birth of both John the Baptist and Jesus are found in two different sections of the Koran, in chapters (or *suras*) III and XIX. The account in chapter III also includes the birth of Mary, agreeing in general with that found in the Protevangelium of James given above, except that Mary's father is here called Imran instead of Joachim. According to Luke's gospel, Zacharias was married to Mary's 'kinswoman', Elizabeth. In the Koran Zacharias is assumed to be Mary's uncle.

THE KORAN

CHAPTER III[9]

The Family of Imran, revealed at Medina ... God hath surely chosen Adam and Noah, and the family of Abraham, and the family of Imran above the rest of the world; a race descending one from another. God is he who heareth and knoweth. Remember when the wife of Imran said, Lord, verily I have vowed unto thee that which is in my womb, to be dedicated to thy service; accept it therefore of me, for thou art he who heareth and knoweth. And when she was delivered of it, she said. Lord, verily I have brought forth a female ... I have called her Mary, and I commend her to thy protection, and also her issue, against Satan ... Therefore the Lord accepted her with gracious acceptance and caused her to bear an excellent offspring. And Zacharias took care of the child; (Though the child happened not to be male, yet her mother presented her to the priests who had the care of the temple, as one dedicated to God; and they having received her, she was committed to the care of Zacharias, and he built her an apartment in the temple.)

Chapter III goes on to tell briefly of the conception and birth of John the Baptist, then Jesus. A somewhat fuller treatment of those events is found in chapter XIX.

CHAPTER XIX[10] [ENTITLED MARY, REVEALED AT MECCA]

A commemoration of the mercy of thy Lord towards his servant Zacharias. When he called upon his Lord, invoking him in secret, and said, O Lord, verily my bones are weakened, and my head is become white with hoarfrost, and I have never been unsuccessful in my prayers to thee, O Lord. But now I fear my nephews, who are to succeed after me, for my wife is barren: wherefore give me a successor of my own body from before thee; who may be my heir, and may be an heir of the family of Jacob. And grant, O Lord, that he may be acceptable unto thee. And the angel answered him, O Zacharias, verily we bring thee tidings of a son, whose name shall be John ... Zacharias said, Lord how shall I have a son, seeing my wife is barren, and I am now arrived at a great age, and am decrepit? And the angel answered him, So shall it be; thy Lord saith: This is easy for me since I created thee therefore, when thou wast nothing. Zacharias answered, O Lord give me a sign. The angel replied, thy sign shall be that thou shalt not speak to men for three nights, although thou be in perfect health. And Zachariah went forth unto his people, from the chamber, and he made signs unto them, as if he should say: Praise ye God in the morning and in the evening.

And we shall say unto his son, O John, receive the book of the law, with a resolution to study and observe it. And we bestowed upon him wisdom, when he was a child, and mercy from us and purity of life; and he was a devout person, and dutiful towards his parents, and was not proud or rebellious. Peace be on him the day whereon he was born, and the day whereon he shall die, and the day whereon he shall be raised to life.

And remember in the book of the Koran the story of Mary (Miriam): When she retired from her family to a place towards the east (to the eastern part of the temple); and took a veil to conceal herself from them; and we sent our spirit Gabriel unto her, and he appeared unto her in the shape of a perfect man (like a full grown but beautiful youth). She said, I fly for refuge unto the merciful God, that he may defend me from thee, if thou fearest him, thou wilt not approach me. He answered, Verily I am the messenger of the Lord and sent to give thee a holy son. She said, How shall I have a son, seeing a man has not touched me, and I am no harlot?

Gabriel replied, So shall it be: thy Lord saith, This is easy with me and we will perform it, that we may ordain him for a sign unto men, and a mercy from us; for it is a thing which is decreed. Wherefor she conceived (for Gabriel blew into the bosom of her shift, and his breath reaching her womb caused the conception).

And Mary went with him in her womb to a different place. (To conceal her delivery she went out of the city by night to a certain high mountain.) And the pains of childbirth came upon her near the trunk of a palm tree. She said, Would to God I had died before this, and become a thing forgotten, and lost in oblivion! And he who was beneath her (the child) called to her, saying, Be not grieved; now God has provided a rivulet under thee; and do thou shake the body of the palm tree, and it shall let fall ripe dates upon thee, ready gathered. And eat and drink and calm thy mind. Moreover if thou see any man, and he question thee, say, Verily I have vowed a fast unto the Merciful; wherefore I will by no means speak to a man this day.

So she brought the child to her people, carrying him in her arms. And they said unto her, O Mary, now hast thou done a monstrous thing: O sister of Aaron, thy father was not a bad man, neither was thy mother a harlot. But she made signs unto the child to answer them; and they said, How shall we speak to him, who is an infant in the cradle? Whereupon the child said, Verily I am the servant of God: he hath given me the book of the gospel and hath appointed me prophet. And he hath made me blessed, wheresoever I shall be; and hath commanded me to observe prayer, and to give alms, so long as I shall live.

And he hath made me dutiful towards my mother, and hath not made me proud, nor unhappy. And peace be on me the day whereon I was born, and the day whereon I die, and the day whereon I shall be raised to life. This was the son of Mary; the word of truth …

It is clear that Mohammed recognised the 'son of Mary' as a prophet, but he totally rejected the Christian belief in Jesus' divinity. He closes the Nativity account with these words:

It is not meet for God, that he should have a son: God forbid!

What does the Koran version contribute to our understanding of the Nativity? It appears to be based more on the apocryphal gospels than Luke or Matthew. The article on 'Maryam' (Mary) in the *New Encyclopaedia of Islam* suggests that Mohammed's account may owe more to the religious folklore of Christians he came in contact with, than to apocryphal sources. Whatever its sources, the Koran's narrative of the infant Jesus portrays the Mohammedan image of Jesus and his place in Moslem beliefs. Since Moslems read the Koran regularly, this picture of the Nativity is the one best known to the millions who make up the Islamic world.

CHAPTER II

The Formation of the Christmas Tradition

Almighty God, you have poured upon us the light of your incarnate Word. Grant that this light, enkindled in our hearts, may shine forth in our lives.

Christmas collect from the Gregorian Sacramentary (7th century)

The church in the west did not generally observe the Nativity as a major feast until the fifth century. In the east the Nativity was initially celebrated on Epiphany (January 6). The first definite reference to a date for Jesus' birthday appears in a calendar of 354 listing Christian martyrs, which states that Jesus was born in Bethlehem seven days before Kalends (January 1). The earliest event recorded as taking place on Christmas day occurred about 360. St Ambrose (d. 397) mentions a sermon given by Liberius (pope between 352 and 366) on *Natali Christi* in St Peter's, when Ambrose's sister took the veil to become a nun. Thirty years later, a far more momentous event took place on the feast of the Nativity in Ambrose's cathedral in Milan.

THE BISHOP AND THE EMPEROR

At the Saturnalia, pagan emperors had exchanged places for a day with a slave, in accord with the 'inversion theme' of the season. What the Christian emperor, Theodosius, did at Christmas 390 represents a vastly different 'inversion'. That year Theodosius was in northern Italy, with his headquarters at Milan, where Ambrose was bishop. During the summer the emperor received word that the people of Thessalonica had rioted against their garrison and murdered its German commander. Infuriated, the emperor determined to wreak a ter-

33

rible vengeance. Although Ambrose, whom Theodosius consulted, urged restraint, Theodosius dispatched a secret order to carry out his fearful punishment of the Macedonian city. The emperor later tried to revoke his command, but it was too late. The inhabitants of Thessalonica were invited to attend an exhibition in the local stadium. After 7,000 had assembled, the garrison moved in and slaughtered the defenceless crowd. Ambrose heard of the massacre while attending a church council. He and his fellow bishops agreed that the church must take a stand against the outrage. In September Ambrose wrote to Theodosius, notifying him of his excommunication. The following is an abridged version of his letter.[1]

Listen, August Emperor. You have zeal for the faith, I own it; you have fear of God, I confess it. But you have a vehemence of temper, which if soothed, may speedily be changed into compassion, but, if inflamed, becomes so violent that you can scarcely restrain it. I would to God that those about you, even if they do not moderate, would at least refrain from stimulating it! This vehemence I have preferred secretly to commend to your consideration rather than run the risk of stirring it up by public act. So I have preferred to seem somewhat slack in the discharge of my duty rather than lacking in respect to my sovereign; and that others should blame me for failure to exercise my priestly power rather than that you should consider me, who am most loyal to you, deficient in reverence. This I have done that you might be free to choose for yourself in calmness the course which you ought to follow.

A deed has been perpetrated at Thessalonica, which has no parallel in history; a deed which I in vain tried to prevent; a deed which I addressed to you beforehand, I declared would be most atrocious; a deed which you yourself, by your later attempt to cancel it, have confessed heinous. This deed I could not extenuate. When the news of it came, a council was in session on account of the arrival of the bishops from Gaul. All the assembled bishops deplored it; not a single one viewed it indulgently. Your act could not be forgiven even if you remained in the communion of Ambrose: on the contrary the odium of the crime would fall more heavily on me, if I were not to declare to you the necessity of becoming reconciled to our God.

Are you ashamed, Sir, to do as did David, who was a prophet as well as a king, and an ancestor of Christ according to the flesh? He, when he had listened to the parable of the poor man's ewe lamb, recognised that he himself was condemned by it and cried, I have sinned against the Lord. Do not, Sir, take it ill if the same words are addressed to you which the prophet addressed to David – *Thou art the man*. For if you give careful heed to them, and answer, *I have sinned against the Lord*, then to you also shall it be said, Because thou repentest, *the Lord hath put away thy sin*.

This I have written, not to confound you, but to induce you, by quoting a royal precedent, to put away this sin from your kingdom. You may do that by humbling your soul before God. You are a man, and temptation has come to you: now get the better of it. Tears and penitence alone can take away sin. Neither angel nor archangel can do it, Nay, the Lord Himself grants no remission of sin except to the penitent.

I advise, I entreat, I admonish. It grieves me that you, who were an example of singular piety, who exercised consummate clemency, who would not suffer individual offenders to be placed in jeopardy, should not mourn over the destruction of so many innocent persons. Successful as you have been in war, and worthy of praise in other respects, yet piety has ever been the crown of your achievements. The devil has grudged you your chief excellence – overcome him, while you have the means. Add not sin to sin by following a course that has proved the ruin of many …

You have my love, my affection, my prayers. If you believe that, follow my instructions; if you believe it, acknowledge the truth of what I say; but if you believe it not, at least pardon me for preferring God to my sovereign.

We do not know exactly what happened after Theodosius received this letter. The emperor appears initially to have resisted the authority of the bishop, and refused to submit to public penance. As Christmas approached, Theodosius became withdrawn and dejected. According to one account, when his chief advisor asked the cause of his grief, Theodosius replied:

You can be cheerful, but I must be sad. God's temple is open to slaves and beggars, who may go freely and pray to their Lord. But to me it is closed, and so must be also the gates of heaven. For I cannot forget the words of Our Lord, 'Whatsoever ye shall bind on earth shall be bound in Heaven.'

The advisor attempted to negotiate a compromise with Ambrose without success. Theodosius finally accepted Ambrose's two stipulations: that he would promulgate a law providing that all death sentences should be suspended for thirty days, and then reconsidered, and that the emperor would do public penance. In the great basilica in Milan, on Christmas day 390, Theodosius, in the presence of many of his subjects, wept and prayed for forgiveness. In the words of Ambrose's modern biographer, this was the first time a minister of the gospel claimed 'power to judge, condemn, punish and finally pardon' a prince for having offended against both God and humanity.[2] The event represented, at least momentarily, the inversion of right over might.

Future Christmas seasons would witness variations of this drama. The anniversary of the humble birth of the world's eternal king served as a reminder of the transitory role of earthly rulers. On Christmas 800, Pope Leo III crowned Charlemagne emperor in St

Peter's in Rome. On Christmas 1066, William the Conqueror had Archbishop Alfred of York crown him king of England. Just after Christmas in 1077, the Emperor Henry IV set off on his journey to seek forgiveness from Pope Gregory VII at Canossa. On Christmas day 1170, four of King Henry II's knights left Normandy for Canterbury, to punish Thomas à Becket for his opposition to Henry. When they arrived four days later, they found the archbishop in the choir of the cathedral. The following account comes from an eye-witness.[3]

The knights: 'Where is the traitor?'
Becket: [No answer]
The knights: 'Where is the archbishop?'
Becket: 'Here. I am not a traitor, but archbishop and priest of God; what seek you?'
The knights: 'Your death – hence traitor!'
Becket: 'I am no traitor, and will not stir hence. Slay me here if you will, but if you touch any of my people you are accursed.'

The four knights assassinated him then and there. By his death Becket became one of the most famous martyrs of the church. Four years later Henry II did penance at Becket's tomb, already one of the most popular shrines in Europe. December 29 became the feast of St Thomas the Martyr and was widely celebrated until the Reformation. Chaucer's pilgrims in the *Canterbury Tales* were on their way to Becket's shrine.

EARLY CHRISTMAS LITURGIES

At the time when the feast of the Nativity was introduced into the church calendar in the fourth century, Christian worship followed written liturgical forms with set readings and prayers. The singing of anthems and hymns dates from about the same time. By the close of the fifth century the Roman church celebrated three masses on the feast of the Nativity: each with its own collect, epistle, gospel, introit and anthems. The first was celebrated at midnight in the church of St Mary Maggiore at a shrine of Christ's crib, the second early in the morning in St Anastatia's at the foot of the Palentine Hill, and the third later in the morning, across the Tiber in the basilica of St Peter. The midnight mass at St Mary Maggiore was in imitation of the mass celebrated on Christmas eve by the church in Jerusalem, which was followed by a procession to the grotto in Bethlehem, the accepted site of Jesus' birth. A Christian lady from southern Gaul, Silvia of Acquitaine, made an extended trip to the Holy Land and wrote an account of the ceremony in Bethlehem in the late fourth century. From her remarks it seems probable that Christians in Palestine had been celebrating the feast of the Nativity since the early fourth century – but on January 6, not December 25. They switched to the latter date about 400.

EARLY CHRISTMAS HYMNS AND ANTHEMS

Soon after the feast of the Nativity was established, St Ambrose composed a hymn glorifying Jesus as the redeemer of mankind, emphasising the virgin birth (translated by Richard Mac Ilwain Frazer, 1996):

> Come redeemer of the nations
> Reveal the birth of the virgin
> Let every age marvel
> Such a birth becomes God

Singing became a regular part of the Advent and Christmas liturgies. One hymn from the fifth century is still sung at lauds (early morning service) on Christmas, and another from the sixth century at vespers on Christmas evening. The next two selections are from hymns derived from two poems of Marcus Prudentius (348-410), a Roman magistrate from Spain who converted to Christianity late in life.[4]

> Of the father's love begotten,
> Ere the worlds began to be,
> He is Alpha and Omega,
> He the source, the ending:
> He, of all things that are, and have been,
> And the future years shall see,
> Evermore and evermore.

> Oh the birth for ever blessed,
> When the Virgin, full of grace,
> By the Holy Ghost conceiving,
> Bare the Saviour of our race:
> And the Babe, the world's Redeemer,
> First revealed his sacred face.
> Evermore and evermore.

> . . . .

> Earth hath many a noble city:
> Bethlehem, thou dost excel.
> Out of thee the Lord from heaven
> Came to rule his Israel.

> Fairer than the sun at morning
> Was the star that told his birth
> To the world announcing
> Seen in fleshly form on earth.

Eastern sages at his cradle
Make oblations rich and rare;
See them give in deep devotion
Gold, frankencense and myrh.

Sacred gifts of mystic meaning:
Incense doth their God disclose,
Gold, the king of kings proclaimeth.
Myrh his sepulcher forshadowes.

Jesus, whom the gentiles worshipped
At the glad Epiphany.
Unto thee, with God the Father
And the Spirit, Glory be.

The following hymn, traditionally sung at lauds during Advent has been attributed to St Jerome (d. 420), but it was probably written in the sixth century.[5]

Hark! a thrilling voice is sounding:
'Christ is nigh,' it seems to say,
'Cast away the works of darkness
O ye children of the day!'

Wakened by the solemn warning
Let the earth bound soul arise
Christ, her Sun, all sloth dispelling,
Shines upon the morning skies.

A verse from a hymn by St Anatolius (5th century):[6]

What gift shall we bring to Thee
O Christ, since Thou as Man on earth
For us has't shewn Thyself?
Since every creature made by Thee
Brings to Thee its thanksgiving?
The Angels bring their song
The Heavens bring their star
The Magi bring their gifts
The shepherds bring their awe,
Earth gives a cave, the wilderness a manger,
And we the Virgin-Mother bring.
God before all worlds, have mercy upon us.

In the first of the above hymns, Prudentius describes Jesus as the 'Alpha and Omega, the source and ending of all things.' Such an emphasis is characteristic of most early Christmas hymns. Their authors shared a theological approach to the incarnation. They strove to teach doctrine, rather than to relate the story of the Nativity to human experience. With few exceptions, such as the verse from St Anatolius, they say little about the holy family seeking shelter in a stable or cave, or of the visit of the humble shepherds. A somewhat later hymn in much the same vein is one by St Germanus, patriarch of Constantinople, 715-30.[7]

A great and mighty wonder
Today on earth is done
Behold a virgin mother
Brings forth God's Son.

The Word now dwells among us,
Made flesh, yet very God;
And cherubims sing anthems
To shepherds all about.

While this they sing your Monarch,
Those bright angelic bands,
Rejoice, ye vales and mountains.
Ye oceans, clap your hands.

Since all he comes to succor,
By all he is adored.
The infant born in Bethl'hem,
The Saviour and the Lord.

Now idol forms shall perish,
Now error shall decay,
And Christ shall wield his sceptre,
Our Lord and God for aye.

Early Advent and Christmas sermons resemble the hymns in their emphasis on doctrine. Some preachers, such as St John Chrysostom (c.347-407) in his homily for the feast of the Nativity, stress a theological approach to the incarnation.

'For with God we look not for the order of nature, but rest our faith in the power of his works.'

Some early sermons express a more down-to-earth point of view. St Caesarius, bishop of Arles, 502-42, observed that if one explained scripture only in the language of the church fathers, 'the food of doctrine could only reach a few learned men, and the rest of the

people, the multitude, would remain famished'.[8] Caesarius became a popular preacher and manuscripts of his homilies have been found in many places, including an eighth-century copy in England.

AN ADVENT SERMON OF CAESARIUS, BISHOP OF ARLES, 502-42 AD

The designation of the period preceding Christmas as Advent appears to have originated in Gaul in the fifth century, where it was observed as a penitential season in preparation for Christ's nativity. In Italy Advent was celebrated more as a joyful time for anticipating the expected birth of Christ. After the Frankish church accepted the Roman liturgy in the eighth century, the two traditions merged.[9]

A homily to be delivered ten or fifteen days before the birthday of our Lord[10]

Through the Divine Mercy, beloved brethren, the day on which we long to celebrate the birthday of our Lord and Saviour is almost at hand. Therefore I pray and advise that with God's help we labour as much as we can, so that on that day we may be able to approach the altar of our Lord with a pure and upright conscience, a clean heart, and a chaste body ...

Although it is fitting for us to be adorned and distinguished by good works at all times, still on the day of the Lord's birth in particular, our good deeds, as he himself said in the Gospel, ought to shine before men. Consider, I beseech you, brethren, a powerful or noble man who wishes to celebrate either his own birthday or that of his son. With what great effort he looks for anything disgraceful in his house many days before. He arranges for it to be cleaned, for anything improper or unsuitable to be thrown away, and whatever is useful or necessary he commands to be displayed. If the house is dirty, it is even whitewashed, the floors are cleaned with brooms, strewn with different kinds of flowers, and adorned; whatever affords delight to the mind and pleasure to the body is provided with every solicitude. What is the purpose of all these preparations, dearest brethren, except to celebrate with joy the birthday of a man who some day will die? Now if you make great preparations on the occasion of your birthday, or on that of your son, what great and what kind of preparations should you make when you are about to begin celebrating the birthday of our Lord? …

If an earthly king or head of a family invited you to his birthday celebration, with what kind of garments would you endeavour to adorn yourself when he approached? Surely with new and shining ones, costly ones whose age and cheapness or ugliness could not offend the eyes of the one who invited you. Therefore with Christ's help strive as much as you can with a like zeal, so that your soul may with an easy conscience approach the solemn feast of the eternal king, that is the birthday of our Lord and Saviour, if it is adorned with the decoration of various virtues. Let it be adorned with the jewels of simplicity and the flowers of temperance, gleaming chastity, shining charity, and joyful almsgiving. For if Christ the Lord recognises that you are celebrating his birthday with such dispositions, he himself will deign to come and not only visit your soul, but also rest and continually dwell in it. As it is written: 'I will dwell with them and walk among them;' and again; 'Here I stand, knocking at the door; if anyone rises up and opens the door, I will enter his house and have supper with him, and he with me.'

How happy is the soul which, with God's help, has striven to direct his life in such a way that he may merit to receive Christ as his guest and indwelling person. On the contrary how unhappy and lamentable with a whole fountain of tears is the conscience which has defiled itself with evil deeds. It has so covered itself with avarice, burned itself with the fire of wrath, polluted itself with continuous dissipation, and ruined itself with the tyranny of pride that Christ does not begin to rest in it, but the devil is starting to prevail. If the remedy of repentance does not quickly come to the aid of such a soul, he is abandoned by the light and occupied by darkness. He is rid of sweetness and filled with bitterness; he is invaded by death and rejected by life. However a man of this kind should not fail to trust in the Lord's goodness. He should not be overcome by deadly despair but should rather have recourse to repentance at once. While the

wounds of his sins are still new and warm, he should apply salutary med-
icines to himself. Our physician is omnipotent, and he is so accustomed to
heal our wounds that he does not allow even a trace of a scar to remain.

A DESCRIPTION OF BETHLEHEM AND NAZARETH IN THE SEVENTH CENTURY

Despite the chaos which came with the disintegration of the Roman Empire, pilgrims
continued to travel to Palestine – even after the Moslem capture of Jerusalem in 638. One
such pilgrim was a bishop from Gaul, named Arculf, who visited Jerusalem and
Bethlehem about 680. Shipwrecked on his return voyage, Arculf ended up in Iona – the
famous site of the Irish monastery off the west coast of Scotland. Adomnán, the learned
abbot of Iona, and biographer of its founder, St Columba, took down the account of
Arculf's pilgrimage. Adomnán's manuscript, entitled *De Locis Sanctis* was commended by
the Venerable Bede, and became well known in Ireland and Britain. Here are the sections
on Bethlehem and Nazareth.[11]

CONCERNING THE SITE OF BETHLEM

In the beginning of this our second book some few things should be set
down briefly concerning the site of the city of Bethlem [*sic*], in which our
Saviour deigned to be born of a holy virgin. Now this city, according to
the account of Arculf, who frequented it, is not so notable by reason of
its site, as it is celebrated by report spread thoughout the churches of all
nations. It is situated on a narrow ridge, which is surrounded by valleys
on every side, and from east to west this ridge of earth stretches for about
a mile. On the level plateau on top a low wall without towers has been
constructed right round the very edge of the hill. It overlooks the little
valleys which lie here and there round about, and the homes of the citizens are scattered in a lengthwise direction within its circuit.

CONCERNING THE PLACE OF THE LORD'S NATIVITY

In the eastern corner of that city is what seems to be a natural half-grotto.
The very innermost portion is called the manger of the Lord in which the
mother laid the child when he was born; another spot. however, close by
the above-mentioned manger, but nearer the entrance, is the traditional
place of the actual nativity of the Lord. Accordingly the whole of that
cave of Bethlem, with the Lord's manger, is completely covered on the
interior with precious marble in honour of the Saviour; and the half-
grotto covered by the stone cenacle, is surmounted by the church of the

holy Mary, a magnificent structure built exactly over the spot where the Lord is said to have been born.

CONCERNING THE ROCK SITUATED OUTSIDE THE WALL

I think that brief mention should be made of the rock situated outside the wall, over which the water of the first ablution of the Lord's little body after the Nativity was poured from the vessel in which it was, which was tilted over from the top of the wall. This water of the sacred washing, when poured from the wall, found a sort of channel hollowed out by nature in the rock lying beneath; which channel, filled by that flow on the first birthday of the Lord, from that day up to our time through the cycle of many centuries one sees to be full without any failing or diminuation of the purest water: our Saviour from the day of his Nativity performing this miracle, of which the prophet sings: 'Who brought forth water from the rock,' and the apostle Paul [said] 'Now the rock was Christ' – he who, contrary to nature, brought a consoling flow for the thirsting people from the hardest rock of the desert. It is the same power and wisdom of God which brought forth water from the rock of Bethlem too, and always keeps its channel filled with water. Our friend Arculf saw it with his own eyes and washed his face in it.

CONCERNING THE TOMB OF THE SHEPHERDS

Concerning the tomb of the shepherds around whom the heavenly brightness shone on the night of the Lord's nativity, Arculf gave us a brief account saying: I visited the three tombs of those three shepherds (who are buried beside the tower of Gader) in a church. They are about a mile distant from Bethlem, towards the east. It is in this very place, near the tower of the flock, where the church containing the sepulchers of the shepherds is built, that, at the Lord's nativity, the brightness of angelic light surrounded them.

CONCERNING NAZARETH AND ITS CHURCHES

The city of Nazareth, as Arculf who lodged in it tells, is situated on a mountain, and, like Capharnaum, has no surrounding walls. It has, however, large stone buildings, and there are two very large churches, one in the centre of the city raised on two piles, where once upon a time was the house in which the Lord, our Saviour, was brought up. This church, as has been said above, is supported upon two mounds with arches between, and there is a very clear fountain underneath, between the mounds. The whole

community of citizens come to draw water from it, and from the same source vessels of water are raised up to the church above by means of pulleys. The second church is constructed on the site of the house in which Gabriel, the archangel, going in to the holy Mary, talked to her alone as he found her there in that hour. We get this information concerning Nazareth from the holy Arculf, who lodged there for two days and two nights.

THE DRAMATIC CHARACTER OF CHRISTMAS LITURGIES

Pope Gregory the Great (590-605) is usually given credit for the introduction of antiphonal, or responsive, singing of the mass and other church services. Antiphonal singing increased the dramatic appeal of the liturgy for the laity as well as the clerical participants. By the ninth century the original Gregorian antiphons had been supplemented by special canticles for the major festivals of the church year, such as Easter, Advent and Christmas. For example, following the introit in the mass for Christmas the choir sung a question which was answered by the congregation. In this way antiphonal singing evolved into drama. Clement Miles gives several examples of early Christmas antiphons in *Christmas Customs and Traditions*, among them a ninth-century trope ascribed to Tutilo of St Gall, Switzerland, and an eleventh-century antiphon also from St Gall.[12]

Today must we sing of a Child, whom in unspeakable wisdom his Father begat before all times, and whom, within time, a glorious mother brought forth.

Who is this Child whom ye proclaim worthy of so great laudations? Tell us that we also may praise him.

This is he whose coming to earth the prophetic and chosen, initiated into the mysteries of God, foresaw and pointed out long before, and thus foretold.

Next followed the introit for the third Mass of Christmas Day:

Unto us a child is born, unto us a son is given.

The later antiphon is less theological and more dramatic.

On the Nativity of the Lord at mass let there be ready two deacons having on vestments, behind the altar saying: 'Whom seek ye in the manger, say, ye shepherds?'

Let two cantors in the choir answer: 'The Saviour, Christ the Lord, a child wrapped in swaddling clothes, according to the angelic word.'

And the deacons: 'Present here is the little one with Mary, his mother, of whom Isaiah the prophet foretold: "Behold, a virgin shall conceive, and shall bring forth a son; and do ye say and announce that he is born."'

Then let the cantor lift up his voice and say: 'Alleluia, alleluia. Now we know indeed that Christ is born on earth, of whom sing ye all, with the Prophet: "Unto us a child is born."'

The two deacons above possibly represent the two midwives found in the *Protevangelium* account of the Nativity given in Chapter I.

CHRISTMAS IN SAXON ENGLAND

In 597 Pope Gregory I sent Augustine to England to become the first archbishop of Canterbury. The next year Augustine reported baptising a large number of converts on Christmas day. The church at Canterbury eagerly accepted Roman liturgical singing, which spread throughout England. By the time of Alcuin of York (735-804) the 'O' antiphons –

sung before and after the magnificat at vespers during Advent – were well established in England. The widely known Advent hymn, 'O come, O come Emmanuel', is based on a combination of several of these antiphons. Some of the 'O' canticles were of Roman origin, others French or Spanish, indicating their widespread use in western Europe.

The next selection contains a Saxon Advent antiphon from the ninth century. Both illustrate the importance of Mary in the religious life of the early medieval period.[13]

Cantor	Response
Hail, O most worthy	in all the world!
Thou purest Maiden	that ever on earth
Through the long ages	lived among men!
Rightly all mortals	in blithe mood
Name thee blessed	and hail thee Bride
Of the King of glory.	The thanes of Christ,
In heaven the highest	carol and sing
Proclaiming thee Lady	of the heavenly legions,
Of earthly orders,	and the hosts of Hell.
Thou only of women	didst purpose of old
To bring thy maidenhood	unto thy Maker,
Presenting it there	unspotted of sin.
Of all mankind	there came no other,
No bride with linked jewels,	like unto thee
With pure heart sending	thy glorious gift.

Germanic converts to Christianity interpreted the church's teachings and traditions in terms they could understand. Jesus' disciples are referred to as *thanes*. A Saxon version of Genesis (like Milton's *Paradise Lost*) follows the Old Testament Apocrypha and includes an account of the revolt of the angels before the temptation of Adam and Eve, thus making treason, rather than disobedience, the first sin – as it was in their warrior society.

In addition to the theatrical appeal of antiphonal singing, churchmen dramatised ecclesiastical celebrations in other ways: with the use of incense, the ringing of bells and with processions. The following excerpt is from a tenth-century book of monastic instructions.

THE MONASTIC AGREEMENT OF THE MONKS AND NUNS OF THE ENGLISH NATION[14]

Of the manner in which the vigil of Christmas shall be kept

On the vigil of Christmas, when the feast itself is announced in chapter by the reader, the brethren shall all rise together and then genuflect, giving thanks for the unspeakable loving kindness of our Lord who came down to redeem the world from the snares of the devil ...

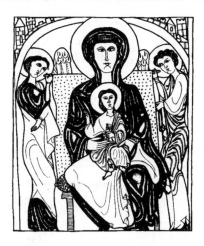

At Nocturnes on Christmas night the fourth response shall, for extra solemnity, be sung by two cantors. After the *Te Deum laudamus* the gospel shall be read by the abbot, as is usual; and when the prayer has been said the ministers shall go out silently, change their shoes, wash and vest quickly; then the bells shall peal and the mass [the first of the three Christmas masses] shall be celebrated. Matins shall follow, after which, if day has not yet dawned, Lauds of All Saints shall be sung in the usual way; if, however, it is already daybreak, that office shall be said after the morrow mass [second Christmas mass] which must itself be said in the early dawn. Then, at the proper time, when the bell rings the brethren shall sing Prime. After Prime they shall assemble for chapter at church, when the words of spiritual edification have been spoken, the brethren shall all, with lowly devotion, beg pardon of the abbot, who takes the place of Christ, and ask forgiveness of their many failings, saying the *Confiteor*. To this the abbot shall answer *Misereatur* and then, prostrate, he himself shall ask pardon of the brethren …

On the days between the feast of the Innocents and the octave of Christmas, since the *Gloria in excelsis Deo* is said at mass on account of the solemnity of such a feast, all the bells shall ring at nocturnes and vespers as at mass, as is the custom among the people of this country. For we have ordained that the goodly religious customs of this land, which we have learned from our fathers before us, be in no wise cast off but confirmed on all hands. For the same reason candles shall be lit at matins and all the bells shall peal and the thurible [incense holder] shall be carried round although the *Te Deum laudamus* is not sung nor the gospel read in the manner of a feast day …

On the Purification of St Mary [February 2, Candlemas Day] candles shall be set out ready in the church to which the brethren are to go to get their lights. On the way thither they shall walk in silence, occupied with the psalms; and all shall be vested in albs if this is possible and if the weather permits. On entering the church, having prayed awhile, they shall say the antiphon and collect in honour of the saint to whom the church is dedicated. The abbot, vested in stole and cope, shall bless the candles, sprinkling them with holy water and incensing them. When the abbot has received his candle from the doorkeeper, the chanting shall begin and the brethren shall receive their candles. During the return procession shall they sing the appointed antiphons until they reach the church doors, and then having sung the antiphon *Responsum accepit Simeon*, with the collect, they shall enter the church singing the response *Cum inducerent Puerum* [Luke 2:26ff].

Next they shall say the Lord's prayer, and Tierce shall follow; after which, if the brethren were not vested for the procession, they shall vest for the mass, during which they shall hold their lighted candles until after the offertory, when they shall offer them to the priest.

HOW DID THE LAITY CELEBRATE CHRISTMAS IN THE EARLY MIDDLE AGES?

The famous historian, the Venerable Bede, writing in 731, suggested that one reason why the Angles accepted Christianity was that they had long begun the new year on December 25, apparently in celebration of the winter solstice. 'That very night which is so holy to us, they called in their tongue *modranect*, that is mother's night.'[15] Bede does not give a source for his remark, but the Germanic peoples did observe the solstice with a feast from which we derive the word *yule*. After they became Christians the Anglo-Saxons kept some of their ancient pagan customs, such as burning the yule log and roasting a boar's head. Just how many, we do not know. There is little information about popular Christmas practices during the first five or six centuries after the Germanic tribes conquered the western Roman empire (400-1000 AD). Almost all of the documentary and artistic evidence from that period is the handiwork of clerics, particularly of monks. Their view of Christmas, illustrated in hymns, poems, illuminated manuscripts and occasionally in chronicles, was essentially theological. While they emphasised most of the motifs listed at the end of Chapter I, they did so in a theological and didactic fashion. Their language tends to be abstract; their metaphors symbolic. They sought primarily to defend the faith against both paganism and heresy.

Until the eleventh or twelfth century church authorities looked upon popular yuletime celebrations as pagan and morally dangerous. The following anecdote, quoted by William of Malmesbury (1090-1143) from an eleventh-century German chronicle, provides an example of this clerical viewpoint.[16]

I, Ethelbert, a sinner, even were I desirous of concealing the divine judgment which overtook me, yet the tremor of my limbs would betray me;

wherefore I shall relate circumstantially how this happened, that all may know the heavy punishment due to disobedience. We were, on the eve of our Lord's Nativity, in a certain town in Saxony, in which was the church of Magnus the Martyr, and a priest named Robert had begun the first mass. I was in the churchyard with eighteen companions, fifteen men and three women, dancing and singing profane songs to such a degree that interrupted the priest, our voices resounded amid the sacred solemnity of the mass. Wherefore, having commanded us to be silent, and not being attended to, he cursed us in the following words, 'May it please God and St Magnus, that you remain singing in that manner for a whole year.' His words had their effect. The son of John, the priest, seized his sister, who was singing with us, by the arm, and immediately tore it from her body; but not a drop of blood flowed out. She also remained a whole year with us, dancing and singing. The rain fell not upon us; nor did the cold, nor heat, nor hunger, nor thirst, nor fatique assail us: we neither wore out our clothes nor shoes, but we kept on singing as though we had been insane. First we sank into the ground up to our knees: next to our thighs; a covering was at length, by permission of God, built over us to keep off the rain. When a year had elapsed, Herbert, bishop of the city of Cologne, released us from the tie wherewith our hands were bound, and reconciled us before the altar of St Magnus. The daughter of the priest, with the two other women, died immediately; the rest of us slept three whole days and nights, some died afterwards, and are famed for miracles; the remainder betray their punishment by the trembling of their limbs. The narrative was given by Lord Pelegrine, the successor of Herbert, in the year of our Lord 1013.

THE CHANGING CHARACTER OF CHRISTMAS IN THE MIDDLE AGES

The same authoritarian approach is found in one of the first miracle stories of the Virgin Mary (from the eleventh-century *Miracles of Peter Venable*).[17] When an evil spirit attempts to enter the monastery at Cluny, a monk, standing before the image of the Virgin and the Christchild, sees the child turn to his mother and tell her how, on the night of his birth, he had been given power to ward off the devil. Hearing this, the evil spirit leaves ... Like the accounts of the child Jesus in the Apocrypha, the anecdote stresses Jesus' divine power; it does not bring Jesus or his mother into a human environment. By the twelfth and thirteenth centuries, most miracle stories are more down to earth. They portray Jesus, Mary and different saints as compassionate intercessors helping people in trouble. The saints, especially Mary, are depicted as loving protectors of the unfortunate, and even the sinful, providing they have faith. In one story the Virgin takes the place of a nun who has broken her vows, until the nun repents and returns. In another, a more martial Mary, jousts in the place of a pious knight who refuses to leave mass in time to participate in a tournament – this at a time when the church officially condemned jousting.

A similar shift to a more humane emphasis occurs in theological writing, even among conservative churchmen. An example is the following selection from St Bernard's (1091-1153) *The Steps of Humility*. Bernard was a dedicated monk, who strove to reform the Cistercian order, known already for its strictness. Extremely conservative, opposed to the new rationalism of men like Abelard, Bernard conceived of the Incarnation in traditional theological terms, yet he explains its human meaning in pragmatic terms.[18]

SAINT BERNARD & INTERPRETATION OF THE INCARNATION

We seek truth in ourselves, in our neighbours, and in its own nature; in ourselves, judging ourselves; in our neighbours, sympathising with their ills; in its nature, contemplating with pure heart. Observe not only the number but the order. First let Truth itself teach you that you should seek it in your neighbours ... For in the list of the Beatitudes which he [Jesus] distinguished in his sermon, he placed the merciful before the pure in heart. The merciful quickly grasp truth in their neighbours, extending their own feelings to them and conforming themselves to them through love, so that they feel *their* joys or troubles as their own. They are weak with the weak; they burn with the offended. They *rejoice with them that do rejoice, and weep with them that weep.* After the spiritual vision has been purified by this brotherly love, they enjoy the contemplation of truth in its own nature, and then bear others' ills for the love of it. But those who do not unite themselves with their brethren in this way, but on the contrary either revile those who weep or disparage those who rejoice, not feeling in themselves that which is in others, because they are not similarly affected – how can they grasp truth in their neighbours? For the popular proverb well applies to them: The healthy do not know how the sick feel, nor the full how the hungry suffer. But sick sympathise with sick, and hungry with hungry, the more closely the more they are alike. For just as the pure see only with a pure heart, so a brother's misery is truly felt with a miserable heart. But in order to have a miserable heart because of another's misery, you must first know from your own; so that you may find your neighbour's mind in your own and know you from yourself how to help him, by the example of our Saviour, who willed his passion in order to learn compassion; his misery to learn commiseration. For just as it is written of him *Yet he learned obedience by the things which he suffered*, so also he learned mercy in the same way. Not that he did not know how to be merciful before, he whose mercy is from everlasting to everlasting; he knew it by nature from eternity, but learned it in time by experience.

Bernard points out that when Christ came into the world, 'He took not on him the nature of angels; but he took on him the seed of Abraham. Wherefore in all things it behoved him to be made like his brethren, that he might be merciful' (Hebrews 2:16-17).

For we do not read that the Word was made angel, but that *the Word was made flesh*, and flesh of the flesh of Abraham ... If you ask what was the necessity, it is answered, *That he might be merciful ... For in that he himself hath suffered being tempted, he is able to succour them that are tempted*. I do not see what can better be understood from these words, than that he wished to partake of the same suffering and temptation, and all human miseries except sin, in order to learn by his own experience how to commiserate and sympathise with those who are similarly suffering and tempted ...

Therefore it should not seem absurd to say, not that Christ began to know anything which he did not know before, but that he knew mercy eternally in one way through his divinity, and learned it temporally in another way through the flesh.

Bernard's reasoning may sound like casuistry, but his emphasis on the need for Christ to share the human experience reflects the more humane approach emerging during the renaissance of the twelfth century. A momentous change in the spirit of western Christendom seems to have occurred in the eleventh and twelfth centuries. Relatively speaking people's lives became less violent, less impoverished, more orderly. Many besides those sheltered in monasteries now enjoyed an existence that was more than a struggle for survival, particularly in the new towns. This change found expression in many different ways – in Gothic art and architecture, in the beginnings of vernacular literature, in the rise of the universities and, in the early thirteenth century, in the founding of the mendicant orders. Instead of retreating from the world, the Franciscan and Dominican friars went out into it to serve and to preach to the laity. St Francis, especially, stressed God's love of common folk, of animals, of God's whole creation. Although Francis did not originate the idea of setting up a Christmas crib or crèche, he gave the custom a new and more universal meaning.

SAINT FRANCIS CELEBRATES THE NATIVITY

The following account is from Thomas of Celano's first Life of St Francis, begun only two years after Francis' death in 1226.[19]

Chapter XXX Of the manger Francis made on the day of the Lord's birth

Francis' highest intention, his chief desire, his uppermost purpose was to observe the holy Gospel in all things and through all things and, with perfect vigilance, with all zeal, with all longing of his mind and all the fervour of his heart: 'to follow the teaching and the footsteps of our Lord Jesus Christ'. He would recall Christ's words through persistent meditation and bring to mind his deeds through most penetrating consideration. The humility of the incarnation, and the charity of the passion occupied his memory particularly, to the extent that he wanted to think of hardly anything else. What he did on the birthday of our Lord Jesus near the little town of Greccio, in the third year before his glorious death, should especially be noted and recalled in reverent memory.

In that place there was a certain man by the name of John [Giovanni Velita, lord of Greccio], of good reputation and an even better life, whom the blessed Francis loved with a special love, for in the place where he lived he held a noble and honourable position in as much as he had trampled upon the nobility of his birth and pursued nobility of soul. Blessed Francis sent for this man, as he often did, about fifteen days before the birth of the Lord, and he said to him: 'If you want to celebrate the present feast of our Lord at Greccio, go with haste and diligently prepare what I tell you. For I wish to do something that will recall to memory the little Child who was born in Bethlehem, and set before our bodily eyes in some way the inconveniences of his infant needs, how he "lay in a manger, how, with an ox and an ass standing by, he lay upon the hay where he had been placed".' When the good and faithful man heard these things, he ran with haste and prepared in that place all the things the saint had told him.

The day of joy drew near, the time of great rejoicing came. The brothers were called from their various places. Men and women of that neighbourhood prepared with glad hearts, according to their means, candles and torches to light up the night that has lighted up all the days and

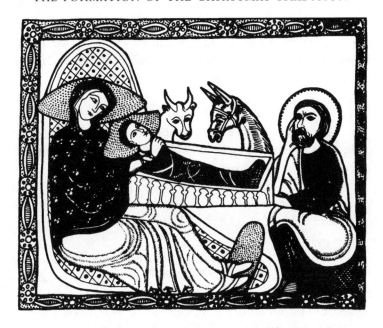

years with its gleaming star. At length the saint of God came, and finding all things prepared, *he saw it and was glad*. The manger was prepared, the hay had been brought, the ox and the ass were led in. There simplicity was honourable, poverty was exhalted, humility was commended, and Greccio was made, as it were, a new Bethlehem. The night was lighted up like the day, and it delighted men and beasts. The people came and were filled with new joy over the new mystery. The woods rang with voices of the crowd and the rocks made answer to their jubilation. The brothers sang, paying their debt of praise to the Lord, and the whole night resounded with their rejoicing. The saint of God stood before the manger, uttering sighs, overcome with love, and filled with a wonderful happiness. The solemnities of the mass were celebrated over the manger and the priest experienced a new consolation.

The saint of God was clothed with the vestments of the deacon, for he was a deacon, and he sang the holy gospel ... And his voice was a strong voice, a sweet voice, a clear voice, a sonorous voice, inviting all to the highest rewards. Then he preached to the people standing about, and he spoke charming words concerning the nativity of the poor King and the little town of Bethlehem. Frequently too, when he wanted to call Christ Jesus, he would call him simply, the *Child of Bethlehem*, aglow with overflowing love for him; and speaking the word *Bethlehem*, his voice was more like the bleating of a sheep. His mouth was filled more with sweet affection than with words. Besides, when he spoke the name *Child of Bethlehem* or *Jesus*, his tongue licked his lips, as it were, relishing and savouring with pleased palate the sweetness of the words.

The gifts of the Almighty were multiplied there, and a wonderful vision was seen by a certain virtuous man. For he saw a little child lying in the manger lifeless, and he saw the holy man of God go up to it and rouse the child as from a deep sleep. This vision was not unfitting, for the Child Jesus had been forgotten in the hearts of many; but, by the working of his grace, he was brought to life again through his servant St Francis and stamped upon their fervent memory. At length the solemn night celebration was brought to a close, and each one returned to his home with holy joy.

The hay that had been placed in the manger was kept, so that the Lord might save the beast of burden and other animals through it as he multiplied his holy mercy. And in truth it so happened that many animals throughout the surrounding region that had various illnesses were freed from their illnesses after eating of this hay. Indeed, even women laboring for a long time in a difficult birth, were delivered safely when some of the hay was placed upon them; and a large number of persons of both sexes of that place, suffering from various illnesses obtained the health they sought. Later, the place on which the manger had stood was made sacred by a *temple of the Lord*, and an altar was built in honor of the most blessed father Francis over the manger, and a church was built, so that where once the animals had eaten the hay, there in the future men would eat unto health of soul and body the flesh of the lamb *without blemish and without spot*, our Lord Jesus Christ, who in the highest and ineffable love gave himself to us, who lives and reigns with the Father and the Holy Spirit, God, eternally glorious, forever and ever. Amen. Alleluja, Alleluja.

Francis' name became so closely linked with the image of Jesus in the manger that by the fifteenth century a legend had grown up that Francis himself had been born in a stable.[20]

CHAPTER III

Christmas Becomes a Communal Festival

This is the day which the Lord hath made,
Let us rejoice and be glad in it.
For the beloved and most holy Child been given to us.
And born for us by the wayside;
And laid in a manger because he had no room in the inn.
Glory to God in the highest, and on earth
Peace to men of good will.

St Francis, Christmas 'Psalm', based on Luke's gospel[1]

As shown in Chapter II, Christmas remained primarily an ecclesiastical feast during the early Middle Ages, celebrated with increasing pageantry by the clergy within the churches, but with little lay participation. Surviving folk traditions associated with the solstice were condemned or discouraged by the church. The new spirit of the twelfth-century renaissance brought about two changes – a more secular outlook, and the growing importance of lay opinion and activity in religious affairs. Between 1300 and 1500 the laity take an increasing part in Christmas celebrations – both within and outside of the church. The church now accepts popular activities, such as carolling, feasting and even dancing. Modern writers and artists may have given us an exaggerated picture of the late medieval Christmas, but it was a colourful and impressive festival. Many of the traditions we associate with the Christmas season come from that period.

MEDIEVAL MIRACLE STORIES

It is appropriate that Celano's account of St Francis' crib should close with the mention of its miraculous hay. In that age of faith people accepted miracles as part of life. They appealed to the imagination and often conveyed an inspiring spiritual message. One of the best known miracle stories from this period is *Our Lady's Tumbler*. Although not a Christmas story, the tale catches the spirit of the image of the Blessed Virgin characteristic of the medieval psyche, a vision of the feminine side of God. Several years ago the story was broadcast on radio as a Christmas reading. It begins with the explanation of how a minstrel and tumbler, tired of worldly life, decided to retire to the monastery of Clairvaux in France. He discovers that, as an illiterate, untrained layman, he has no service to perform that was of any use to the communal life of the monastery. Unhappy with his inability to contribute, he withdraws to the crypt below the church instead of attending matins. Finding himself in the crypt, he seeks sanctuary by an altar dedicated to the Virgin.[2]

OUR LADY'S TUMBLER

Above the altar was carved the statue of Madame St Mary. Truly his steps had not erred when he sought that refuge: nay but rather, God, who knows his own, had led him thither by the hand. When he heard the bells for mass he sprang to his feet all dismayed. 'Ah!' said he, 'now am I betrayed. Each adds his mite to the great offering save me. Like a tethered ox, naught can I do but chew the cud, and waste good victuals on a useless man. Shall I speak my thought? Shall I work my will? By the Mother of God, thus am I to do. None is here to blame. I will do that which I can, and honour with my craft the Mother of God in her monastery. Since others honour her with chant, then I will serve with tumbling.'

He takes off his cowl, and removes his garments, placing them near the altar, but so that his body is not naked he dons a tunic, very thin and fine, of scarce more substance than a shirt. So, light and comely of body, with gown girt closely about his loins, he comes before the Image right humbly. Then raising his eyes, 'Lady,' said he, 'to your fair charge I give my body and soul. Sweet Queen, sweet Lady, scorn not the thing I know, for with the help of God I will essay to serve you in good faith, even as I may. I cannot read your Hours, nor chant your praise, but at least I can set before you what art I have. Now will I be as the lamb that skips and plays before its mother. Oh, Lady, who are nowise bitter to those who serve you with a good intent, that which thy servant is, that he is for you.'

Then commenced his merry play, leaping low and small, tall and high, over and under. Then once more he knelt upon his knees before the statue, and meekly bowed his head. 'Ha!' said he, 'most gracious Queen, of your pity and your charity scorn not my service.' Again he leaped and played, and for holiday and festival made the somersault of Metz. Again he bowed before the Image, did reverence, and paid all honor that he might. Afterwards he did the French vault, then the vault of Champagne,

then the Spanish vault, then the vault they love in Brittany, the vault of
Lorraine, and all these feats he did as best he was able. Afterwards he did
the Roman vault, and then, with his hands before his brow, he danced
daintily before the altar, gazing with a humble heart at the statue of God's
Mother. 'Lady,' said he, 'I set before you a fair play. This travail I do for
you alone; so help me God, for you Lady, and your Son. Think not I
tumble for my own delight; but I serve you, and look for no other
[reward] on my carpet. My brothers serve you, and so do I, Lady. Scorn
not your villein, for he toils for your good pleasure; and, my Lady, you
are my delight, and the sweetness of the world' ...

Then when the chants rose louder from the choir, he, too, forced the
note and put forward all his skill. So long as the priest was about that mass,
so long his flesh endured to dance, and leap and spring, till at the last, nigh
fainting, he could stand no more upon his feet, but fell for weariness on
the ground. From head to heel sweat stood upon him. drop by drop, as
blood falls from meat turning upon the hearth. 'Lady,' said he, 'I can do
no more, but truly will I seek you again.' He took his habit once more,
and when he was wrapped therein, he rose to his feet, and bending low
before the statue, went his way. 'Farewell,' said he, 'gentlest Friend. For
God's love take it not to heart, for so I may, I will soon return ...'

In this fashion passed many days ... His service was so much to his
mind that never once was he too weary to set out his most cunning feats
to distract the Mother of God, nor did he ever wish for other play than
this. Now, doubtless, the monks knew well enough that day by day he
sought the crypt, but not a man on earth – save God alone – was aware of

aught that passed there; neither would he, for all the wealth of the world, have let his goings on be seen, save by the Lord his God alone. For truly he believed that were his secret once espied he would be hunted from the cloister and flung once more into the foul sinful world ...

Thus things went well with this good man for a great space. For more years than I know how to count of, he lived greatly at his ease, but the time came when the good man was sorely vexed, for a certain monk thought upon him, and blamed him in his heart that he was never seen in choir for Matins. The monk marvelled much at his absence, and said within himself that he would never rest until it was clear what manner of man this was, and how he spent the Hours, and for what service the convent gave him bread. So he spied and pried and followed till he marked him plainly, sweating at his craft in just such fashion as you have heard.

'By my faith,' said he, 'this is a merry jest, and a fairer festival than we observe altogether. Whilst others are at prayers, and about the business of the house, this tumbler dances daintily, as though one had given him a hundred silver marks. He prides himself on being so nimble of foot, and thus he repays us what he owes. Truly, it is this for that; we chant for him, and he tumbles for us. We throw him largess; he doles us alms. We weep for his sins, and he dries our eyes. Would that the monastery could see him, as I do, with their very eyes; willingly therefore would I fast till Vespers. Not one could refrain from mirth at the sight of this simple fool doing himself to death with his tumbling, for on himself he has no pity. Since his folly is free from malice, may God grant it to him as penance. Certainly I will not impute it to him as sin, for in all simplicity and good faith, I firmly believe, he does this thing so that he may deserve his bread.' So the monk saw with his very eyes how the tumbler did service at all Hours, without pause or rest, and he laughed with pure mirth and delight, for in his heart was joy and pity.

The monk went straight to the abbot and told him the thing from beginning to end, just as you have heard. The abbot got him on his feet, and said to the monk, 'By holy obedience I bid you hold your peace, and tell not this tale or speak of this matter to none, save me. Come now, we will go forthwith to see what this can be, and let us pray the Heavenly King, and his very sweet, dear Mother, so precious and so bright, that in her gentleness she will plead with her Son, her Father, and her Lord, that I may look on this work – if thus it pleases him – so that the good man be not wrongly blamed, and that God may be more beloved ... Then they secretly sought the crypt, and found a privy place near the altar, where they could see, and yet not be seen. From there the abbot and his

monk marked the business of the penitent. They saw the vaults he varies so cunningly, his nimble leaping, and his dancing, his salutations to Our Lady, and his springing and his bounding, till he was nigh to faint. So weak was he that he sank to the ground, all outworn, and the sweat fell from his body upon the pavement of the crypt. But presently, in this his need, came down to him from the vault a Dame so glorious, that certainly no man had seen one so precious, nor so richly crowned. She was more beautiful than the daughters of men, and her vesture was heavy with gold and gleaming stones. In her train came the hosts of heaven, angel and archangel also, and these pressed close about the minstrel. and solaced and refreshed him … Then the sweet and courteous Queen herself took a white napkin in her hand and with it gently fanned her minstrel before the altar, courteous and debonair, the Lady refreshed his neck, his body and his brow. Meekly she served him as a handmaid in his need. But these things were hidden from the good man, for he neither saw nor knew that about him stood so fair a company …

This marvel the abbot and his monk saw at least four times, and thus at each Hour came the Mother of God with aid and succour for her man. Never did she fail her servants in their need. Great joy had the abbot that this thing was made plain to him. But the monk was filled with shame, since God had shown his pleasure in the service of this poor fool. His confusion burnt him like fire. 'Dominus,' said he to the abbot, 'grant me grace. Certainly this is a holy man, And since I have judged him amiss, it is very right that my body should smart. Give me now fast or vigil or the scourge, for without question he is a saint. We are witnesses to the whole matter, nor is it possible that we can be deceived.' But the abbot replied, 'You speak truly, for God has made us to know that he has bound him with the cords of love. So I lay my commandment upon you, in virtue of obedience, and under pain of your person, that you tell no word to any man of what you have seen, save only to God alone and to me.' 'Lord,' said he, 'thus will I do.'

The widespread interest in and worship of Mary during the Middle Ages had its origins during the time when Christmas first became an official church feast. As noted in the first chapter, there was a shift of emphasis from the extended to the nuclear family in the Roman world during the fourth and fifth centuries. The Christian church encouraged the change and taught its Germanic and Celtic converts to adopt a similar approach. In addition to the emphasis on the nuclear family, the world of late antiquity fostered the worship of a number of goddesses, particularly divine mother figures. German mythology also possessed similar deities. It was thus natural that Mary, as the mother of God, should become an important figure in popular worship. Church leaders resisted at first, but by the eighth century had come to accept Mary in the role of mediatrix or intercessor. In the early twelfth century Guilbert of Nogent recorded three miracles of Mary. By the thirteenth century she had become by far the most popular of all the saints, as the dedication of countless abbeys, cathedrals, churches and chapels attests.[3]

Among miracle tales popular in the thirteenth century were a number about St Nicholas, whom we now associate so closely with Christmas. St Nicholas' day is December 6 and came to be celebrated in the Middle Ages as a children's festival. St Nicholas was a fourth-century bishop of Myra, on what is now the southern coast of Turkey, above Cyprus. As a saint he was seen as a protector of children, of maidens and of sailors. Nicholas became one of the most popular saints in the medieval calendar. A biography of him appeared in the ninth century, and a special liturgy was composed for December 6 in his honour.[4]

According to one legend Nicholas saved two young scholars whose father had sent them to receive his blessing before going to study in Athens. Arriving late in Myra, they decided to spend the night in a hostelry. Their wicked host murdered them, disposing of their dismembered remains in a barrel of pickled pork, and kept their money and belongings. In a dream that night the bishop had a vision of their murder, arose and sought out the innkeeper, who confessed and asked for forgiveness. In response to his penance and the bishop's prayers, the boys reappeared, alive (and in one piece). This miracle was one basis for considering Nicholas the patron saint of children. Several of his other miracles, as related in the thirteenth-century *Golden Legend*, constitute the next selection. The English translation, with a few modernisations, is that of William Caxton (d. 1491). It was one of the first books printed in the English language.

MIRACLES OF SAINT NICHOLAS[5]

Nicholas, citizen of the city of Patras, was born of rich and holy parents ... He was begotten in the flower of their age, and from that time on they lived in continence and led a heavenly life. The first day that he was washed and bathed Nicholas addressed himself right up in the basin, and he would not take the breast nor the pap but once on the Wednesday and once on the Friday. In his young age he eschewed the plays and japes of other young children. He used and haunted gladly holy church; and all that he might understand of holy scripture he executed it in deed and work after his power. And when his father and mother departed this life, he began to think how he might distribute his riches, not to the praising of the world, but to the honour and glory of God. One of his neighbours had three daughters, virgins, and he was a nobleman: but for the poverty of them together, they were constrained to abandon them to the sin of lechery, so that by the gain and winning of their prostitution they might be sustained. And when the holy man Nicholas knew hereof he had great

horror of this villainy, and threw by night into the house of the man a mass of gold wrapped in a cloth. And when the man arose in the morning and found the gold, he rendered to God therefor great thanksgivings, and therewith married his eldest daughter. And a little while after, this holy servant of God threw in another mass of gold, which the man found, and thanked God, and purposed to wake, in order to discover who had aided him in his poverty. And after a few days, Nicholas doubled the mass of gold, and cast it into the house of this man. He awoke at the sound of the gold, and followed Nicholas, who fled from him. And he said to him: Sir, flee not away so but that I may see and know thee. Then he ran after him more hastily, and knew that it was Nicholas; and anon he kneeled down, and would have kissed his feet, but the holy man would not let him, but required him not to tell nor discover this thing as long as he lived...

It is read in a chronicle that the blessed Nicholas was at the council of Nicea; and on a day, as a ship with mariners was perishing on the sea, they prayed and required devoutly Nicholas, servant of God, saying: If those things that we have heard of thee be true, prove them now. And anon a man appeared in his likeness and said: Lo, see ye me? Ye called me, and then he began to help them in their exploit of the sea, and anon the tempest ceased. And when they were come to his church, they knew him without anybody to show him to them, and yet they had never seen him. And then they thanked God and him of their deliverance. And he bade them to attribute their safety to the mercy of God, and to their belief, and nothing to his merits.

It was so on a time that all of the province of St Nicholas suffered great famine, in such wise that victual failed. And then this holy man heard say that certain ships laden with wheat were arrived in the haven. And anon he went thither and prayed the mariners that they would succour the perished at least with a hundred muyes of wheat of every ship. Father we dare not, for it is meted and measured, and we must give reckoning thereof in the garners of the Emperor in Alexandria. And the holy man said unto them: Do this that I have said to you and I promise in the truth of God, that it shall not be lessened or diminished when ye shall come to the garners. And when they delivered so much out of every ship, they came to Alexandria and delivered the measure that they had received. And then they recounted the miracle to the ministers of the Emperor, and worshipped God and his servant Nicholas. Then this holy man distributed the wheat to every man according to his need ...

There was a man that had borrowed of a Jew a sum of money, and swore upon the altar of St Nicholas that he would render and pay it again as soon as he might, and gave no other pledge. And this man held this money so long, that the Jew demanded and asked for his money, and he said that he had paid him. Then the Jew made him go before the law in judgment, and the oath was given to the debtor. And he brought with him a hollow staff, in which he had put the money in gold, and he leant upon the staff. And when he should make his oath and swear, he delivered his staff to the Jew to keep and hold whilst he should swear, and then swore that he had delivered to him more than he owed to him. And when he had made the oath, he demanded his staff again of the Jew, and he nothing knowing of his malice had delivered it to him. Then this deceiver went his way, and anon after he became very sleepy, and lay himself by the road, a cart with four wheels came with great force and slew him, and brake the staff with the gold so that it spread abroad. And when the Jew heard this, he came thither sore moved, and saw the fraud. And many said to him that he take to him the gold; and he refused, saying: If he that was dead were not raised again to life by the merits of St Nicholas, he would not receive it. But if he came again to life, he would receive baptism and become Christian. Then he that was dead arose, and the Jew was christened.

Stories of miracles were understandably popular in the Middle Ages. In the play, *Saint Joan*, G.B. Shaw has the bishop of Beauvais define a miracle as an act which creates faith, regardless of whether the act has a natural or supernatural explanation. In the chaotic world of the collapsing Roman empire, and for centuries after that, people were confronted with so much insecurity and so many unforeseen events that they lost faith in natural explanations; a miraculous interpretation seemed far more credible. It, at least, explained why an event had occurred. Before the scientific revolution, people were far more interested in *why* than in *how* things happened. What meaning can a modern reader find in these legends from the past?

One way to interpret St Nicholas' miracle of the two scholars, is to assume that somehow Nicholas did save the boys from being robbed and possibly murdered. Worried by their failure to arrive, he searched for them and found them staying with an innkeeper of bad repute, who had robbed them and held them captive. Whatever actually occurred, Nicholas, being a conscientious and caring person, saved the boys from harm. While it may be difficult to accept some miracle stories on any grounds, the best way to appreciate them is to look for their moral and /or religious purpose. How, and in what way, do they strengthen faith?

MEDIEVAL CELEBRATIONS OF
SAINT NICHOLAS' DAY

Santa Claus appears to have little in common with the original St Nicholas. Several medieval customs, stressing Nicholas' concern for children, provide a link between the kindly bishop of late antiquity and his modern descendant. One was having children take a leading part in religious worship during the Christmas season. On St Nicholas' day, in a number of European cathedrals, choir boys elected one of their members boy-bishop, to take part in the services on that feast and on Holy Innocents' day (December 28). Boy-bishops could not say mass, but they wore episcopal vestments, walked in processions, led prayers and preached. A few of their sermons have survived. As is shown in the next chapter, the practice of having boy-bishops gave rise to mockery and disorder, and was suppressed at the time of the Reformation. But originally, boy-bishops were taken seriously, as a symbol of Christ's love for children and his respect (as the gospels bore witness) for their simple faith. The detailed instructions, in Latin, for the vestments, conduct and liturgical role of the boy-bishops of Salisbury, clearly show that the whole procedure was meant to be done with dignity. The following selection is taken from the *Processionale ad usum insignis et preclare Ecclesie Sacrum*, dated 1566, but based on long usage.[6]

On the eve of Holy Innocents' day, the boy-bishop was to go in solemn procession with his fellows to the altar of the Holy Trinity and All the Saints in their copes with burning tapers in their hands. The bishop beginning and the other boys following ... The chorister bishop, in the meantime, fumed the altar, then the image of the Holy Trinity. Then the bishop chanted the verse, 'Laetamini', and the response was, 'Et gloriamini etc.' [Next, the boy-bishop said the collect for the day, after which the procession returned from the altar singing] ... The procession went into the choir, by the west door, in such order that the dean and canons were foremost; the chaplains next; the bishop with his little prebendaries, in the last and highest place. The bishop took his seat, and the rest of the children disposed themselves upon each side of the choir, upon the uppermost ascent, the canons resident bearing the incense and the book; and the petit canons the tapers, according to the rubric. And from this hour to the end of the next day's procession no clergy took a place above the children.

The choosing of the boy-bishop is another example of the persistence of the inversion theme. The practice goes back at least to the thirteenth century at Salisbury and other English cathedrals, and earlier on the continent.

An even more ancient and widespread practice associated with St Nicholas was presenting gifts to children and attributing them to him. Rudolf Hospinian (1547-1626), in a work on the origins of Christian festivals, says that this custom grew out of St Nicholas' gift of a dowry to the three maidens related above. Children were told that St Nicholas, on the eve of his day, went up and down through towns and villages, and miraculously came through doors and windows to distribute his presents.

Two other traditional accounts also attribute the custom of giving children presents to St Nicholas' generosity to the three maidens.[7]

Saint Nicholas money used to give to maidens secretly,
Who, that he may still use his wonted liberality,

The mothers all their children on the Eve do fast.
And when they every one in senseless sleep are cast,
Both apples, nuts and pears they bring, and other things beside,
As caps, and shoes, and petticoats, which secretly they hide.
And in the morning found, they say, this St Nicholas brought.

1570 version of a traditional rhyme

St Nicholas was venerated as the protector of virgins; and there are, or were until lately, numerous fantastical customs observed in Italy and parts of France, in reference to that peculiar patronage. In several convents it was customary on the eve of St Nicholas, for the boarders to place each a silk stocking at the door of the apartment of the abbess, with a piece of paper enclosed, recommending them to the *great St Nicholas of her chamber.* The next day they were called together to witness the Saint's attention, who never failed to fill all the stockings with sweetmeats, and other trifles of that kind, with which these credulous virgins made a great feast.[8]

Many scholars, following the noted Belgian historian, Philippe Aries, believe that in Europe children received little attention or understanding before the seventeenth or eighteenth centuries. That viewpoint is now being questioned. The medieval celebration of St Nicholas' day would seem to support a revision of Aries' thesis.

MEDIEVAL CHRISTMAS PLAYS

Like the ancient Greek theatre, that of medieval Europe grew out of the pageantry of religious worship. The Christian church, which had condemned classical drama, itself gave birth to a form of liturgical drama in which the clergy enacted stories from scripture. Dramatisations of scripture came to be called mysteries, from the Latin *mysterium* – a church service. Similar presentation of stories based on the lives of the saints were called miracle plays. Among the oldest surviving miracle plays are a number about St Nicholas, further evidence of his popularity in the Middle Ages. Both mystery and miracle plays appeared in France and Germany around 1300, about a generation later in England. Their antecedents, however, may well go back to the Advent antiphons of 500 years earlier. The Saxon antiphon between Mary and Joseph found in Chapter II is thought to be the earliest written dialogue in Old English. By the fourteenth century the miracle and mystery plays were being presented outside churches by guildsmen, and eventually by troupes of travelling actors.[9] A number of English collections of these plays were preserved in several different places, such as Chester, Coventry, Townley and York.

The abridged *Redemption* below is from a fifteenth-century Nativity play based on an earlier version, belonging to the Coventry cycle of plays. It has a more theological approach than most such plays; possibly it was performed by a troupe of friars rather than laymen. The play provides a theological interpretation of the Nativity in terms compre-

hensible to ordinary people. The first scene describes the Fall of Man, thus explaining the need for human redemption. In the second scene Truth, Mercy, Justice and Peace discuss man's fate. They conclude that man can be saved only by God's sacrifice. At this juncture, God the Father calls on his Son to ordain some plan whereby man may win salvation. The selection begins with Christ's reply.[10]

THE MYSTERY OF THE REDEMPTION

Christ	Father, he who shall do this must be god and man;
	Let me see how I may wear that weed,
	And since in my wisdom he began
	I am ready to do this deed.
The Holy Spirit	I, the Holy Ghost, from you two proceed
	Taking this charge at once on me:
	I, Love, to your lover shall give you speed:
	This is the consent of our unity.
The Father	Go, Angel Gabriel, as our breath
	Into the country of Galilee.
	The name of the city is Nazareth,
	A wedded maiden you shall see
	The wife of Joseph, and verily
	She is of the house which David bore.

> The name of this maid of glee
> Is Mary, who shall all restore.

Christmas *Christ*

> Say that she is sinless and full of grace
> And that I, the Son of God, shall be her son
> Hasten that you may arrive apace,
> Or I shall be present ere you have begun.
> I have great haste to see this done.
> And to be born of a maid whom spirits adore.
> Tell her that by her is won
> All which your angels lost before.*

The Holy Spirit

> And if she ask how it may be.
> Tell her that I, the Holy Ghost, do this
> She shall be saved through our unity,
> In token her barren cousin Elizabeth is
> Quick with child in her old age indeed.
> Tell her nothing is impossible for God to do.
> Her body shall be filled with bliss
> She shall soon believe this message true.

Gabriel

> On this high embassy, Lord, I shall fly,
> It shall be done, even as a thought,
> Behold, dear God, how true am I,
> I take my flight and linger not!

Gabriel passes from Heaven to the house of Mary.

> Ave Maria, gratis plena, Dominum tecum.
> Hail full of Grace! God is with thee, I say!
> Among all women blessed art thou!
> Here the name of Eva is turned to Ave.
> That is to say, without sorrow as thou art now.

Mary

> Ah, merciful God, this is a marvellous greeting!
> The angel's words are dreadful to hear,
> I am much troubled by this strange meeting,
> Angels indeed daily appear.

* A reference to the revolt of the angels, mentioned in the introduction to the play

But not in forms of man, and that is my fear,
Also to be given so high a name,
When I am unworthy of this heavenly cheer,
Gives me much dread and greater shame.

Gabriel   Mary, for this have no dread,
For God's grace has fallen on thee,
Thou shalt conceive and in maidenhead
Bear the Son of the Trinity.
And Joseph shall give him his father David's seed.
Reigning in the house of Jacob whose reign shall have
    no end.

Mary   Angel, I ask you now
In what manner this thing can be?
As for knowledge of a man, I have none now;
I ever have kept, and ever shall keep, virginity.
I cannot doubt what you say to me
But I ask, so that I may know –.

Gabriel   From on high the Holy Ghost shall fall on thee
And the virtue of the Highest shall shadow so,
Of the holy Spirit thou shalt shortly bear
God's Son, who shall be called the Sapient One.
And see, thy cousin Elizabeth there
In her old age has conceived a son.
Her six months of bearing have run,
Her barrenness has passed away –
Nothing is impossible which God will have done;
We listen to hear what thou shalt say.

{A pause}

Mary   With all meekness I incline to their accord,
Bowing down my face with all benignity,
See here the handmaid of our Lord:
According to thy word, be it done to Me!

Gabriel   Gramercy, my lady free,
Gramercy for thy word of might,
Gramercy for thy great humility,
Gramercy, thou lantern of light!

Here the Holy Ghost descends with three beams of light to Our Lady; the Son of God shines with three beams upon the Holy Ghost, and God the Father with three beams upon the Son. And all three enter her bosom.

Mary

Ah, now I feel in the body of me
Perfect God and perfect man,
And the form of a child's carnality
And all at once, thus God began
I cannot tell what joy and bliss
I find through all my body fly;

Angel Gabriel, I thank thee for this;
Most meekly commend me to my Father on high.

Gabriel

At thy will, Lady, it shall be,
Thou gentlest of blood, and highest of race,
Reigning on earth in any degree
Through the high occasion of heaven's grace.
I commend myself to thee, throne of the Trinity,
O mother of Jesus, and meekest maid!
Queen of heaven, lady of earth, empress of hell, these three,
And succour of the sinful who cry for aid.
Through thy blessed body our bliss is remade,
To thee, mother of mercy, I humbly cry!
And as I began with an Ave I fade,
Joining heaven to earth, and ascend on high,

The angels in heaven sing the sequence: 'Ave Maria, gratia plena, Dominum tecum, virgo serena.'

The medieval image of Mary and the holy family is a combination of the celestial and the commonplace. *Our Lady's Tumbler* depicts Mary as the richly adorned Queen of heaven, yet she acts as the 'handmaid' of the tumbler. In the next scene we have a humorous account of a dialogue between Mary and Joseph – yet one with a religious meaning, The concern here is with Joseph, and his relationship to Mary. Joseph's ambiguous position, as Jesus' apparent father, posed a problem. Joseph is usually portrayed sympathetically, as someone ordinary people can identify with. Joseph was first venerated as a saint by Coptic and Palestinian Christians, but his popularity quickly spread to the west.

SCENE IV: THE CHERRY TREE

On the road to Bethlehem. A bare tree on one side of the stage. Enter Joseph and Mary travelling to Bethlehem.

Joseph   Lord, what trouble is made for man!
          Rest in this world is given to none
          For our lord and Emperor Octavi
          Demands a tribute from every one.
          In every city the order's the same.
          I, a poor carpenter of David's kin,
          Must obey the commandment or fall in sin,
          Coming to bitter blame.
          Now, Mary, my wife, what have thou to say?
          I must surely go from you.
          To the city of Bethlehem far away;
          The journey is hard and the comforts few.

Mary   My husband, I will take it too,
          For there live some of my family,
          Bethlehem is a city I long to view
          And my friends will be great joy to me.

Joseph   Wife, I think of your baby, I greatly fear
          That you would suffer crossing the wild.
          You know I would gladly give you cheer,
          Though women are moody whenever with child.
          But come, let us go as fast as you may.
          And Almighty God speed us upon our way.

Mary   Ah, my sweet husband, what do I see?
          What tree is standing upon that hill?

Joseph   Why, Mary, that is a cherry tree;
          At one time of the year you might eat your fill.

Mary   Look again, husband, more carefully;
          Its blossoms are brighter than ever I saw.

Joseph   Mary, come to the city speedily
          Or we shall suffer the hand of the law.

Mary   Now, my husband, look once again.
          How lovely cherries cling to the tree,
          And though I would not cause you pain,
          I wish you would pick a few for me.

Joseph   I shall try to do what you desire.
    [*He tries awkwardly to reach a bunch, but fails.*]
    Oh, to pick these cherries I won't be beguiled.
    The tree is so high I can easily tire;
    Let *Him* pluck your cherries who got you with child!

Mary   Now, good Lord, grant this boon to me.
    To have these cherries, if such is Your will.
    [*The tree bows*]
    Now I thank Thee, God, Thou hast bowed the tree
    And I may gather and eat my fill.

Joseph   Ah, I well know I have offended my God the Trinity
    In speaking to Mary so unkind a word as this,
    For now I believe it can only be
    That Mary bears the Son of the King of Bliss.
    May he help us in our need! ...

Mary   Thank you, husband, for what you say
    And first let us go on to our journey's end.
    Almighty Father, comfort us I pray,
    And the Holy Ghost in glory be our friend. They go out.

SCENE V: THE ADORATION OF THE SHEPHERDS

The three shepherds, Manfras, Bosenbace and Mois lie on a hill. An angel appears.

Angel   Joy to God who reigns in heaven
    And peace to men on earthly ground!
    A Child is born to be your leaven;
    Through him the folk shall be unbound.
    Sacraments there shall be seven
    Won through that child's wound.
    Therefore I sing to him you believe in:
    The flower of friendship now is found.
    God who rules the earth and sea,
    Descends from heaven above to win
    Man below and heal his sin,
    Peace is come to all his kin
    Through God's subtlety.

First Shepherd   Manfras, Manfras, fellow mine,
I saw a light like silver shine,
I never saw so strange a sign
Shaped upon the skies.
Brighter than the sun's beam
On Bethlehem I saw it stream
And over all this region gleam,
Thrice I saw it rise.

Second Shepherd   You are my brother Bosenbace;
I saw this miracle take place,
I know it is a sign of grace
Shining before dawn.
Balaam come to prophesy
A light should sparkle in the sky
When maid Mary's son should lie
In Bethlehem new born.

Third Shepherd   Though I love best silent joys,
A herdsboy whom men name as Mois,
In Moses' law I heard a voice
Calling on the cross.
Of a maid a babe is born;
On a tree he shall be torn,
Saving folk who lie forlorn;
This Child shall heal that loss.

Here the Angel sings 'Gloria in excelsis'.

First Shepherd   Eh, Eh, that was a wonderful note
Which now was sung above the sky.
I have the music all by rote ...

Third Shepherd   The song, I thought, retold the story,
And afterwards I heard him say
The child that was born shall be Prince of glory.
And we should seek him straight-away.

Second Shepherd   Let us follow with all our worth
Going along with song and mirth
To worship with joy at that blessed birth

> The Lord of all our throng.
> Let us march on speedily
> To honor that babe worthily
> With mirth, song and melody.
> [*They arrive at Bethlehem.*]
> Now stay, and sing this song.

First Shepherd   Hail, Flower of flowers, the fairest found,
> Hail, Peerless pearl, the rose we prize,
> Hail, Bloom, by whom we'll be unbound
> With thy bloody wounds in wondrous wise.
> To love thee is my delight !
> Hail, Flower fair and free,
> Light from the Trinity,
> Hail, blessed mayst thou be,
> Hail, Maiden, Mother of Might !

As the mystery plays moved out of the churches they became more diverse, mixing contemporary and comic elements with the biblical stories. The shepherds' role in the Nativity plays became a vehicle for popular protest and comedy, sometimes as a separate drama by itself. For example, in the second shepherd's play in the Townley cycle (published in several modern anthologies of English literature) one of the supposed shepherds is a thief in disguise. The dialogue between him and the shepherds includes folk humour and sharp comments on unjust taxes, oppressive government and avaricious landlords. The mystery plays presented to observe Holy Innocents' day (December 28) depict King Herod as the epitome of the cruel and wicked ruler with an enthusiasm which suggests familiarity with capricious rulers. Both England and France had their share of arbitrary kings in the late Middle Ages.

Some communities held a pageant on Holy Innocents' day, enacting the flight of the holy family into Egypt, in which Joseph led a donkey carrying Mary and the Baby Jesus up to the high altar. A French carol, written for the occasion contains this verse.[11]

> Conquering kings their titles take
> From the foes they captive make:
> Jesus by a noble deed
> From the thousands he has freed.

EARLY CHRISTMAS CAROLS

Carols represent the musical expression of the new more human and earthly interpretation of Christmas which emerged in the later Middle Ages. They were mostly of folk origin, designed primary for group singing – more often out of church than in it. The term *carol* comes from an old French, and originally classical, word for dancing. The carols depict the Nativity in a realistic and often informal manner. Even more than the Nativity plays, the carols of the late medieval and early modern periods articulate the ideas and feelings of the laity about Christmas. Below are six carols representing different popular themes. The first two are about the Virgin Mary: the first as a metaphorical image, the second describing the holy family's reception in Bethlehem. The third carol, like the second, deals with the lowly circumstances of Jesus' birth. The fifth expresses the sense of immediacy with which a French village celebrated Noel. The last carol gives voice to the exuberance of popular festivities.[12]

SONG OF THE SHIP

Es Kommt ein Schiff (German, earliest known text, 1470)

There comes a ship asailing
With angels flying fast;
She bears a splendid cargo
And has a mighty mast.

This ship is fully laden,
Right to her highest board;
She bears the Son from Heaven,
God's high eternal Word.

Upon the sea unruffled
The ship moves in to shore,
To bring us all the riches
She has within her store.

And the ship's name is Mary
Of flowers the rose is she,
And brings to us her baby
From sin to set us free.

The ship made in this fashion,
In which such store was cast,
Her sail is Love's sweet passion'
The Holy Ghost her mast.

A VIRGIN MOST PURE

A virgin most pure, as the prophets do tell,
Hath brought forth a baby, as it hath befel,
To be our Redeemer from death, hell, and sin,
Which Adam's transgression hath wrapped us in:

At Beth'l'em in Jewry a city there was,
Where Joseph and Mary did pass,
And there to be taxed with many one mo',
For Caesar commanded the same should be so:

But when they had entered the city so fair,
A number of people so mighty was there,
That Joseph and Mary, whose substance was small,
Could find in the inn no lodging at all:

Then they were constrained in a stable to lie,
Where horses and asses they used for to tie,

Their lodging so simple they took it no scorn;
But against the next morning our Saviour was born:

The King of all kings to this world being brought,
Small store of fine linen to wrap him was sought;
And when she had swaddled her young son so sweet,
Within an ox manger she laid him to sleep:

Then God sent an angel from heaven so high,
To certain poor shepherds in fields where they lie,
And bade them no longer in sorrow to stay,
Because that our Saviour was born on this day:

Then presently after the shepherds did spy
A number of angels that stood in the sky;
They joyfully talked, and sweetly did sing,
To God be all glory, our heavenly King:

IN THE TOWN
Nous voici dans la ville (French, before 1450)

Joseph   Take heart, the journey's ended:
          I see the twinkling lights,
          Where we shall be befriended
          On this night of nights.

Mary   Now praise the Lord that led us
          So safe unto the town
          Where men will feed and bed us.
          And I can lay me down.

Joseph   And how then shall we praise him?
          Alas, my heart is sore
          That we have no gifts to take him
          Who are so very poor.

Mary   We have as much as any
          Who on the earth do live.
          Although we have no penny,
          We have ourselves to give.

Joseph   Look yonder, wife, look yonder!
A hostelry I see
Where travellers that wander
Will very welcome be.

Mary   The house is tall and stately
The door stands open thus;
Yet, husband, I fear greatly
That inn is not for us.

Joseph   God save you gentle master,
Your littlest room indeed
With plainest walls of plaster
Tonight will serve our need.

Host   For lordings and for ladies
I've lodging and to spare
For you and yonder maid is
No closet anywhere.

Joseph   Take heart, take heart, sweet Mary,
Another inn I spy,
Whose host will not be chary
To let us easy lie.

Mary   Oh, aid me, I am ailing
My strength is nearly gone;
I feel my limbs are failing,
And yet we must go on.

Joseph   God save you, Hostess, kindly!
I pray you house my wife,
Who bears beside me blindly
The burden of her life.

Hostess   My guests are rich men's daughters
And sons, I'd have you know!
Seek out the poorer quarters
Where ragged people go.

Joseph   Good sir, my wife's in labour
Some corner let us keep.

Host   Not I! Knock up my neighbour,
As for me, I'll sleep.

Mary   In all the lighted city
Where rich men welcome win,
Will not one house for pity
Take two poor strangers in?

Joseph   Good woman, I implore you,
Afford my wife a bed.

Hostess   Nay, nay, I've nothing for you
Except the cattle shed.

Mary   Then gladly in the manger
Our bodies we will house
Since men tonight are stranger
Than asses are and cows.

Joseph   Take heart, take heart, sweet Mary,
The cattle are our friends;
Lie down, lie down, sweet Mary,
For here our journey ends.

Mary   Now praise the Lord that found me
The shelter in the town,
Where I with friends around me
May lay my burden down.

The theme of the holy family seeking a room in an inn came to be acted out as a pageant with processions going from place to place in the evenings before Christmas. Such pageants were popular in Spain and later Latin America. For a description of one, see below Chapter VI.

THE HOLY WELL

As it fell out one May morning,
And upon a bright holiday,
Sweet Jesus asked of his dear mother
If he might go to play. (*twice*)
To play, to play, sweet Jesus shall go
And to play now get you gone

78

And let me hear of no complaint
At night when you come home. (*twice*)

Sweet Jesus went down to yonder town.
As far as the Holy Well.
And there did see as fine children
As any tongue can tell.
He said, 'God bless you every one.
And your bodies Christ save and see
And now, little children, I'll play with you
And you shall play with me.'

But they made answer to him, 'No,
Thou art meaner than us all;
Thou art but a simple fair maid's child
Born in an ox's stall.'
Sweet Jesus turned him round about,
Neither laughed, nor smiled, nor spoke
But the tears came trickling from his eyes
Like waters from the rock.

Sweet Jesus turned him round about
To his mother's dear home went he
And said, 'I have been in yonder town
As after you may see:
I have been in yonder town
As far as the Holy Well:
There did I meet with as fair children
As any tongue can tell.'

I said, 'God bless you every one,
And your bodies Christ save and see,
And now, little children, I'll play with you,
And you shall play with me.'
But they made answer to me, 'No.'
They were lords' and ladies' sons,
And I the meanest of them all,
Born in an ox's stall.

'Though you are but a maiden's child
Born in an ox's stall
You are the Christ, the king of heaven
And Saviour of them all.
Sweet Jesus, go down to yonder town,
As far as the Holy Well,
And take away those sinful souls
And dip them deep in hell.'

'Nay, nay,' sweet Jesus smiled and said,
'Nay, nay, that may not be,
For there are too many sinful souls
Crying out for the help of me.'
Then up spoke the angel Gabriel,
Upon a good set steven
'Although you are but a maiden's child,
You are the King of Heaven.'

WAKING TIME
Voisin, d'ou venait ce grand bruit? (French)

Neighbour, what was the sound, I pray
That did awake me as I lay,

And to their doorways brought the people?
Everyone heard it like a chime
Pealing for joy within a steeple,
'Get up, good folk, 'tis waking time!
Get up, good folk, 'tis waking time!'

Nay then, young Martin, know you not
That it is this our native spot
Sweet Love has chosen for his dwelling?
In every quarter rumors hum.
Rumors of news beyond all telling:
'Wake up, good folk! Wake up for Christ is come.
Wake up, good folk for Christ is come.'

Neighbours, and is it really true,
True that the babe so small and new
is lying even now among us?
What can we lay upon his knees –
He whose arrival angels sung us.
What can we give,
What can we give the child to please?

Dickin shall bring a ball of silk,
Peter, his son, a pot of milk,
And Tom a sparrow and a linnet,
Robin a cheese, and Ralf the half
Part of a cake with cherries in it,
And jolly Jack,
And jolly Jack a little calf.

I think this child will come to be
Some sort of workman such as we,
So he shall have my tools and chattels.
My well-set saw, my plane, my drill,
My hammer that so merry rattles,
And planks of wood,
And planks of wood to work at will.

When we have made our offerings.
Saying to him the little things

Whereof all babies born are witting.
Then we will leave and go.
Bidding goodnight in manner fitting –
Hush, hush wee lamb,
Hush, hush, wee lamb, dream sweetly so.

TORCHES
(A Spanish Christmas carol)

Torches, torches, run with torches
All the way to Bethlehem!
Christ is born and now lies sleeping:
Come and sing your song to him!

Ah, ro-ro, ro-ro my baby,
Ah, ro-ro, my love, ro-ro:
Sleep you well, my heart's own darling,
While we sing you our ro-ro.

Sing, my friends, and make you merry,
Joy and mirth and joy again:
Lo, he lives, the King of heaven,
Now and evermore. Amen.

MACARONIC HYMNS AND CAROLS

The word *macaronic* was coined by Italian writers in the fifteenth century. Initially the term referred only to Latin verse which included vernacular phrases, usually introduced for comic or satirical effect. Over time the definition of *macaronic* expanded and today it is employed to describe almost any combination of two (or more) languages in a song or a poem. Many macaronic hymns, poems and carols became popular in the medieval period. Scholars have advanced a number of explanations for their origin. Some believe that clerics, knowing the Latin liturgy simply borrowed quotations from biblical texts, canticles, hymns or prayers and combined them with their every day language. Others think the authors were mostly laymen who were familiar, as were most educated people, with some Latin. Local conditions could also encourage the mixture of other languages. After the Norman conquest of England the upper classes generally spoke a version of French and the populace Old English until the mid fourteenth century. In Ireland and Wales four languages (the Celtic vernacular, French, English and Latin) were all in use at that period.

Macaronic Christmas hymns date from at least as early as the thirteenth century and, along with less formal carols, had become widely popular by the fifteenth. Here are a few examples. The first is a translation of a part of a Latin hymn, with the last line of each verse still in Latin.[13]

There is no rose of such virtue,
As is the rose that bare Jesu,
Alleluia!

For in this rose contained was
Heaven and earth in little space,
Res miranda [a marvelous thing]!

By that rose we may well see,
There be one God in Persons Three,
Pares forma [equal in form].

The following hymn to the Virgin, written in Middle English, has six verses. Each verse starts with the greeting *Heil*, and the last line of each verse is in Latin. Below, the first and last lines are given for verses 1-5, along with the last verse in full. The English has been modernised and the Latin translated.[14]

I
Hail be thou, Mary, the mother of Christ,
...
Ave regina celorum [Hail queen of Heaven]!

II
Hail comely queen, comforter of care!
...
Mater regis angelorum [Mother of the king of angels]!

III
Hail crowned queen, fairest of all!
...
O maria, flos virginum [O Mary, flower of virgins].

IV
Hail fairest that ever god found,
...
Velud rosa vel lilium [Like a rose or lily].

V
Hail be thou goodly ground of grace!
...
Funde preces ad filium [Pour forth prayers for the son].

VI

Hail be thou virgin of virgins!
Hail blessed mother! hail blessed may [maiden]!

Hail nourisher of sweet Jesus!
Hail chiefest of chastity, forsooth to say!
Lady, keep us so in our last day
That we may come to thy kingdom!
For me and all Christians you pray,
Pro salute fidelium. [For the salvation of the faithful.] Amen

One popular medieval legend was that animals could talk to each other on Christmas eve.
According to the following traditional carol (date unknown), they spoke in Latin.

The cock crowed, *Christus natus est.* [Christ is born]
The raven asked, *Quando?* [when]
The crow replied, *Hoc nocte.* [this night]
The ox cried out, *Ubi, ubi?* [where, where]
The sheep bleated out, *Bethlehem;*
And a voice from Heaven sounded, *Gloria in Excelsis.*

Macaronic carols were not exclusively religious. One of the most widely known honoured the ancient custom of serving a boar's head for Christmas dinner, which had pagan
origins.[15]

Solo The Boar's head in hand bear I,
Bedecked with bays and rosemary;
And I pray you my masters, be merry,
Quot estis in convivio [As many as are at the dinner].

chorus

Caput apri defero [I offer the head of a boar],
Reddens laudes Domino [Rendering praise to the Lord].

The Boar's head, as I understand,
Is the bravest dish in all the land;
When thus bedeck'd with a gay garland,
Let us *servire cantico* [serve it with a song].

chorus

Oure steward hath provided this
In honour of the King of Bliss;
Which on this day to be served is
In Regimensi Atrio [In the abbey's hall].

chorus

CHAPTER IV

Christmas Celebrations, Feasts and Revels from the Late Middle Ages to the 18th Century

The bittre frostes, with sleet and reyn'
Destroyed hath the grene in every yerd
Janus sit by the fyr, with double berd
And drynketh of his bugle horn the wyn;
Biforn hym stant brawen of tusked swyn.
And 'Nowel' crieth every lusty man.

Chaucer, *Franklin's Tale*

Two of the carols in the previous chapter illustrate how ordinary people celebrated Christmas with music, processions and dancing. Although most carols express a sense of sincere religious feeling, a few were purely secular. One of the earliest Anglo-Norman carols was a thirteenth-century drinking song. By then, and probably much earlier, the feast of the Nativity had become an occasion for merrymaking as well as worship. The term *merry*, so closely associated in our minds with Christmas, comes from the Saxon word for *mirth*.

MANORIAL CHRISTMAS DUES & FEASTS

Christmas was the major rural festival in medieval England. It came after all the crops had been harvested, during a pause in the agricultural year. It was a time of leisure and of rel-

86

ative abundance. Animals that could not be fed during the lean winter months were butchered and eaten. At Christmas tenants were bound to bring the lord a *lok* or gift, such as so many chickens or so much brewed ale. In return the lord gave them a Christmas dinner. The following excerpt, from a Somerset manor roll of 1314, is as an example. One John de Chappe, with a partner and tenants, held two and a half yardlands. Upon presenting his gifts at Christmas, he along with two others were to receive bread, beef, bacon, chicken and all the beer they could drink in a day, along with fuel to cook the food and two candles 'to burn from dinner to even'.[1]

Such communal Christmas dinners were well established by the close of the thirteenth century. They must go back at least a century or two, maybe to Anglo-Saxon times; *Lok* is a Saxon word. The custom long continued. In his *Hundreth Good Points of Husbandrie*, London 1557, Thomas Tusser remarks:[2]

At Christmas be merry, and thankfull withall,
And feast thy poore neighbors, the great with the small.

In the 1680s Sir John Reresby gave his tenants Christmas dinners, and a hundred years later Parson Woodforde regularly invited the poor old men of his parish to share his ample Christmas fare and gave them each a shilling as well.

Medieval kings and courtiers, as well as lords and peasants, celebrated the feast of the Nativity. An early biography of William the Conqueror states that he liked to give sumptuous feasts to his nobles on the high festival days of the year – Easter, Whitsunday and Christmas. By the fourteenth century the English court observed Christmas with elabo-

rate festivities. In his *Description of London* (1598), John Stow includes what appears to be a contemporary account of the entertainment provided the young Richard II in 1377 by a group of London mummers.[3]

LONDON MUMMERS ENTERTAIN RICHARD II

In the night one hundred and thirty citizens disguised, and well horsed, in a mummery, with sound of trumpets, sackbuts, cornets, shalmes, and other minstrels. And innumerable torch lights of wax, rode from Newgate, through Cheape over the bridge, through Southwarke, and so to Kennington beside Lambeth, where the young prince [Richard II] remained with his mother, the Duke of Lancaster his uncle, ... with divers other lords. In the first rank did ride forty-eight in the likeness and habit of esquires, two and two together, clothed in red coats and gowns of say or sandal, with comely visors on their faces: after them came riding 48 knights in the same livery of colour and stuff. There followed one richly arrayed like an emperor; and after him some distance, one stately attired like a pope, then followed twenty-four cardinals, and after them eight or ten with black visors, not amiable, as if they had been legates from some foreign princes. These maskers, after they had entered Kennington, alighted from their horses, and entered the hall on foot: which done the prince, his mother, and the lords, came out of the chamber into the hall, whom the mummers did salute, showing a pair of dice upon the table their desire to play with the prince, which they so handled that the prince did always win when he cast them. Then the mummers set to the prince three jewels, one after the other, which were a bowl of gold, a cup of gold and a ring of gold, which the prince won at three casts. Then they set to the prince's mother, the duke, the earls, and the other lords, to every one a ring of gold, which they did also win. After which they were feasted, and the music sounded, the prince and the lords danced on the one part, and the mummers which did also dance, which jollity being ended, they were again made to drink, and thus departed as they came.

The next selection, while not written until the late eighteenth century, is like Stow composed largely of transcriptions of earlier documents, chronicles and histories. It too approaches a contemporary source in its language and tone. For example, the first part is drawn from King Edward III's wardrobe accounts; most of the rest from Tudor sources. The author, Joseph Strutt (d. 1802), was an engraver, antiquarian and a pioneer in the field of social history. The excerpts all come from his last book, *The Sports and Pastimes of the People of England*, published in 1801.[4]

CHRISTMAS AT THE ENGLISH COURT

There was another species of entertainment which differed materially from any of the pastimes mentioned, the plays exhibited at court in the Christmas holidays: we trace them as far back as the reign of Edward III (d. 1377). The preparations made for them at that time are mentioned without the least indication of novelty, which admits of the supposition that they were still more ancient. From the numeration of the dresses appropriated in 1348, which consisted of various kinds of disguisements, they seem to have merited rather the denomination of mummeries than of theatrical divertisments. The king then kept his Christmas at his castle in Guildford; the dresses are said to be *ad faciendum lodos domini regis* (made for the king's plays) and consisted of eighty tunics of buckram of various colours; forty-two visors of different similitudes, namely, fourteen of faces of women, fourteen faces of men, and fourteen heads of angels made with silver; twenty-eight crests; fourteen mantles embroidered with heads of dragons; fourteen white tunics wrought with the heads and wings of peacocks; fourteen with the heads of swans with wings, fourteen tunics painted with the eyes of peacocks; fourteen tunics of English linen painted; and fourteen other tunics embroidered with stars of gold. How far these plays were enlivened with dialogue ... is not known; but probably they partook more of the feats of pantomime than colloquial excellency, and were more calculated to amuse the sight than to instruct the mind.

The magnificent pageants and disguisings frequently exhibited at court in the succeeding times, and especially in the reign of Henry VIII (1509-1547) no doubt originated from the *ludi* above mentioned. These mummeries ... [had as] their chief aim to surprise the spectators by the ridiculous and exaggerated oddity of their visors, and by the singularity and splendour of the dresses; every thing was out of nature and propriety ...

The reader may form some judgment of the appearance the actors made upon these occasions from the following engravings ... taken from a beautiful manuscript in the Bodleian Library, written and illuminated in the reign of Edward III.

The performance seems to have consisted chiefly in dancing, and the mummers were usually attended by minstrels playing upon different kinds of musical instruments.

Many of these stately shows are described at length by Hall and Holinshed; and, as some of my readers may not have those authors near at hand, I will subjoin the account of two of them in Hall's own words. [Strutt gives the original spelling; here it has been modernised.]

> In the fifth year of the reign of Henry VIII, his majesty kept Christmas at Greenwich and, according to custom, there came into the great hall, a mount called rich mount. This mount was full of rich flowers of silk, and especially of broom slips full of pods, the branches were green satin and the flowers flat gold of damask which signifies Plantagenet; on the top stood a goodly beacon giving light. Round about the beacon sat the king and five others all in coats and caps of bright crimson velvet, embroidered with flat gold of damask, their coats set full of spangles of gold. And four woodhouses drew the mount 'till it came before the queen, and the king and his companions descended and danced. Then suddenly the mount opened, and out came six ladies all in crimson satin and plunket, embroidered with gold and pearl, with French hoods on their heads, and they danced alone. Then the lords of the mount took the ladies and danced together, and the ladies reentered, and the mount closed, and so was conveyed out of the hall.

The woodhouses, in the preceding quotation, or wodehouses, as they are sometimes called, were wild or savage men; and in this instance, men dressed up with skins, or rugs resembling skins, so as to appear like savages.

THE LORD OF MISRULE

It is said of the English, that formerly they were remarkable for the manner in which they celebrated the festival of Christmas; in which season they admitted variety of sports and pastimes not known, or little practised in other countries. The mock prince, or lord of misrule, whose reign extended through the greater part of the holidays, is particularly remarked by foreign writers, who consider him as a personage rarely to be met with out of England; and, two or three centuries back, perhaps this observation might be consistent with the truth; but I trust we shall upon due examination be ready to conclude, that anciently this frolicksome monarch was well known upon the continent, where he probably received his first honours [his origins possibly go back to the Roman Saturnalia]. In this kingdom his power and his dignities suffered no diminution, but on the contrary were established by royal authority ... In some great families, and also sometimes at court, this officer was called the Abbot of Misrule. Leland says, 'This Christmas [1489] saw no disguisings at court, and right few players: but there was an abbot of misrule that made much sport, and did right well his office.' In Scotland he was called the Abbot of Unreason, and prohibited there in 1555 by the parliament.

Holinshed, speaking of Christmas [says that], 'there is always one appointed to make sport at courts called commonly lord of misrule, whose office is not unknown to such as have been brought up in noblemen's houses and among great housekeepers, which use liberal feasting in the season.' Again: 'At the feast of Christmas,' says Stow, 'in the king's court wherever he chanced to reside, there was appointed a lord of misrule, or master of merry disports; the same merry fellow made his appearance at the house of every nobleman and person of distinction, and among the rest the lord mayor of London and the sheriffs had severally their lord of misrule, ever contending, without quarrel or offence, who should make the rarest pastimes to delight the beholders. This pageant potentate began his misrule at All-Hallows' eve, and continued the same till the morrow of the feast of the Purification [February 2]; in which space there were fine and subtle disguisings, masks and mummeries.'

This master of merry disports was not confined to the court nor to the

houses of the opulent, he was also elected in various parishes, where indeed, his reign seems to have been of shorter date. [Strutt here quotes Philip Stubbs, a late sixteenth-century writer.]

First of all, the wild heads of the parish flocking together, choose them a grand captain of mischief, whom they ennoble with the title of Lord of Misrule; and him they crown with great solemnity, and adopt for their king. This king annointed chooseth forth twenty, forty, threescore, or a hundred lusty men like himself; to wait upon his lordly majesty, and to guard his noble person. Then every one of these men he investeth with is liveries of green, yellow, or some other light, wanton colour, and, as though they were not gaudy enough, they bedeck themselves with scarfs, ribbons and laces, hung all over with gold rings, precious stones, and other jewels. This done, they tie about either leg twenty or forty bells with rich handkerchiefs in their hands, and sometimes laid accross their shoulders and necks, borrowed, for the most part of their pretty mopsies and loving Bessies. Thus all things set in order, then have they their hobby horses, their dragons, and other antiques, together with their bawdy pipers and thundering drummers, to strike up the devil's dance with all. Then march this heathen company towards the church, their pipers piping, their drummers drumming, their stumps dancing, their bells jingling, their handkerchiefs fluttering, about their heads like mad men, their hobby horses and other monsters skirmishing amongst the throng. And in this sort they go to the church, tough the minister be at prayer or preaching, dancing and singing like devils incarnate, with such a confused noise that no man can have his own voice. Then the foolish people they look, they stare, they laugh, they fleer [grimace], and mount upon the forms and pews to see these goodly pageants solemnized. Then after this, about the church they go again and again, and so forth into the church yard, where they have commonly their summer-halls, their bowers, arbours, and banqueting-houses set up, wherein they feast, banquet, and dance all that day, and peradventure all night too …

For the further ennobling of this honourable lord, they have certain papers wherein is painted some childish, or imaginary work, and these they call my Lord of Misrule's badges or cognizanes. These they give to every one that will give them money to maintain them

in this their heathenish devilry; and who will not show himself
buxom to them and give them money, they shall be mocked and
flouted shamefully; yea, and many times carried upon a cowlstaff,
and dived over head and ears in water, or otherwise most horridly
abused. And so besotted are some that they not only give them
money, but wear their badges or recognizances in their hats or caps
openly. Another sort of fantastical fools bring to these hellhounds,
the Lord of Misrule and his complices, some bread, some good ale,
some new cheese, some old cheese some custards, some cracknels
[biscuits], some cakes, some flauns [cheese cakes], some tarts, some
cream, some meat, some one thing, some another.

THE KING OF THE BEAN AND THE ORIGIN OF KING CAKES

The King of the Bean's reign commenced upon the vigil of Epiphany, or
upon the day itself. [Sir William Dugdale wrote in 1666 that] 'it was a
common Christmas gambol in both our universities, and continued to be
usual in other places, to give the name of king or queen to that person
whose extraordinary good luck it was to hit upon that part of a divided
cake which was honoured above others by having a bean in it.' The
reader will readily trace the vestige of this custom, though somewhat dif-
ferently managed, and without the bean, in the present [1800] method of
drawing, as it is called, for king and queen upon Twelfth day.

Another vestige of this custom, or a related one, which apparently began in medieval
France, survives today in New Orleans. From Epiphany to Ash Wednesday people serve
king cakes in homes and offices. In each cake is a minute baby doll. Whoever happens to
find the baby in his or her piece of cake is supposed to bring the *king cake* to the next
party.

THE FESTIVAL OF FOOLS

Strutt goes on to describe other versions of the lord of misrule tradition. One was the
Festival of Fools, popular in medieval France and probably also in England. The festivals,
he says, were always exhibited at Christmas-time or near to it.

In each of the cathedral churches there was a bishop, or an archbishop of
fools, elected: and in churches immediately dependent upon the papal see
a pope of fools. These mock pontiffs had usually a proper suit of ecclesiastics who attended upon them, and assisted at the divine service, most of
them attired in ridiculous dresses resembling pantomimical players and

buffoons. They were accompanied by large crowds of the laity, some being disguised with masks of monstrous fashion, and others having their faces smutted; in one instance to frighten the beholders, and in the other to excite their laughter. And some, again, assuming the habits of females, practised all the wanton airs of the loosest and most abandoned of the sex.

During divine service this motley crowd were not contented with singing of indecent songs in the choir, but some of them ate, and drank, and played at dice upon the altar, by the side of the priest who celebrated the mass. After the service they put filth in the censers, and ran about the church, leaping, dancing, laughing, singing, breaking obscene jests and exposing themselves in the most unseemly attitudes with shameless impudence …

The bishop, or the pope of fools, performed the divine service habited in the pontifical garments, and gave the benediction to the people before they quitted the church. He was afterwards seated in an open carriage, and drawn about to the different parts of the town, attended by a large train of ecclesiastics and laymen promiscuously mingled together; and many of the most profligate of the latter assumed clerical habits in order to give their impious fooleries the greater effect; they had also with them carts filled with ordure [manure], which they threw occasionally upon the populace assembled to see the procession.

THE BOY-BISHOP

The election and the investment of the boy-bishop was certainly derived from the festival of fools. It does not appear at what period this ceremony was first established, but probably it was ancient, at least we can trace it back to the fourteenth century. In all of the collegiate churches, at the feast of St Nicholas, or of the Holy Innocents, and frequently at both, it was customary for one of the children of the choir, completely apparelled in the episcopal investments, with a mitre and crosier, to bear the title and state of a bishop. He exacted a ceremonial obedience from his fellows, who being dressed like priests, took possession of the church, and performed all of the ceremonies and offices which might have been celebrated by a bishop and his prebendaries.

Warton, and the author of the manuscript he has followed, add 'the mass excepted'; but the proclamation of Henry VIII, for the abolition of the custom, proves they did 'singe mass'.

Colet, dean of St Paul's, though he was a wise and good man, countenanced this idle farce and, in the statutes for his school at St Paul's, expressly orders that the scholars 'shall, every Childermas, that is, Innocents-day, come to Paul's church, and hear the Child Bishop's sermon, and after be at high mass, and each of them offer a penny to the child bishop; and with them the masters and suvyors of the school … After having performed divine service, the boy-bishop and his associates went about to different parts of the town, and visited the religious houses, collecting money. These ceremonies and processions were formally abrogated by proclamation from the king in council in 1542 [but revived by Queen Mary]. In the second year of her reign an edict, dated November 13, 1554, was issued from the bishop of London to all the clergy of his diocese, to have a boy-bishop in procession. The year following, 'the child bishop of Paul's church, with his company,' were admitted into the queen's privy chamber, where he sang before her on St Nicholas-day and upon Holy Innocents'-day. Again the next year, says Strype, 'on Saint Nicholas-even, that is a boy habited like a bishop in pontificalibus, went abroad in most parts of London, singing after the old fashion; and was received with many ignorant but well-disposed people into their houses, and had as much good cheeres ever was wont to be had before.' After the death of Mary this silly mummery was totally discontinued.

It is evident that Strutt, and some of the historians he quotes, shared a Protestant antipathy for many of the Catholic traditions inherited from the medieval period.

The Puritan point of view could not comprehend how people could combine satire and even sacrilegious behaviour with deep faith. The conflict between older customs and beliefs and Puritanism grew in intensity after Mary's death in 1558, eventually culminating in the civil wars of the next century. During Elizabeth's reign the buoyant spirit of the renaissance counterbalanced the intensity of religious conflict with a worldly *joie de vivre*.

Christmas celebrations continued unchecked well into the Stuart period. The degree to which the season's festivities had become institutionalised is illustrated by the following excerpts from Gerald Leigh's description (published in 1576) of Christmas ceremonies at the Middle Temple, one of the inns of the court where London lawyers resided and trained candidates for the legal profession.

HOW ELIZABETHAN LAWYERS CELEBRATED CHRISTMAS[5]

Christmas Eve. The Marshall at dinner is to place at the highest table's end, and next to the library, all on one side therof, the most antient persons in the company present: the Dean of the Chapel next to him; then an Antient or Bencher, beneath him. At the other end of the table the Sewer [official in charge of serving the dinner], Cup-bearer, and Carver. At the upper end of the bench-table, the King's Serjeant and Chief Butler; and when the Steward hath served in, and set the on the table the first mess, then he is also to sit down.

Also at the upper end of the other table, on the other side of the Hall, are to be placed the three Masters of the Revels: and at the bench-table are to sit, the King's Attorney, the Ranger of the Forest, and the Master of the Game. And at the lower end of the table, in the other side of the Hall, the fourth Master of the Revels, the Common Serjeant, and Constable-Marshall. And at the upper end of the Utter-Barrister's table, the Marshall sitteth, when he hath served in the first mess; the Clark of the Kitchen also, and the Clark of the Sowce-tub, when they have done their offices in the kitchen, sit down. And at the upper end of the Clark's table, the Lieutenant of the Tower, and the attendant to the Buttery, are placed ...

At the first course the minstrels must sound their instruments, and go before; and the Steward and Marshall are next to follow together; and after them the Gentlemen Server; and then cometh the meat. Those three officers are to make altogether three solemn curtesies, at three several times, between the skreen and the upper table ...

When the first table is set and served, the Steward's table is next to be served. And after him the Master's table of the Revells, then that of the Master of the Game ... all which time the musick must stand right above the harth side, with the noise of their musick; their faces direct towards the highest table; and that done, to return to the Buttery with their musick sounding.

At the second course every table is served, as at the first course, in every respect; which performed, the Servitors and Musicians are to resort to the place assigned for them to dine at; which is the Valects or Yeoman's table, beneath the skreen. Dinner ended, the Musicians prepare to sing a song at the highest table ...

Then, after a little repose, the persons at the highest table arise, and prepare to revells; in which time, the Butlers, and other Servants with them, are to dine in the library ...

At night, before supper, are revels and dancing, and so after supper, during the twelve daies of Christmas. The antienest Master of the Revels is, after dinner, to sing a carol or song; and command other gentlemen then there present to sing with him and the company; and so it is very decently performed.

Christmas Day. Service in the Church ended, the Gentlemen presently repair to the Hall to breakfast, with brawn, mustrad and malmsley.

At dinner the Butler, appointed for the Grand Christmas, is to see the tables covered and furnished: the ordinary Butlers of the House are decently to set bread, napkins, and trenchers, in good form, at every table; with spoons and knives.

At the first course is served in a fair and large boar's head, upon a silver platter, with minstralsye. Two Gentlemen in gowns are to attend at supper, and to bear two fair torches of wax, next before the Musicians and Trumpetters, and stand above the fire with the musick, till the first course be served in through the Hall. Which performed, they with the musick, are to return into the Buttery. The like course is to be observed in all things during the time of Christmas.

Leigh goes on to describe variations in the ceremonies to mark: St Stephen's day, St John's day, Childermas [Holy Innocents' day]. He states that New Year's day is 'Banqueting Night', as solemn an occasion as Chistmas eve.

It is proper to the Butler's office, to give warning to every House [Inn] of Court, of this banquet; to the end that they, and the Innes of Chancery, be invited thereto, to see a play and mask. The Hall is to be furnished with scaffolds to sit on, for Ladies to behold the sports, on each side. Which ended, the Ladyse are to be brought into the Library, unto the banquet there.

Leigh does not say what plays were given at the Temple on New Year's Day; very possibly they were of classical origin or inspiration. Renaissance enthusiasm for the classical heritage led to a keen interest in Roman festivals such as the Saturnalia and Kalends. Christmas plays performed by the lawyers at Gray's Inn and by the fellows and students of several Oxford colleges featured the Roman holidays. A lengthly manuscript recounting the Christmas revels at St John's College, Oxford, 1607-8 (the same year the settlers in Jamestown endured their first winter) provides an example of the extent to which a Christmas celebration could become a totally secular, and essentially pagan festival.

REVELS AT ST JOHN'S COLLEGE OXFORD, 1607-1608

Philip Bliss published parts of the manuscript under the title *The Christmas Prince* in the nineteenth century. The manuscript itself bears no title; it simply begins with the statement: *A true and faithfull relation of the risinge and fall of Thomas Tucker, Prince of Alba Fortunae, Lord of St John etc., with the occurrents which happened throughout his Domination.*

The narrative starts with the election of 'the Prince or Lord of the Revells' on All Saints' day, November 1, 1607. His installation as prince took place on St Andrew's day, November 30; his reign came to an end on Shrove Tuesday, February 9, 1608. The manuscript contains nine plays (originally ten, one was lost) and two interludes. The prince's enthronement and dethronement are the subjects of the first and last plays; *Ara Fortunae* and *Ira Fortunae*. Six of the dramatic pieces are in Latin, three in English. The play, performed on December 25, was a Latin drama called *Saturnalia*, It begins with the inversion theme, a slave changes places with his master; then, borrowing from the Roman playwright Macrobius, goes on to relate how Hercules instituted the *Saturnalia* by erecting an altar to Saturn in thanks for the god's aid. None of the nine plays has any connection with the Nativity except that the prologue to *Saturnalia* attributes the origin of Christmas candles to the Roman festival, and the epilogue points out similarities between the *Saturnalia* in its purified form and Christmas. The six Latin plays seem to have been composed primarily to display the urbane wit and classical scholarship of the authors, actors and academic audience. Much the same can be said of the three English plays, although one of them, *Time's Complaint*, has a contemporary touch, two everyday comic characters – a drunken cobbler and thief, Humphrey Swallow, and a woman pub-keeper, Goodwife Spiggot. *Time's Complaint* was appropriately presented on New Year's day. The selections below give a sample of the play's style. Time, who unwittingly falls asleep next to the loot Swallow has stolen from Goodwife Spiggot, is accused of theft. At the opening of the play poor Time is waiting to appeal to the Prince for justice.

SELECTIONS FROM 'TIME'S COMPLAINT'[6]

Enter the Prince, Lord Chamberlain, Lord Treasurer and other members of the royal procession.

Ld. Chamb.	What would this old man have?
Time	God save your honour
	I have a poore petition to the Prince.

Ld. Chamb.	I will preferre it to him.
Time	O noe my Lord I can doe that my selfe.
Ld. Chamb.	Avaunt base peasant, doting foole bee gone,
	Doest thou refuse my kindness?
Time	Noe not soe, but I suspect when great men soe soone move,
	'Tis rather for advantage than for love.
Ld Chamb.	The Prince will not receave petitions now,
Time	Who told you soe? God bless your Majestie
	O pitie mee, pitie distressed Time.
Ld. Treas.	Awaie thou bawling varlet ...

Time succeeds in presenting his petition to the Prince.

Prince	Is thy name Time?
Time	Yes, and 't like your grace.
Ld. Treas.	A most lewd fellowe full of all disorders
	Whom all the land complaines of.
Time	But unjustlie
	As I shall shew; if you will heare mee speake.
Prince	Speake freelie man, we graunt thee libertie.
Time	Sound out my woes, sad solemn harmony;
	For Time and Musick alwaies well agree.

After a flourish of music Time presents his prologue, explaining how he has been unjustly blamed for crimes and calamities, such as Caesar's death:

> Here are a fearful Ides of March indeed,
> The morning cleere, good words in all men's mouths.
> All haile and Ave Caesar at the gates,
> My acclamations in the market place,
> And yet before the glorious Sunne attain'd,
> The middle poynt of this our Hemi-sphere:
> The daie was overcast, the world was chang'd
> Time curst with piteous out-cries: when as rather
> They should have curst the sonne that kild the father.

The play is concerned with time on two levels. Literally speaking, the plot deals with Time's alleged theft of Goodwife Spiggot's belongings. Metaphorically, it shows how time is blamed for all our failings and misfortunes. In the final act Time's daughter, Veritas, disposes of both charges.

Enter Studioso, Veritas, Opinion, Errour, Bellicos [a cashiered soldier] Clineas [a bankrupt yeoman].

Studioso addresses Veritas.

Studioso	Faire creature doe not still goe hudwinckt thus,
	Unmaske thy bewty to a Schollers eies
	Who doth adore thy sacred deitie,
	Let not the world in a perpetuall night
	Involved lie because it wants your light.

Veritas	Schollars I graunt love mee and speake mee faire
	But there hard fortune is to plaine a baite
	To sharpe a hooke for truth to nibble at.

At this point Opinion and Errour demand to be consulted. Bellicose extolls Opinion's merits and Clineas the virtues of Errour. Studioso defends Veritas, appealing to her to help her father.

Studioso	Come Una Veritas and goe with mee
	To see thy aged and afflicted Sire
	Afflicted for thy absence prittie maide.
Veritas	Alas I cannot helpe or comfort him,
	I alwaies lookt for comfort at his hands
	But have found none; for dutie yet I'le goe.
Errour	Doe not believe him:
Clineas	No in faith not,
	I alwaies tooke him for a smooth tongued rascall.
Opinion	Doe not believe him Sir:
Bellicos	Not I by Mars
	I knowe him for a most white-livered coward
	I will maintaine my brave Opinion
	Through all the world:
Veritas	My father, oh my father
	Who hath thus us'de thee?
Studioso	What is Time a-sleep?
	No marveile then if Truth sit downe and weepe.
	Rise up faire maide I will rouze up this Time
	This sluggish age, and hallowe in his eares
	The scourge of vice. So, ho, what Time I say
	Soe overwhelm'd with vaine securitie?
	Awake for shame looke upp. and see thy self.

Studioso goes on to recount the evils of the times: drunkeness, gluttony, avarice, lust, theft, murder – all active while time, unheeding, slept on.

Time	I am amaz'd; Nay, am I not asleepe

	Is not all this a dreame, a vision?
Studioso	Noe good Time all is true, your daughter too;
Time	What Veritas my daughter:
Veritas	A blessing father,
Time	Now Jove and bright Apollo shine on thee,
	That all the world may see thy beauties grace,
	Truth doth not hide her face, why hid'st thou thine?
Veritas	Errour did give mee this brave gaudie scarfe
	To cover my faire face, my tender browe
	From the hot scorching slanders of the world.
Time	Alas pore infaint, how art thou misled?
	To feare the scorching heat of slanderous tongues?
	The sunne is not so bright as thou my daughter.
	Thy piercing beames could scatter Errours mists
	Then for thy fathers sake unmaske thyselfe.
	And live with him. that dies for lacke of thee.
	Shew mee what chance hath brought these sinnes uppon mee
	Which I my selfe am no waie guiltie of.

Enter Justice Philonices, Servus, Swallow and Spiggot.

Philonices	Where is this aged Time thou toldst mee of
	Who is the sole maintainer of all faults?
Servus	Looke where he stands, with all his crimes about him.

Time tells the Justice he has no cause to deal severely with 'afflicted Time'.
Philonices replies:

Doe not upbraide mee with thy benefits,
I have done much for thee; thy daughter Truth
I have maintained openly gainst wrongs
False perjuries, deep slanders; *Verit.* Nay Forbeare
And now let Veritas once shew her selfe.
I must confesse you often are my friend
And help a true cause with a true defence,
Yet I owe you but little thankes for that,
Unlesse my evidence bee plaine and good.
Alas too often with many broiles and jarres
In the crosse waies of discord I am lost.
And sometimes feare, sometimes affection,
Confound mee quite and will not let me speake.

Then doe not boast what you have donne for truth.
This for my selfe. My father thus I quit
This lump of fleshe whome you imagine dead
Is but deaths image drowsie Morpheus prisoner,
Which weariness and sloth hath brought him to.
This drunken man [*Swallowe*] to all sinnes allied
First stole these goods from her [*Spiggot*] then left them here.
It is an old excuse for each new crime
To laie all blame uppon corrupted Time.

Swallowe escapes punishment because he has married Spiggot and thus her goods are his. Time, cleared of all charges thanks his daughter, pleads with her to stay with him. Veritas refuses, the world is too full of deceit. In the play's closing speech, Time replies:

... Nay stay thou hast my hart
A father and his childe must not soe parte.
Rather than thus thou shouldst abandon mee
I doubt not but this present company,
Some honourable patron will afford.
But where? O where? O where? Bright Majestie
Looke downe uppon perplexed miserie,
Repeale concealed truth from banishment,
Ane cure sicke Times consuming lanquishment.
O helpe thou onlie which canst helpe afford,
All may be mended by a Prince's worde.

In all probability, among those watching the performance on January 1, 1608, was a recently appointed fellow of St John's College, William Laud, future archbishop of Canterbury. If so, Laud must have been pleased with its concluding appeal, for he became a strong advocate of the divine right of kings.

CHRISTMAS MASQUES AT THE ROYAL COURT

One of the ways in which the court of King James I and his queen consort, Anne of Denmark, celebrated Christmas was to present a masque, a short musical, allegorical play. In their emphasis on elaborate costumes and dancing the masques resembled the earlier mummers' plays, but were more sophisticated. The early seventeenth century was England's great dramatic age. People of all classes loved nothing better than watching a good show, unless it was being part of one. Queen Anne with her ladies in waiting and courtiers, wearing masks and costumes, were the chief performers. The staging was lavish and spectacular, designed to catch the eye – in short, baroque. The apparel and behaviour of the participants sometimes bordered on the risqué, and drew sharp criticism from

Puritans. The first masque put on by the Court, enacted on Twelfth Night 1605, entitled Masque of Blackness, was written by the gifted playwright and poet Ben Jonson. The theme reflects the fascination of the age with exotic lands and peoples.

SELECTIONS FROM THE MASQUE OF BLACKNESS[7]

First for the scene was drawn a *landtschap* [landscape] consisting of small woods, and here and there a void place filled with huntings; which falling, an artificial sea was seen to shoot forth, as if it flowed to the land, raised with waves which seemed to move, and in some places the billows to break, as imitating that orderly disorder which is common in nature. In front of this sea were placed six Tritons [with trumpets], in moving and sprightly actions, their upper parts human, save their hairs were blue, as partaking of the sea-colour: their disinent parts fish … From their backs were borne out certain light pieces of taffeta, as if carried by the wind, and their music made out of wreathed shells. Behind these, a pair of sea-maids, for song, were as conspicuously seated; between which, two great sea-horses, as big as life, put forth themselves; the one mounting aloft, and writhing his head from the other, which seemed to sink forward; so intended for variation, and that the figure behind them might come off better; upon their backs, Oceanus and Niger were advanced.

Oceanus presented a human form, the colour of his flesh blue; and shadowed with a robe of sea-green; his head grey and horned, as he is described by the ancients; his beard of the like mixed colour: he is garlanded with alga, or sea-grass; and in his hand a trident.

Niger [the African river], in form and colour of an Aethiop; his hair and rare beard curled, shadowed with a blue and bright mantle: his front, neck and wrists adorned with pearl, and crowned with an artificial wreath of cane and paper-rush.

These induced, the masquers, which were twelve nymphs, negroes and daughters of Niger, attended by so many of the Oceanae, which were their light-bearers. The masquers were placed in a great concave shell, like mother of pearl, curiously made to move on those waters and rise with the billow; the top thereof was stuck with a chevron of lights, which ... struck a glorious beam upon them, as they were seated one above the other ...

The attire of the Masquers alike in all, without difference: the colours azure and silver; but returned on the top with a scroll and antique dressing of feathers and jewels interlaced with ropes of pearl. And for the front, ear, neck and wrists, the ornament was of the most choice and orient pearl; best setting off the black [the Queen and her ladies blackened their faces and arms for the performance]. For the Light-bearers, sea-green, waved about the skirts with gold and silver; their hair loose and flowing, garlanded with sea-grass, and that stuck with branches of coral.

Jonson's instructions for the setting and costuming go on for several more paragraphs. Shakespeare's plays may have been presented at the *Globe* without scenery; the court masques were flamboyant in their staging. The text of the masque itself begins with a song.

> Sound, sound aloud
> The welcome of the orient flood,
> Into the West;
> Fair Niger, son to great Oceanus,
> Now hounour'd thus,
> With all his beauteous race;
> Who, though but black in face,
> Yet are they bright,
> And full of light and life.
> To prove that beauty best,
> Which, not the colour, but the feature
> Assures unto the creature.

> *Oceanus*   Be silent, now the ceremony's done,
> And, Niger, say, how comes it, lovely son,
> That thou, the Aethiop's river, so far East

Art seen to fall into the extremest West
Of me, the King of floods, Oceanus,
And in mine Empire's heart, salute me thus?

…

Niger   To do a kind and careful father's part.
In satisfying every pensive heart
Of these my daughters, my most loved birth:
Who, though they were the first form'd dames of Earth,
And in whose sparkling and refulgent eyes,
The glorious Sun did still delight to rise;
Though he, the best judge, and the most formal cause
Of all dames beauties, in their firm hues, draws
Signs of his fervent love; and thereby shows
That in their black, the perfect'st beauty grows;

…

Despite these lines affirming the beauty of their complexion, Niger attributes their black skin to the scorching heat of the Sun and explains that his daughters wish to change it. Niger felt powerless to help them until the daughters told him they had seen a vision of a face 'all circumfused with light' who said to them:

That they a land must forthwith seek
Whose termination of the Greek,
Sounds *Tania*; where bright Sol, that heat
Their bloods, doth never rise or set,
But in his journey passeth by,
And leaves that climate of the sky,
To comfort of a greater light,
Who forms all beauty with his sight.

Niger   In search of this, have we three Princedoms past
That speak out Tania in their accents last;
Black Mauritania, first; and secondly,
Swarth Lusitania; next we did descry
Rich Aquitania: and yet cannot find
The place unto these longing nymphs design'd.
Instruct and aid me, great Oceanus,
What land is this that now appears to us?

Oceanus This land, that lifts into the temperate air
His snowy cliff, is Albion the fair

In 'this blest isle', Britannia, Niger's daughters discover how to change their color and Niger leaves them to return home. This masque must have been impressive to watch; yet despite Jonson's artistry, the masque is obviously more show than substance. It is probably a mistake to see it as a manifestation of either racial tolerance or bigotry.

THE MASQUE OF CHRISTMAS[8]

In 1616 Ben Jonson presented the royal court with a masque with a more popular theme, the defence of Chistmas against Puritan attacks.

The Court being seated,

Enter *Christmas*, with two or three of the guard, attired in round hose, long stockings, a close doublet, a high crowned hat, with a brooch, a long thin beard, a truncheon, little ruffs, white shoes, his scarfs and garters tied cross, and his drum beaten before him.

Why, gentlemen, do you know what you do? Ha! would you have kept me out? CHRISTMAS, old Christmas, Christmas of London, and captain Christmas? Pray you, let me brought before the lord chamberlain, I'll not be answered else: *'Tis merry in hall, when beards wag all:*
I have seen the time you have wish'd for me, for a merry Christmas; and now you have me, they would not let me in: I must come another time! a good jest, as if I could come more than once a year: Why I am no dangerous person, and so I told my friends of the guard. I am old Gregory Christmas still, and though I come out of Pope's-head alley, as good a Protestant as any in my parish. The truth is, I have brought a Masque here, out o' the city, of my own making, and do present it by a set of my sons, that come out of the lanes of London, good dancing boys all ...

Enter his sons and daughters (ten in number) led in, in a string, by CUPID, who is attired in a flat cap, and a prentice coat, with wings at his shoulders.
    MISRULE, in a velvet cap, with a sprig, short cloak, great yellow ruff, like a reveller, his torch-bearer bearing a rope, a cheese, and a basket
    CAROL, a long tawney coat, with a red cap, and a flute at his girdle, his torch-bearer carrying a song-book open.
    MINCED-PIE, like a fine cook's wife, drest neat; her man carrying a pie, dish and spoons.
    GAMBOL, like a tumbler, with a hoop and bells, his torch-bearer arm'd with a colt-staff, and a binding cloth.
    POST AND PAIR, with a pair-royal of aces in his hat; his garment all done over with pairs and purses; his squire carrying a box, cards and counters.
    NEW YEAR'S GIFT, in a blue coat, serving-man like, with an orange, and a sprig of rosemary gilt on his head, his hat full of brooches, with a collar of ginger bread, his torch-bearer carrying a march-pane with a bottle of wine on either arm.

MUMMING, in a masquing pied suit, with a vizard, his torch-bearer carrying the box and ringing it

WASSEL, like a neat sempster and songster, his torch-bearer bearing a brown bowl, drest with ribands and rosemary.

OFFERING, in a short gown, with a porter's staff in his hand, a wyth born before him, and a basin, by his torch-bearer.

BABY-CAKE, drest like a boy, in a fine long coat, biggis bib, muckender, and a little dagger; his usher bearing a great cake, with bean and a pease.

The children of Jonson's *Christmas* account for most of the ways people celebrated the season in early seventeenth-century England: the lord of misrule, caroling, feasting, dancing, drinking, playing games, mumming. The presence of *New Years Gift* suggests that most gifts were then exchanged on New Year's Day, a custom which survives in Scotland and France. Queen Elizabeth I's accounts show that she gave presents to courtiers and servants on New Year's day. On the other hand, in 1557 Tusser wrote:

> At Christmas of Christ many carols we sing
> And give many gifts in the joy of that King.

POPULAR CHRISTMAS CELEBRATIONS

The following poems by Wither and Herrick, and Breton's comments on popular activities during December and on Christmas day, also show that most people celebrated the yule season with singing, feasting, drinking, dancing and games.

CHRISTMAS CARROLL[9]
George Wither (1588?-1667)

Lo! now is come our joyful'st Feast !
Let every Man be jolly.
Each Roome with Yvie leaves is drest,
And each Post with Holly.
Now, all our Neighbours' Chimneys smoke,
And Christmas Blocks are burning;
Their Ovens they with bak't Meats choke
And their Spits are turning.
Without the Doors let sorrow lie;
And if, for cold, it hap to die,
Wee'l bury't in a Christmas pie,
And ever more be merry.

Now, every Lad is wondrous trimm,
And no man minds his Labour.

Our Lasses have provided them
A Bagpipe and a Tabor.
Ranke Misers now doe sparing shun:
Their Hall of Musicke soundeth:
And Dogs thence with whole Shoulders run,
So all Things there aboundeth.
The Countrey Folke themselves advance;
For crowdy muttons come out of France:
And Jack shall pipe, and Jyll shall daunce,
And all the Towne be merry.

CEREMONIES FOR CHRISTMASSE[10]
Robert Herrick (1591-1674)

Come bring with a noise,
My merrie merrie boyes,
The Christmas log to the fire;
While my good Dame, she
Bids you all be free
And drink to your heart's desire

With the last yeere's brand
Light the new block, and
For good success in his spending [burning],
On your psalters play
That sweet luck may
Come while the log is tending,

Drink now the strong beere
Cut the white loaf here,
The white meat on the shredding
For the rare mince-pie
And the plums stand by
To fill the paste that's a kneading.

Selections from *Fantasticks*, by Nicholas Breton[11] (1575?-1626). The spelling and punctuation have been modernised.

DECEMBER

It is now December, and he that walks the streets shall find dirt on his shoes, except he go all in boots. Now doth the lawyer make an end to his harvest, and the client of his purse. Now capons and hens, besides turkeys, geese and ducks, besides beef and mutton, must all die for the great feast, for in twelve days a multitude of people will not be fed with a little. Now plums and spice, sugar and honey square it among [contend with] pies and broth. And 'Gossip I drink to you, and your are welcome, and I thank you, and how do you, and I pray you be merry.'

Now are the tailors and tiremakers [headdress makers] full of work against the holidays; and music must be in tune or else never: the youth must dance and sing, and the aged sit by the fire. It is the Law of Nature, and no contradiction in reason. The ass that hath borne all the year must now take a little rest, and the lean ox must feed till he be fat.

The footman now shall have many a foul step, and the ostler have work about the heels of the horses, while the tapster, if he take not heed, will lie drunk in the cellar. The prices of meat will rise apace, and the apparel of the proud will make the tailor rich. Dice and cards will benefit the butler; and if the cook does not lack wit, he will sweetly lick his fingers. Starchers and launderers will have their hands full of work, and periwigs and painting will not be a little set by. Strange stuffs will be well sold, strange tales well told, strange sights much sought, strange things much bought ... To conclude, I hold it [December] the costly purveyor of excess and the after breeder of necessity, the practice of Folly and the Purgatory of Reason.

CHRISTMAS DAY

It is now Christmas, and not a cup of drink must pass without a carol. The beasts, fowl and fish come to a general execution, and the corn is ground to dust in the bakehouse, and the pastry. Cards and dice purge many a purse. The youth show their agility in shoeing the wild mare [to exact a fine, called footing, from a newcomer, a colt or greenhorn]. Now 'good cheer and welcome, and God be with you, and I thank you.' And against the New Year provide for the presents.

The Lord of Misrule is no mean man for his time, and the guests at the high table must lack no wine. The lusty bloods must look about them like men, and piping and dancing puts away much melancholy. Stolen venison is sweet, and a fat coney is worth money. Pit-falls are now set for small birds, and a woodcock hangs himself in a gynne [snare]. A good fire heats all the house and a full alm's basket makes the beggar's prayers. The maskers and the mummers make the merry sport, but if they lose their money, their drums go dead. Swearers and swaggerers are sent away to the ale-house, and unruly wenches are in danger of judgment. Musicians now make their instruments speak out, and a good song is worth the hearing. In sum, it is a holy time, a duty in Christians, for the remembrance of Christ, and custom among friends, for the maintenance of good fellowship. In brief, I thus conclude of it: I hold it a memory of Heaven's love, and the world's peace; the mirth of the honest, and the meeting of the friendly.

Breton clearly considered Christmas a time for merrymaking and feasting as well as a religious holiday – a time 'of Heaven's love and the world's peace'. So did Robert Herrick. In addition to *Ceremonies for Christmasse* Herrick wrote a Christmas carol which closed with the following two verses:[12]

> The darling of the world is come
> And fit it is we find a room
> To welcome him. The nobler part
> Of all the house here is the heart.
>
> Which we will give him, and bequeath
> This holly and this ivy wreath,
> To do him honour who's our King,
> And Lord of all this revelling.

The carol was part of a Christmas play, *Hesperides*, which Herrick presented to King
Charles at Whitehall, possibly in December 1647, when Charles, defeated by the parliamentary armies, was a prisoner in his own palace. A year later, in December 1648,
Parliament tried him for treason and condemned him to death. He was executed in front
of Whitehall on January 30, 1649.

PURITAN SUPPRESSION OF CHRISTMAS

Puritan attempts to eliminate Christmas as a holiday began in London in 1643 and became
official policy after the overthrow of the monarchy. The Puritan regime, which governed
England during the interregnum (1649-60), consistently opposed Christmas celebrations
and, as is described below, eventually outlawed them. In 1656 the Revd Hezekiah
Woodward wrote a pamphlet denouncing Christmas as:[13]

The old Heathen feasting Day, in honour to Saturn, their Idol-God, the
Papist's Massing Day, the Profane Man's Ranting Day, the Superstitious
Man's Idol Day, the Multitude's Idle Day, Satan's Working Day, the
True Christian's Fasting Day ... We are persuaded no one thing more
hindereth the Gospel work all the year long than doth the observance of
that Idol Day once a year, having so many days of cursed observation

with it.

That year the English House of Commons met on Christmas like any other business day. One of its members recorded the following incident in his diary.[14]

Thursday, December 25, 1656

Major General Disbrowe stood up, but the orders of the day were called for.

Colonel Mathews The House is thin; much, I believe, occasioned by observation of this day. I have a short Bill to prevent the superstition for the future. I desire it to be read.

Mr Robinson I could get no rest all night for the preparation of this foolish day's solemnity. This renders us, in the eyes of the people, to be profane. We are, I doubt [suspect] returning to Popery.

Sir William Strickland It is a very fit time to offer the Bill, this day, to bear your testimony against it, since people observe it with more solemnity than they do the Lord's-day. I desire it may be read.

Major-General Kelsey and *Major Morgan* If this had been ten days since, it might have been in good time; but let not this business jostle out great and eminent business, you having a twelve-month's time to provide this law. It is too late now to make a law against it.

Major-General Packer, Major Audley and *Sir Gilbert Pickering* If ever a bill was welltimed this bill is. You see how the people keep up these superstitious observations to your face; stricter in many places, than they do the Lord's day. One may pass from the Tower to Westminster and not a shop open, not a creature stirring. It is a fit time now.

They desired it might be read.

Mr Godfrey If this Bill had not been moved to be read, I should not have passed it; but seeing you have admitted it to a debate, and at this time, I hope we will all witness against it [the observance of Christmas]: otherwise it will be said abroad that these superstitious days have favourites in this House.

An Act for abolishing and taking away festivals, commonly called holydays, read the first time.

Sir William Strickland proposed that it might be read the second time tomorrow.

The bill passed its second and third readings and became law. The next Christmas the government dispatched troops to arrest anyone attending Christmas services. But abolishing Christmas proved beyond the power of the revolutionary regime, which was now approaching its end. Within two years Cromwell was dead and in the spring of 1660 Charles II landed at Dover. Both the monarchy and the established church were restored;

so too were the season's traditional feasting and celebrations. A Christmas carol appearing in *Poor Robin's Almanack* for 1695 reflects the holiday spirit of England after the restoration of the monarchy.[15]

> Now thrice welcome Christmas, which brings us good Cheer,
> Minced Pies and Plumb porridge, good Ale and strong Beer;
> With Pig, Goose, and Capon, the best that may be.
> So well doth the Weather and our stomachs agree.
>
> Observe how the Chimneys do smoak all about,
> The Cooks are providing for Dinner, no doubt;
> But those on whose tables no Victuals appear,
> O may they keep Lent all the rest of the Year!
>
> With Holly and Ivy so green and so gay;
> We deck up our Houses as fresh as the Day,
> With Bays and Rosemary, and Laurel compleat.
> And every one is a king in conceit.

In 1698, the French traveller, Misson, described the English celebration of Christmas in glowing terms:[16]

From Christmas Day till after Twelfth Day is a time of Christian rejoycing; a mixture of devotion and pleasure. They wish one another happiness; they give treats, and make it their whole business to drive away melancholy. Whereas little presents from one another are made only on the first day of the year in France, they begin here at Christmas; and they are not so much presents from friend to friend, or from, equal to equal (which is less practis'd in England now then formerly) as from superior to inferior. In the taverns the landlord gives part of what is eaten and drank in his house.

Although Puritan attempts to make Christmas into a fast day survived well into the eighteenth century in New England, in England itself they had long become a memory. John Thomlinson noted in his diary for Christmas 1717 that the holiday had been set aside during the civil wars:[17]

And a severe inquisition was set out against the usual fare of this feast, mince pies and plum pudding.

Not only plum puddings and mince pies survived the Puritan era, so did Christmas revels and theatricals, including those of the obstreperous mummers. In December 1773, Horace

Walpole remarked that David Garrick had brought out a new play (*A New Dramatic Entertainment called a Christmas Tale, in Five Parts*). 'It is believed to be Garrick's own, and a new proof that it is possible to be the best actor and the worst author in the world.'[18] Despite Walpole's criticism the play, set in an enchanted island with fairies and evil spirits, was an impressive spectacle with beautiful painted scenery – in the tradition of the royal masques of an earlier age. A new type of dramatic performance appeared at the close of the eighteenth century, the Christmas pantomime.

In 1717, John Rich, the owner of Lincoln's Inn Theatre in London, produced a pantomime, derived from Italian *commedia del'arte*. Various types of pantomime soon became popular in England. One spin-off of the form, was a kind of burlesque with stock characters and situations, superimposed on a children's nursery rhyme or fairy tale. Initially such pieces were performed at several different times of the year, as well as Christmas, but soon they became a distinctly seasonal tradition. Leigh Hunt (1784-1859) wrote that not to like pantomime was:[19]

Not to like motion; not to like love; not to like jest upon dullness and formality; ... not to fancy; not to like a holiday; not to know the pleasure of sitting up at Christmas; not to sympathize with one's own children; not to remember that we have been children ourselves.

While Christmas pantomimes have changed in many ways since Hunt's day, they still retain much of the same spirit. As A.E. Wilson wrote in 1935, the Christmas panto defies 'all theatrical conventions' and gives the actors the chance to 'lead you into the realm that knows nothing of time, space, and human bondage to tyrant nature and its laws'.[20] The Christmas pantomime is possibly an offshoot of the English mummers as well as Italian comedy. Panto actors display many of the attributes of mummers, including cross dressing. The mummers themselves, still common in the eighteenth century, were becoming increasingly rare in the Victorian era, although they survived in rural areas.

MUMMERS' PLAYS

It seems appropriate to close this chapter with the text of a mummers' play which survived into the late nineteenth century. Its text was published by the American Folklore Society in 1909. The play was brought to the attention of a St Louis high school teacher by one of her students who had written down her father's recollection of its wording, The father came from the English midlands, where, as a boy, he had been one of the actors. The cast was trained by an older man (who sometimes played the part of Father Christmas). The troupe went around the neighbourhood stopping in farmhouses. The account explains that:[21]

In old English farmhouses there are usually two kitchens. The back kitchen was used as a waiting room; the front kitchen was the place where the play was given. The kitchen floors were of smooth white stone. Both rooms were heated by means of large open fireplaces, and lighted by large brown candles, usually set in 'horn lanterns' fastened to the walls. The costumes of the players were very crude, intended merely to suggest the characters. Old Father Christmas wore a fur cap and fur gloves, a long red coat and top boots. He had a wig and a beard of long white hair, and the end of his nose was reddened. Beelzebub wore a large black hat, called a dripping pan, and a long black coat, and in his hand carried a club. The Italian Doctor wore a top hat and a swallow-tail coat. The Valiant Soldier wore a blue soldier's suit and a soldier's cap. Little Dick Nipp. wore a hat with a very wide brim, a short coat, and carried a long stick on the end of which a pig's bladder was tied. He was the 'fool' or fun-maker of the play. St George wore a small hat with a feather in it, a dark red coat, knee-breeches, and low shoes, and carried a sword.

From the cast and the costumes it is apparent that the play represented a jumble of characters and historical periods. The presence of the King of Spain (whose outfit is not described) probably goes back to the time of the Spanish armada (1588). Although St George, of course, is older, his red coat and knee-breeches date from the eighteenth century. Perhaps the Italian doctor had his origins in the renaissance period, but his swallow-tail coat comes from the early nineteenth century. The plot of the drama, if it can be called that, is a hodge-podge of popular myths and traditions, some very old, others quite new.

The play has two parts. After the performance, the players were usually rewarded with hot spiced ale or cider and bread and cheese, and in addition to this a sum of from two to five shillings was collected.

PART I

Enter Father Christmas

> In comes I,
> Old Christmas, Christmas, or Christmas not,
> I hope old Father Christmas will never be forgot,
> Christmas comes but once a year.
> And when it comes, it brings good cheer,
> Roast beef, plum pudding, and mince pie.
> There's no old Father Christmas loves better than I.

Enter Beelzebub

> A room, a room, brave gallant boys!
> And give us room to reign,
> For we have come to show our bold activity,

Here on a merry Christmas time –
Activity of youth, activity of age,
The like was never acted upon any stage,
If you don't believe what I say,
Enter in St George, and clear the way.

In comes St George

St George, that man of courage bold,
With sword and spear all by my side,
Hoping to gain the twelve crowns of gold.
'T was I who slew the fiery dragon,
And brought him to the slaughter
And by those fiery means I hope
To gain the Queen of Egypt's daughter
Seven long years I was kept in a close cave,
Where I made my sad and grievous mourn.
I have led the fair Sarepa from the snake,
Which neither man nor mortal would undertake,
I brought them all most couragely,
And still I gain the victory.
Show me the man who dare me!

Enter the Turkish Knight

I am the man who dare fight thee,
The Turkish Knight,
Come from my own Turkish land to fight.
I will fight St George, that man of courage bold.
If his blood is hot I will quickly make it cold.

St George and the Turkish Knight fight with back swords.
Turkish Knight, dropping on one knee

Hold, hold, St George! Another word
From thee I have to crave,
Spare me this time, and I will arise
To be your Turkish slave.

St George   Arise, arise, thou Turkish Knight!
Go over to thine own Turkish lands and fight.

Tell them there the champions grow in England.
Tell them the wonders I have done,
I have slain ten thousand for thy one.

Turkish Knight No, rather than tell them that,
I cut thee, hew thee, as small as flies,
And send thee to Jamaica to make mince pies.

St George Mince pies I do not like.
But another battle then, and I will fight.

St George kills the Knight. Enter Beelzebub

A room! a room!
And let the prudent King of Spain come in!

St George Thou prudent King of Spain,
Hast thou come here to fight?

King of Spain Yes, bold champion, and I think it is my right,
And with thee I have come to fight.

St George Firstly, thou has challenged me, King,
Secondly, thou hast challenged me.
Stand forth! thou figure of a tree,
And see who gains the victory!

King of Spain is killed. Enter Beelzebub

A room! a room!
And let the valiant soldier in.

Enter Soldier

In comes the valiant soldier,
Cut and Slasher is my name,
All from the fiery wars of Spain.
'T was I and seven more
Who slew eleven score,
And could have slain twelve thousand more,
All brave marching men of war,
Many a battle have I been in,

And still fight St George, that noble King.

Soldier killed by St George. Enter Beelzebub

A room! a room!
And let the Italian doctor walk in.

Enter Italian Doctor

In comes the little Italian doctor,
Lately come from Rome, France and Spain.
I carry a little vial bottle
In the waist of my break, with which I can cure.

Beelzebub   What canst thou cure?

Italian Doctor What thou canst not cure, old Dad.

Beelzebub   Old Dad, what's that?

Italian Doctor Rheumatic gout,
Pains within, and pains without.
Bring me an old woman
Of three score years and ten
With knuckle of her little toe broke.
And I can set it again..

Beelzebub   Set it then.

Italian Doctor goes round the slain, who all lie on the floor, and says over each –

Drop on thy brow,
Drop on thy heart,
Arise up, Jack,
And take thy part,

All arise and are cured.

PART II

Sweet Moll walks into the room.

St George   Sweet Moll, Sweet Moll, where are you going,

So early and so soon?
I have something to thee to say,
If yet that thou canst stay.

Sweet Moll   What hast thou got to say?
Pray tell me now,
For I am spending all my time
In what I can't tell how.

St George   Sweet Moll, thy parents and mine had well agreed
That married we should be,
So pull down thy lofty looks,
And fix thy love on me.

Sweet Moll   But I must have a little boy
Who speaks a peevish tongue;
A pair of silver buckles
That ladies do have on;
And I must have some butcher's meat
Of every sort and kind;
And in the morn a cup of tea,
At night, a glass of wine.

St George   Won't bacon serve thy turn, Sweet Moll,
Some good fat powder puffs?
And in the morn a cup of milk,
And that's the farmer's cut.
Sweet Moll, thou hast no cause
To talk of silver things,
For thou wast not brought up in palaces
Amongst lords, dukes and kings.
And the little thou hast learnt
Thou hast almost forgot;
If thou wilt not marry me,
Thou canst go to rot!

Exit Sweet Moll. Enter Little Dick Nipp

In comes I, Little Dick Nipp,
With my big head, and my little wit,
My head is so big, and my body so small,

> Yet I am the biggest rogue of all,
> My forehead is lined with brass,
> My head is lined with steel,
> My trousers touch my ankle bones,
> Pray doctor come and feel.

Doctor   Yes, yes.

St George   A room! a room! A gallant room!
             And let old Beelzebub come in.

Enter Beelzebub

> In comes old Beelzebub,
> On my shoulder I carry my club,
> In my hand my dripping pan.
> Don't you think I'm a jolly old man?
> A mug of good ale will make us merry and sing.
> And a few of your half-crowns and five-shilling pieces
> In our pockets would be a very fine thing.

A collection is taken up and the players dance and sing

> Here's health to her stock,
> Likewise to his flock;
> We'll take this small cup
> And we'll drink it all up,
> And there's enough to fill it again.

There appear to have been many renditions of this play. In his memoirs, *Good Neighbours* (1942), the English writer, Walter Rose, includes a shorter and somewhat different version. St George is now King George and Beelzebub's role is played by 'Johnny Jack'. The opening of both plays create a similar atmosphere:[22]

    The first player, flinging open the door, boldly announces:

> A room! A room! Brave gallants, room!
> I come to show you merry sports and sights
> upon this dark and wintry night.
> New activity; old activity;
> such activity as never was seen before
> and perhaps will never be seen no more.

Come in, my next head man.

Thereupon entered *Old Father Christmas*, bent with age and with a beard hoary from the passage of years. Thumping his gnarled stick heavily on the floor, he said:

In comes I, Old Father Christmas!
Welcome or welcome not.
I hope Old Father Christmas will never be forgot.
For in the room there will be shown
The dreadfulest battle that ever was known ...

In comes I, King George, King George,
The man of courage is.
With this, my broad sword, in my hand,
I won ten pounds in gold.
I fought the fiery dragon
And drove him to the slaughter.
And by means of that I won
The King of Egypt's daughter.
Let e'er man defy me, I'll hack him to the finest dust
and send him to college to make mince pie crust ...

In comes I, the Turkish Knight.
From Turkey's land I've come to fight.
Fight thee, King George, thou man of courage bold.
And if thy blood be hot, I'll quickly fetch it cold.

After a further exchange of challenges, the knight wounds King George. Arising, the king exclaims:

No! Think I've done with thee, Turkish Knight?
I will arise and show my might.
So guard your head and guard your nose
and guard your body, and down you goes.

In the play recalled by Rose, George fights only the Turkish knight, then the doctor arrives and revives his slain opponent.

Mummers have nearly disappeared from the Christmas scene except in a few localities. The most notable of these in the United States is Philadelphia, where the Mummers' parade on New Year's day has become an annual carnival. Mummers still parade in Ireland and in Scotland and can be called upon to provide entertainment at a variety of festivals.

CHAPTER V

The Persistence of Religious Traditions

Merciful God, give us grace that we may cast away the works of darkness, and put upon us the armour of light, now in the time of this mortal life in which thy Son Jesus Christ came to visit us in great humility; that in the last day, when he shall come again in his glorious majesty to judge both the quick and the dead, we may rise to the life immortal.

Collect for the first Sunday in Advent from
the English *Book of Common Prayer*, 1549

As shown in Chapter II, the mystery plays and carols of the late Middle Ages manifested a growing lay participation in the religious as well as the secular celebration of Christmas. The Franciscans and the Dominicans emphasised preaching in the vernacular and encouraged the education of the laity. Increasing literacy created a demand for translations of scripture. Both a French and a Middle English Bible appeared in the fourteenth century. The English translation was the work of John Wycliffe (d. 1384). A Christmas sermon by him or one of his disciples closely follows the biblical story of the Nativity and stresses, like St Francis, the humble circumstances of Jesus' birth.

A WYCLIFFITE SERMON: 'IN DIE NATALIS DOMINI'[1]

This day men sing three masses in worship of the Trinity, but the third and the most is of the manhood of Christ, which is both God and man for the love of mankind. The gospel of the first mass, and of the second also, tell what things befell in the birth of this child ...

'And Joseph went from Nazareth, that was a town in Galilee, into the town of Bedlem that was in Judea. For both Joseph and our Lady were of the house of David,' and the city of Bedlem was David's, for David was born in that city, as the book of Kings telleth. And so Joseph went with Marie, that was his wife, into Bedlem. They brought an ox and an ass with them, as men say, for this reason; Marie was great with child; therefore she rode upon an ass; the ox they brought with them for to sell, for Jews hate begging. And Bedlem was full of men before they came to the town; and so they had no harbor but dwelt in a common stable, and these two beasts with them, 'til time came to use them.

'And it fell, while they were there, our Lady bear her child,' that which was her first child, for him she bore and none other ... 'And she wrapped Christ with cloths and put him in the creche,' for she had no better place to put him in ... And so men sing and tell, Christ lay before an ox and an ass, and the breath of these two beasts kept him hot in this cold time.

'And shepherds were in this same country, waking, and keeping the watch of the night over their flock,' for this was the manner in Judea, when the night was longest, to keep their sheep and watch that night. And so men say that Christ was born at the middle of the night ... 'And, lo, the angel of our Lord stood by these shepherds and the clearness of God shined about them, and they dreaded with a great dread. But the angel said to them: "Be not afraid, for lo, I tell you a great joy that shall be to all people. For this day is born a saviour, that is Christ the Lord, in

the city of David, and this shall be a token to you, ye shall find the child wrapped with cloths, and put in the creche." And suddenly there was with this angel a multitude of heavenly knights, praising God, and saying, "Glory be to God in highest heaven, and peace be to men in earth which be of good will".'

Here may we see how Christ loved common poverty in many ways, for he chose to be harboured in a common place, without pride, and without worldly help of either men or women. And he chose a poor cradle that the child was put in. But he had a privilege in many things, for he was born without pain or sorrow of his father or mother. For as he broke not Marie's cloister when she was made with child, so he broke not his mother's womb when he came out of this cloister. And so these just folk before God were better than many worldly people, kings or lords and ladies, with much wealth of this world ... The second comfort of Christ's birth was the many angels, for they were better than many lords, and their song a great comfort. Oft-times, in the Old Testament, angels appeared to men, but not in such a multitude, nor in such a joyful speech.

The preacher goes on to remark that at his birth Jesus had the company of his father and mother, who were devout, and of the shepherds:

That lived a simple and holy life ... nigh the state of innocence; for God loveth Abel better than Cain that was his brother. And the first was a herdsman, and the other a tilling man; and tilling men are craftier than shepherds in their deeds. And as God loved Jacob's sons, that were all herdsmen, so he loved these shepherds that come to visit Christ.

The author of this sermon does not simply take a verse or two from the Bible as his text, he repeats most of the gospel account, embellishing it with homespun explanations, that could be understood by ordinary folk. Wool was then England's primary product and sheepherding a common occupation. The shepherds have an important role in all of the English Christmas plays.

Wycliffe followers, who were called Lollards, stressed the importance of the Bible. Individual interpretations of scripture, at first by clergy and then by laymen, challenged the authority of the church and eventually helped to precipitate the Protestant Reformation.

The hostility of radical Protestants to the observance of Christmas was just one aspect of the religious conflicts which divided Europe in the sixteenth and seventeenth centuries. It was an age of intolerance, persecution and sectarian warfare. At the same time, it was an age of genuine concern about moral and religious values. Ordinary people, not just theologians and philosophers, were deeply interested in such questions as original sin, pre-destination, the real presence. They discussed them in their homes, in the market place, in the tavern. Churchgoers not only endured, but demanded, long and involved sermons, especially in Protestant churches. The Reformation emphasised preaching more than worship. The Reformation also encouraged a growing literate public to read the Bible in the vernacular, now available in print. In response, Catholics put renewed emphasis upon preaching and produced their own versions of the Bible. For English speaking peoples the Catholic Douai and the Protestant King James provided eloquent translations.

CHRISTMAS SERMON BY JOHN DONNE

It is difficult for us today to comprehend the atmosphere of the period. A selection from a sermon, written in 1624, by the English poet, John Donne, will help us to recapture the spirit of the seventeenth century. Donne (1573-1631) was raised a Catholic but became a clergyman in the Church of England. He delivered this sermon in St Paul's cathedral in London (the old Gothic cathedral, not Wren's later structure), where he was dean. Donne took as text a verse from the Old Testament lesson for Christmas afternoon, Isaiah 7:14.[2]

Therefore the Lord shall give you a sign; Behold a Virgin shall conceive, and beare a Son, and shall call his name IMMANUEL.

Donne begins with this introduction:

St Bernard [1091-1153] spent his consideration upon three remarkable conjunctions, this Day. First, a conjunction of God and Man in one person, Christ Jesus; Then a conjunction of the incompatible Titles, Maid and Mother, in one blessed woman, the blessed Virgin Mary; And thirdly a conjunction of Faith, and the Reason of man, that so believes, and comprehends those two conjunctions. Let us accompany these three with another strange conjunction, in the first word of this Text, *Therefore*; for that joins the anger of God, and his mercy together. God has the prophet chide and rebuke King Achaz [as described in the reading from Isaiah]. He is angry with him, and therefore says the text, because he is angry, he will give him a sign, a seal of mercy ... This *therefore*, shall therefore be the first part of this Exercise. That God takes any occasion to show mercy; And a second shall be, the particular way of his mercy, declared here, *the Lord shall give you a sign*: And then a third and last, what this sign was, Behold a Virgin etc.

  In these three parts, we shall walk by these three steps: Having made our entrance into the first, with that general consideration, that God's mercy is alwaies in season ... In the second, ... that God persists in his own ways, goes forward with his own purpose. And then what his way, and his purpose here was, he would give them a sign ... In the third we have more steps to make; First, what this sign is in general, it is that there is a Redeemer given. And then how?

Donne points out that the text states that a Virgin shall conceive, and bear a son who, he explains, shall be both God and man:

of her substance, not only man, but man of her: And this Virgin shall call this Son *Immanuel, God with us*, that is, God and man.

Donne notes that Joseph was instructed to call the son Jesus, but only Mary was told to name him Immanuel.

The Blessed Virgin saw more than this; not only that he should be such a Jesus [saviour] as should save them from their sins, but she saw the manner how, that he should be *Immanuel, God with us*, God and man in one Person; That so, being Man, he might suffer, and being God, that should give infinite value to his sufferings ...

Having finished his introductory summary, Donne takes up the first topic of his sermon: God's mercy.

We begin with that which is elder than our beginning, and shall over-live our end, The mercy of God. When we fixe our selves upon the meditation and modulation of the mercy of God, even his judgements cannot put us out of tune, but we shall sing, and be cheerful, even in them. As God made grasse for the beasts, before he made beasts, and beasts for man before he made man: As in that first generation, the Creation, so in the regeneration, our re-creating, he begins with that which was necessary for that which followes. Mercy before Judgement. Nay, to say that mercy was first, is but to post-date mercy; to preferre mercy but so, is to diminish mercy; The names first and last are but ragges of time, and his mercy hath no relation to time, no limitation in time, it is not first or last, but eternal, everlasting. Let the Devill make me so desperate as to conceive a time when there was no mercy, and he hath made me so far an Atheist, as to conceive a time when there was no God; if I despoile him of his mercy, any one minute, and say, now God hath no mercy, for that minute I discontinue his very Godhead, and his being. Later grammarians have wrung the name mercy out of misery: *Misericordia praesumit miseriam*, say these, there could be no subsequent mercy if there were no precedent misery; But the true roote of the word mercy through all the Prophets is *Racham*, and *Racham* is *diligere*, to love; as long as there has been love (and *God is love*) there hath been mercy; And mercy considered externally, And in the practice and the effect, began not at the helping of

man, when man was fallen and become miserable, but at the making of
man, when man was nothing. So then, we consider not mercy as it is rad-
ically in God, and an externall attribute of his, but productively in us, as
it is an action, a working upon us, and more especially, as God takes all
occasions to exercise that action and to shed mercy upon us ...

We call not upon you from this Text, to consider God's ordinary
mercy, that which he exhibits to all in the ministry of his Church; nor the
miraculous mercy, his extraordinary deliverances of States and Churches;
but we call upon particular Consciences, by occasion of this Text, to call
to minde God's occassionall mercies to them; such mercies as a regener-
ate man will call mercies, though a naturall man would call them acci-
dents, or occurrences, or contingencies. A man wakes at midnight full of
unclean thoughts, and he heares a passing Bell; this is an occasionall
mercy, if he call that his own knell, and consider how unfit he was to be
called out of this world then, how unready to receive that voice, *Foole,
this night they shall fetch away thy soule* ...

After giving biblical examples of God's occasional mercy, Donne, who had recently
recovered from a very serious illness, continues:

If I should declare what God hath done (done occasionally) for my soule,
where he instructed me for feare of falling, where he raised me when I
was fallen, perchance you would rather fixe your thoughts upon my illness, and wonder at that, than at God's goodnesse, and glorifie him in
that; rather wonder at my sins, than at his mercies, rather consider how
ill a man I was, than how good a God he is. If I should inquire upon
what occasion God elected mee, and writ my name in the book of Life,
I should sooner be afraid that it were not so, than finde a reason why it
should be so. God made Sun and Moon to distinguish seasons, and day,
and night, and we cannot have the fruits of the earth but in their seasons;
But God hath made no decree to distinguish the seasons of his mercies;
In paradise the fruits were ripe, the first minute, and in heaven it is
alwaies autumne, his mercies are ever in their maturity. We ask *panem
quotidianum*, our daily bread, and God never sayes you should have come
yesterday, he never sayes you must come tomorrow, but *to day if you will
heare his voice*, to day he will have you ... He brought light out of darkness, not out of lesser light; he can bring thy Summer out of Winter,
though thou have no Spring; though in the wayes of fortune, or understanding, or conscience, thou have been benighted till now, wintred and
frozen, clouded and eclypsed, damped and benummed, smothered and

stupified till now, now God comes to thee, not as the dawning of the day, not as the bud in the spring, but as the Sun at noon to illustrate all shadowes, as the sheaves in harvest, to fill all penuries, all occasions invite his mercies, and all times are his seasons.

This abridged selection, comes from only the first third of Donne's full sermon. By modern standards the sermon is not only long, it develops three different and involved themes and is replete with learned allusions and subtle reasoning. Donne draws not only on the Bible and St Bernard, he quotes theologians from many periods. In the third part, in discussing the virgin birth and the incarnation he recapitulates views of Tertullian, Augustine, other patristic writers, as well as those of Calvin and Luther. As a Christmas message, perhaps the sermon's most remarkable concept (taken from St Bernard) is seeing the incarnation and the virgin birth, not as *inversions* of the natural order, but as *con-joined* or linked together. God becoming man, a virgin giving birth, though apparent contradictions represent a higher reality.

Like his poems, Donne's homilies express deep thought as well as eloquent imagery. They also reveal a breadth of vision lacking among most of his contemporaries – Protestant or Catholic. He once wrote to a friend:[3]

You know I never fettered nor imprisoned the word religion, ... immuring it in a Rome or a Wittenberg or a Geneva. They are all beams of the same sun, and whenever they find clay hearts they harden them into dust.

As shown in the last chapter, the English Puritans attempted to outlaw Christmas. The Roundhead Parliament initiated its campaign against the holiday in 1645 by declaring Christmas a fast day. In response, the poet, John Taylor, published the following satire.

THE COMPLAINT OF CHRISTMAS[4]

Christmas day speakes

Can any Christian man tell poore old Christmas day where he is? Is this England or Turkey that I am in? or is this London or Constantinople that gives me no better Entertainment? I was on the 15 day of December [December 25 by the new Gregorian calendar adopted in Continental Europe in 1582: England remained on the Julian calendar until 1752] in France, Spain, Italy, Germany, and in most of the Kingdomes of the Christian World, and in all places I was joyfully received with mirth and merry cheere. The Rich did feast me; the Poore rejoiced, and all sorts of people in every house made me heartily welcome, and my company made them as heartily merry; and all their mirth and jocundity was in Venerable Thankfull Remembrance kept and solemnized amongst all Christians these 1645 yeares past, in a pious gratitude for our Blessed Saviour, and Redeemer's Nativity. But in this tract of Time and yeares, there was never any Kingdome or People did afford me better welcome than *England*, where I landed (as I was accustomed every yeare) on the 25th of December, expecting the like treatment that I was wont to have. But (alas) the case was alter'd, and the whole frame of the Kingdome turn'd quite Topsy Turvy, upside downe, or (as I might say) with the Bottome upwards. I wish this were a Lye. I gazed about me, and with astonishment I saw Churches, and Steeples, and Houses, and Chimneys. But I could heare no sound of any Bell, or so much smoke as might put me on Comfort that there was any fire in the Kingdome. These unexpected symptomes put me in a *Browne* study [Robert Browne was a leading Puritan preacher] ...

Thus I, being old, cold, weather-beaten, frost-bitten and hungry, began to view certaine Townes and Cities, such as London, Gloucester, Yarmouth, Newbury, ... where as soone as I entered, I was more and more amazed, for I could perceive no signe or token of any Holy day; the

Shops were open, the Markets were full, the Watermen rowing, the Carmen were a loading and unloading. the Porters bearing, and all Trades were forbearing to keepe any respectful memory of me, or of Christ, in whose memory I was first instituted by the Church so many ages and yeares foregone. After I had walked through every Streete, Lane, and Alley, the weather being cold, and my entertainment colder, I went to a Cobbler's stall, and demanded of him what harme old *Christmas* had done them, and wherefore he was banished so suddenly? The cobbler replied, that it was a pity that ever Christmas was borne, and that I was a Papist, and an Idolatrous Brat of the Beast; and an old Reveller sent from Rome into England, and that the latter end (or last syllable of my name) was Popish, as other superstitious daies were, such as are *Candlemas, Lammas, Michaelmas, Hallowmas, Martinmas, etc.* But that now, he praised the Lord, and the godly Parliament, that their eyes were opened to perceive and see their Antichristian errours, and that now the cleare sunshine of the Word hath (by the operation of the Spirit) illuminated their understandings, and enlightened them out of Aegyptian darkness.

Thus I stood quaking with cold, whil'st the Cobbler was pipeing hot with zeale; so that if I had not tooke him off with a short answer, I might have been serv'd with a foure or five houres Lecture. I asked him if he knew what the word *Masse* meant? He said the very word *Masse* was abominable, detestable, Babylonian, Idolatrous, Romish. Superstitious, Blasphemous, Anti-Christian etc. with other impertinent words and Epithets. I told him againe that the word *Masse* was no other but a dismission, or a giving the People to understand, that such and such service or prayers and thanksgiving were ended as were appointed by the Church for that day. And that the Congregation might all depart and be gone about their other lawful Affaires. And that the Prayers and Service ordained on *Christmas* day by the Primitive church were to give thankes to God the Father, our Creator, for sending his Sonne our Redeemer.

Taylor's Puritan cobbler like other radical Protestants opposed Christmas because of its association with Catholicism as well as with revelry and idleness. Calvinists were not moved by the image of God as a helpless baby, and they vehemently rejected the medieval veneration of the Virgin. While Taylor, as an Anglican, repudiated the papacy and some Catholic doctrines, he had a love for tradition and a deep respect for Mary. In 1630 he published a poem entitled *The Life and Death of the Most Blessed amongst all women, the Virgin Mary*. In the poem (like the author of the redemption play in Chapter III) Taylor observes that Mary redeemed Eve's original sin.[5]

And as a woman tempted Man to vice
For which they both were thrust from Paradice

So from a woman was a Saviour's birth,
That purchas'd Man a Heaven for losse of Earth

Taylor's description of the Nativity may be closer to doggerel than poetry, yet it depicts a vivid scene, a popular image of Jesus' birth.

Through winters weather, frost & wind, and snow,
Foure weary daies in travell they bestow.
But when to Bethlem they approached were,
Small friendship, & less welcome they found there;
No chamber, nor fire to warme them at,
For harbor only they a Stable gat.
The Inne was full of more respected guests,
Of Drunkards, Swearers, and of godlesse beasts:
Those all had roomes, whilst Glory and all Grace
(But among beasts) could have no lodging place.
There (by protection of the Almighties wings)
Was borne the Lord of Lords, and King of Kings.
...

There did the humane nature and divine,
The Godhead with the Manhood both combine:
There was this Maiden-mother brought to bed,
Where Oxen, Kine, and Horses lodg'd and fed:
There this bright Queene of Queenes with the heave'ly joy,
Did hug her Lord, her Life, her God, her Boy
Her Sonne, her Saviour, her immortal Blisse,
Her sole Redeemer, she might rocke and kiss,
Oh blessed Lady, of all Ladies blest;
Blessed for ever, for thy sacred brest
Fed him that all the famisht soules did feed.

CHRISTMAS POEMS AND HYMNS FROM THE REFORMATION TO THE AGE OF THE ENLIGHTENMENT

As noted above, Lutherans and Anglicans, as well as Catholics, continued to use traditional Christmas anthems and hymns. Furthermore, despite the antagonism between the different branches of the Christian community following the Reformation, members of opposing denominations wrote new Christmas poems and hymns which articulated the same Christmas themes discussed in the Introduction.

MARTIN LUTHER (1483-1546)

Luther customarily prepared entertainment for his family on Christmas Eve. The following hymn was written for this Weihnachts celebration, probably in 1534.[6]

The Angel's Message

From heaven high I come to you
I bring you tidings good and new,
Good tidings of great joy I bring
Thereof will I both say and sing

For you a little child is born:
Of God's own chosen maid this morn:
A fair and tender baby bright,
To be your joy and your delight

Lo he is Christ the Lord indeed,
Our God, to guide you in your need
And he will be your saviour strong
To cleanse thee from all sin and wrong

The Children's Response

Now let us all right merry be,
And, with the shepherds, go to see
God's own dear Son, within the stall;
His gift bestowed upon us all.

Mark well, my heart; look well mine eyes;
Who is it in the manger lies:
What child is this, so young and fair?
It is my Jesus lieth there

Ah, dearest Jesus, be my guest:
Soft be the bed where thou will rest,
A little shrine within my heart,
That thou and I may never part.

ROBERT SOUTHWELL (1561-95)[7]

The Burning Babe

As I in hoary winter's night stood shivering in the snow,
Surprised I was with sudden heat which made my heart to glow;
And lifting up a fearful eye to view what fire was near,
A pretty Babe all burning bright did in the air appear;
Who, scorched with excessive heat, such floods of tears did shed,
As though his floods should quench his flames which with his tears
    were fed.
'Alas!; quoth he, 'but newly born in fiery heats I fry,
Yet none approach to warm their hearts or feel my fire but I,
My faultless breast the furnace is, the fuel wounding thorns:
Love is the fire, and sighs the smoke, the ashess shame and scorn;
The fuel justice layeth on, and merry blows the coals.
The metal in the furnace wrought are men's defiled souls:
For which, as now on fire I am to work them to their good,
So I will I melt into a bath to wash them in my blood'
With this he vanished out of sight and swiftly shrunk away,
And straight I called unto mind that it was Christmas day.

BEN JONSON (1573?-1637)[8]

A hymn to the Nativity of My Saviour

I sing the birth was born tonight,
The author both of life and light;
The angels so did sound it,
And like, the ravished shepherds said,
Who saw the light and were afraid,
Yet searched, and true they found it.

The Son of God, the Eternal King,
That did us all salvation bring,
And freed the soul from danger;
He whom the whole world could not take,
The Word, which heaven and earth did make,
Now laid in a manger.

The Father's wisdom willed it so,
The Son's obedience knew no No,
Both wills were in one stature;
And as that wisdom had decreed,
The Word was now made flesh indeed,
And took on him our nature.

What comfort by him do we win,
Who made himself the price of sin.
To make us heirs of glory!
To see the babe, all innocence,
A martyr born in our defence,
Can man forget this story?

WILLIAM DRUMMOND OF HAWTHORNDEN (1585-1640)

Nativity[9]

Run shepherds, run, where Bethlehem blest appears,
We bring the best of news, be not dismayed:
A Saviour there is born, more old than years,
Amidst heaven's rolling heights this earth who stayed;
In a poor cottage inned, a virgin maid,
A weakling, did him bear who all upbears'

This is he, poorly swaddled, in a manger laid.
To whom too narrow swaddlings are our spheres.

Run shepherds, run, and solemnise his birth,
This is the night – no, day grown great with bliss,
In which, the power of Satan broken is;
In heaven be glory, peace unto the earth.
Thus singing through the air the angels swam,
And cope of stars re-echoed the same.

JOHN MILTON (1608-1674)

Milton supported the parliamentary and Puritan side in the English civil wars and became a propagandist for the revolutionary government; yet Christmas had a deep spiritual meaning for him. In 1645 he published a collection of his poems. He chose this Nativity ode, which he had written in December 1629, the month of his twenty-first birthday, as the first poem in the book. Milton 's approach to the Nativity, like that of the redemption play in Chapter III, is theological. He depicts the incarnation with cosmic rather than human imagery. His interpretation is close to that of early hymn writers, like Prudentius.[10]

On the Morning of Christ's Nativity

This is the month, and this the happy morn
Wherein the Son of heaven's eternal king,
Of wedded maid and virgin mother born,
Our great redemption from above did bring;
For so the holy sages once did sing,
That our deadly forfeit should release
And with his Father work us a perpetual peace.

That glorious form, that light unsufferable,
And that far-beaming blaze of majesty
Wherewith he wont at heaven's high counsel-table
To sit the midst of trinal unity,
He laid aside; and here with us to be,
Forsook the courts of everlasting day,
And chose with us a darksome house of mortal clay.

Say heavenly Muse, shall not thy sacred vein
Afford a present to the infant God?
Hast thou no verse, no hymn, or solemn strain,
To welcome to this his new abode,

Now while the heaven by the sun's team untrod
Hath took no print of the approaching light
And all the spangled host keep watch on squadrons bright.

See how from far upon the eastern road
The star-led wizards haste withe odours sweet,
O run, prevent then with thy humble ode,
And lay it lowly at his blessed feet;
Have the honour first thy Lord to greet.
And join thy voice unto the angel choir,
From out his secret altar touched with hallowed fire.

The hymn

I

It was the winter wild
While the heaven-born child
All meanly wrapped in the rude manger lies;
Nature in awe to him
Had doffed her gaudy trim.
With her great Master so to sympathize:
It was no season then for her
To wanton with the sun her lusty paramour.

II

Only with speeches fair
She woos the gentle air
To hide her guilty front with innocent snow,
And let her naked shame,
Pollute with sinful blame,
The saintly veil of maiden white to throw,
Confounded, that her Maker's eyes
Should look so near upon her foul deformities

III

But he her fears to cease,
Sent down the meek-eyed Peace,
She crowned with olive green came softly sliding
Down through the turning sphere
His redy harbinger,

With turtle wing the amorous clouds dividing.
And waving wide her myrtle wand
She strikes a universal peace through sea and land.

IV

No war, or battle's sound
Was heard the world around:
The idle spear and shield were high up hung,
The hooked chariot stood
Unstained with hostile blood.
The trumpet spake not to the armed throng,
And kings sat still with awful eye,
As if they surely knew their sovereign Lord was by.

V

But peaceful was the night
Wherein the Prince of light
His reign of peace upon the earth began:
The winds with wonder whist.
Smoothly the waters kissed,
Whispering new joys to the mild ocean,
Who now hath quite forgot to rave,
While birds of calm sit brooding on the charmed wave.

VI

The stars with deep amaze
Stand fixed in steadfast gaze,
Bending one way their precious influence,
And will not take their flight,
For all the morning light,
Or Lucifer that often warned them thence;
But in their glimmering orbs did glow,
Until their Lord himself bespake, and bid them go.

VII

And though the shaddy gloom
Had given day her room,
The sun himself withheld his wonted speed,
And hid his head for shame.
As his inferior flame

The new enlightened world no more should need;
He saw a greater Sun appear
Than his bright throne, or burning axle-tree could bear.

VIII

The shepherds on the lawn,
Or ere the point of dawn,
Sat simply chatting in a rustic row;
Full little thought they than
That the mighty Pan
Was kindly come to live with them below;
Perhaps their loves, or else their sheep,
Was all that did their silly thoughts so busy keep.

IX

When such music sweet
Their hearts and ears did greet,
As never was by mortal finger strook.
Dively-warbled voice
Answering the stringed noise,
As all their souls in blissful rapture took:
The air such pleasure loath to lose,
With thousand echoes still prolongs each heavenly close

XII

Such music (as 'tis said)
Before was never made,
But when of old ihe sons of morning sung
While the Creator
His constellations set
And the well-balanced world on hinges hung,
And cast the dark foundations deep.
And bid the weltering waves their oozy channel keep.

XV

Yea, Truth and Justice then
Will down return to men,
Orbed in a rainbow; and, like glories wearing
Mercy will sit between
Throned in celestial sheen,

With radiant feet the tissued clouds down steering,
And heaven as at some festival
Will open wide the gates of her high palace hall.

XVI

But wisest Fate says no,
This must not yet be so,
The babe lies yet in smiling infancy
That on the bitter cross
Must redeem our loss,
So both himself and us to glorify:
Yet first to those chained in sleep
The wakeful trump of doom must thunder through the deep.

When this final day of judgment comes 'with such a horrid clang as on Mount Sinai rang', the old pagan gods and nymphs and such become powerless and are condemned to destruction. Milton closes his list of doomed deities with Osiris.

XXIV

Nor is Osiris seen
In Memphian grove, or green
Trampling the unshowered grass with lowings loud:
Nor can he be at rest
Within his sacred chest,
Naught but profoundest hell can be his shroud,
In vain with timbrelled anthems dark
The sable-stoled sorcerers bear his worshipped ark,

XXV

He feels from Judah's land
The dreaded infant's hand,
The rays of Bethlehem blind his dusky eyn;
Nor all the gods beside.
Longer dare abide,
Not Typhon huge ending in snaking twine:
Our babe to show his godhead true,
Can in his swaddling hands control the damned crew.

XXVI

So when the sun in bed.
Curtained with clouds red,

Pillows his chin upon an orient wave,
The flocking shadows pale,
Troop to the infernal jail,
Each fettered ghost slips in his several grave,
And yellow-skirted fays,
Fly after the night steeds, leaving their moon-loved maze.

XXVII

But see the virgin blest.
Hath laid her babe to rest.
Time is our tedious song should here have ending:
Heaven's youngest-teemed star [star of Bethlehem]
Hath fixed her polished car,
Her sleeping Lord with handmaid lamp attending:
And all about the courtly stable,
Bright-harnessed angels sit in order serviceable.

At twenty-one Milton was already thinking of life and religion in cosmic terms. He treats the Nativity as a metaphor, embracing the creation, man's fall and redemption and the last judgement. His allusions and images are drawn from classical mythology, the Bible and Christian, especially Calvinist, theology. His imaginative vocabulary sometimes seems affected; at other times it has the splendour of *Paradise Lost* – which he began some twenty years later. Milton certainly did not reject Christmas as a superstitious or sinful holiday, but the Nativity ode suggests that he shared the Puritan view that the world (of nature as well as man) was sinful.

RICHARD CRASHAW (1613?-1649)

A Hymne of the Nativity, Sung by the Shepherds[11]

Chorus
Come we shepherds whose blest Sight
Hath mett love's Noon in Nature's night;
Come lift we up our loftyer Song
And wake the Sun who lyes too long.

To all our world of well-stoln joy
He slept; and dream't of no such thing.
While we found our Heaven's fairer eye
And kis't the Cradle of our King.
Tell him he rises now too late
To show us ought worth looking at

Tell him we now can show him more
Then he e're show'd to mortall Sight;
Then he himselfe e're saw before;
Which to be seen needes not his light,
Tell him, Tityrus, where th'hast been
Tell him, Thyrsis, what th'hast seen.

Tityrus. Gloomy night embrac't the Place
Where the noble Infant lay.
The Babe look't up and show'd his Face'
In spite of Darkness, it was DAY,
It was DAY day, SWEET! and did rise
Not from the East, but from thine Eyes.

Chorus It was from Thy day, Sweet

Thyrsis WINTER chidde aloud; and sent
The angry North to wage his warres.
The North forgott his fierce Intent:
And left perfumes in stead of carres.
By those sweet eyes' persuasive powrs
Where he mean't frost, he scatter'd flowrs.

Chorus By those sweet eyes' …

Both We saw thee in thy balmy Nest
Young dawn of our eternall DAY!
We say thine eyes break from the EASTE
And chase the trembling shades away.
We saw thee, and we blest the sight
We saw thee by thine own sweet light

Tityrus POOR WORLD (said I) what wilt thou doe.
To entertain this starry STRANGER?
Is this the best thou canst bestow?
A cold, and not too cleanly, manger?
Contend, ye powers of heav'n and earth.
To fitt a bed for this huge birthe.

Chorus Contend ye powers …

Full Chorus Welcome, all wonders in one sight!
Aeternity shutt in a span,

Summer in Winter, Day in Night.
Heaven in earth, and God in Man,
Great little one! whose all-embracing birth
Lifts earth to heaven, stoops heav'n to earth.

For Crashaw, as for Milton, Jesus' Nativity is an event embracing all eternity, yet his poem
is more one of personal devotion than cosmic drama. The next three shorter poems come
from seventeenth-century Ireland.

LUKE WADDING (1558-1657)

Christmas Day Is Come[12]

Christmas Day is come, let's all prepare for mirth
Which fills the heav'ns and earth at this amazing birth.
Through both the joyous angels in strife and hurry fly,
With glory and hosannas, All Holy' do they cry
In heaven the Church triumphant adores with all her choirs,
The militant on earth with humble faith admires.

But why shuld we rejoice? Should we not rather mourn
To see the Hope of Nations in a stable born?
Where are his crown and sceptre, where his throne sublime?
Where is his train majestic that should the stars out shine?
Is there not sumptuous palace nor any inn at all
To lodge his Heav'nly mother but in a filthy stall?

ROGER BOYLE, EARL OF ORRERY (1621-1679)

On Christmas Day[13]

Hail, glorious day which miracles adorn,
Since 'twas on thee eternity was born!
Hail, glorious day, on which mankind did view
The saviour of the old world and the new!

Hail glorious day, which defies man's race,
Birth-day of Jesus, and through him, of grace!
On thy blest light the world once did see
Proofs of his Godhead and humanity.

To prove him man, he did from woman come
To prove him God, 'twas from a virgin's womb.

Man ne'er could feign, what his strange birth prov'd true,
For his blest mother was a virgin too.

While as a child he in the manger cries,
Angels proclaim his Godhead from the skies;
He to so vile a cradle did submit,
That we, through faith in him, on thrones might sit.

Oh prodigee of mercy, which did make
The God of Gods our human nature take!
And through our vaile of flesh, his glory shine,
That we thereby might share in the divine.

Hail, glorious virgin, whose triumphant womb
Blesses all ages past and all to come!
Thou more than heal'st the sin of Adam's wife,
She brought in death, but thou brought'st endless life,

No wonder in the world could be,
Than thou to live in it and heaven in thee.
All generations still shall call thee blest.
To thee that title is most justly paid,
Since by thy Son we sons of God are made!

LUKE WADDINGE, THE YOUNGER (1600–1691)

For Christmas Day[14]

This Christmas Day you pray and sing,
My carol to our new-born King,
A God made Man, the Virgin's Son,
The Word made Flesh, can this be done?
Of me I pray no more require
Then this great Mystery to admire.

Whom Heaven of Heavens cannot contain,
As Scripture doth declare most plain,
In a poor stable is born this day
Lay'd in a manger wrapt in hay,
Of me I pray no more require
Then this great Mystery to admire.

Heaven's great treasures are now but small!
Immensity no extent at all,
Eternity's but one day old
Tho' Almighty feeleth the Winter cold,
Of me I pray no more require
Than this great Mystery to admire.

Following are two Christmas carols from Canada. The first, 'Twas in the moon of the wintertime', was originally written in Huron Indian by Fr Jean de Brebeue and appears here in translation by J.E. Middleton. The second, 'Whence Art Thou, My Maiden', is a traditional French carol, translated by William McLennan in 1866.[15]

FATHER JEAN DE BREBEUE (1593-1649)

'Twas in the Moon of the Wintertime

Twas in the moon of the wintertime when all the birds had fled.
That mighty Gitchi manitou sent angel choirs instead.
Before their light the stars grew dim,
And wandering hunters heard the hymn:
'Jesus, your King, is born.
Jesus is born. *In excelsis gloria.*'

Within a lodge of broken bark the tender Babe was found.
A ragged robe of rabbit skin enwrapped his beauty round.
And as hunter braves drew nigh,
The angel song rang loud and high:
'Jesus, your King, is born.
Jesus is born. *In excelsis gloria.*'

The earliest moon of wintertime is not so round and fair,
As the ring of glory on the helpless Infant there.
While Chiefs from far before him knelt,
With gifts of fox and beaver pelt.
'Jesus, your King, is born.
Jesus is born. *In excelsis gloria.*'

O children of the forest free, O sons of Manitou,
The Holy Child of earth and Heav'n is born today for you.
Come, kneel before the radiant Boy,
Who brings you beauty, peace and joy.
'Jesus, your King, is born.
Jesus is born. *In excelsis gloria.*'

TRADITIONAL FRENCH CAROL, 1600S

Whence Art Thou, My Maiden?

'Whence art thou, my maiden,
whence art thou?
Whence art thou, my maiden,
whence art thou?'
'I come from the stable where,
this very night
I, a shepherd maiden,
saw a wondrous sight.'

'What sawst thou, my maiden
What sawst thou?
What sawst thou, my maiden
What sawst thou?'
'There, within a manger,
a little Child I saw
Lying, softly sleeping
On a bed of straw.'

'Nothing more, my maiden
nothing more?
Nothing more, my maiden
nothing more?'
'I saw ass and oxen,
kneeling meek and mild,
with their gentle breathing
warm the holy Child.'

'Nothing more, my maiden
nothing more?
Nothing more, my maiden
nothing more?'
'there were three bright angels
come down from the sky,
Singing forth sweet praises
To our God on high.'

The authors of this series of Christmas hymns and poems held a variety of religious views.
Robert Southwell was a Catholic priest and martyr, who was executed for 'treason' at

Tyburn late in Elizabeth's reign. Richard Crashaw, the son of a Puritan father, became a Catholic and died in Rome. Ben Johnson belonged to the Church of England, William Drummond to the Scottish Kirk. Milton, of course, was an avowed Puritan. Luke Wadding was a Franciscan friar who became president of the Irish College in Salamanca. In 1618 he went to Rome, where he founded the Irish College of St Isidore. The younger Luke Waddinge, possibly of the same family, but not closely related, was a Catholic bishop in Ireland who wrote a number of popular poems. Roger Boyle, son of the English-born first earl of Cork, was a Protestant political leader and dramatist. The eighteenth-century authors, whose selections conclude this chapter, reflect the same diversity. Isaac Watts, was a Protestant Dissenter of Puritan background. Charles Wesley, was an evangelical Anglican, who helped his brother, John, to launch the Methodist movement. John Francis Wade, the man who published and possibly wrote *Adeste, Fidelis*, was an English Catholic resident in France.

ISAAC WATTS (1674-1748)

Joy to the World (1719)[16]

Joy to the world! the Lord is come:
Let earth receive her king:
Let every heart prepare his room,
And heav'n and nature sing.

Joy to the world! the Saviour reigns;
Let men their songs employ,

While fields and floods, rocks, hills and plains,
Repeat the sounding joy.

No more let sins and sorrows grow,
Nor thorns infest the ground;
He comes to make his blessing flow
Far as the curse is found,

He rules the world with truth and grace,
And makes the nations prove
The glories of his righteousness,
And wonders of his love.

CHARLES WESLEY (1707–1788)

Hymn for Christmas-Day (1739)[17]

Hark how all the Welkin rings
Glory to the King of Kings,*
Peace on Earth, and Mercy mild.
God and Sinners reconcil'd!

Joyful all ye Nations rise,
Join the Triumph of the Skies.
Universal Nature say
CHRIST the LORD is born to Day!

CHRIST, by highest Heav'n ador'd
CHRIST, the Everlasting Lord,
Late in Time behold him come,
Offspring of a Virgin's Womb.

Veil'd in Flesh, the Godhead see,
Hail th' Incarnate Deity!
Pleas'd as Man with Men t'appear
JESUS, our *Immanuel* here!

---

* The first two lines were changed to 'Hark! the Herald Angels sing, Glory to the new-born King' in 1787. Most modern versions have other alterations as well. Charles Wesley wrote a number of other Christmas hymns, among them the following, now often sung in Advent.[18]

Hail the Heave'nly Prince of Peace!
Hail the Sun of Righteousness!
Light and Life to All he brings,
Ris'n with Healing in his Wings.
Mild he lays his Glory by,
Born – that Man no more may die,
Born – to raise the Sons of Earth,
Born – to give them second Birth.

Come, Desire of Nations, come,
Fix in Us thy humble Home,
Rise, the Woman's Conquering Seed,
Bruise in Us the Serpent's Head

Come, Thou long-expected JESUS,
Born to set thy people free,
From our Fears and Sins relieve us,
Let us find our Rest in Thee:
Israel's Strength and Consolation,
Hope of all the Earth Thou art,
Dear Desire of every Nation,
Joy of every longing Heart.

Born they People to deliver,
Born a Child and yet a King,
Born to reign in Us for ever,
Now they gracious Kingdom bring;
By thy own eternal Spirit
Rule in all our Hearts alone,
By thine all-sufficient Merit
Raise us to they glorious Throne

The eighteenth century, the 'Age of Reason,' distrusted the mysticism, intolerance and superstition of the past, and viewed the 'gothic' architecture and life style of the Middle Ages as benighted. Yet the hymns of Watts and Wesley, as well as a number of others from the period, convey a deep religious feeling, illustrating the continuity of Christmas religious traditions. More surprisingly, several hymns which were first published in the eighteenth century seem almost medieval in spirit. For example:

God rest you merry gentlemen,
Let nothing you dismay,
Remember Christ our Saviour
Was born on Christmas Day;
To save us from Satan's power
When we were gone astray.
O tidings of comfort and joy;
O tidings of comfort and joy!

first published in *Roxburghe Ballads, c.* 1770[19]

Another eighteenth-century favourite with an antique flavour is:

While Shepherds watched their flock by night,
All seated on the ground,
The angel of the Lord came down.
And glory shone around.
'Fear not,' said he, for mighty dread had seized their troubled mind.
Glad tidings of great joy I bring
To you and all mankind.'

This simple paraphrasing of Luke's gospel first appeared in a *New Version of the Psalms by Dr Brady and Mr Tate* (1708), compiled by two Irish Protestants. It quickly became popular and was translated into Latin and several modern languages. It was one of a couple of dozen hymns bound with the first edition of the *American Prayer Book* (Episcopal) in 1789.[20]

For many people today one of the most beloved and, most of us would say, oldest Christmas hymns is *Adeste, fideles* or *O Come, All Ye Faithful*. Actually the earliest extant text of the hymn dates from 1746. It was written in Latin by an English Catholic exile, John Francis Wade (1711–1786), who lived in Douai and made his living copying and selling beautifully executed manuscripts of plainsong and other music. The tune seems to have come from a Paris vaudeville piece 'Air Anglois' (1744). It is possible the words come from an unidentified manuscript source; more probably Wade wrote them himself, inspired by medieval sources.

The Christmas music of the eighteenth century, especially Handel's *Messiah*, shows deep religious feeling, and both the music and the words of the period's hymns and carols crossed sectarian boundaries, finding acceptance among many denominations. As the Irish bishop, George Berkeley, explained:[21]

Christ's religion is spiritual and supernatural; and there is an unseen cement of the faithful, who draw grace from the same source ... And this although they may be members of different political or visible congregations, may be estranged, or suspected, or even excommunicated to each other.

CONTINUITY OF RELIGIOUS THEMES & MOTIFS

Although some secular customs associated with Christmas go back to pre-Christian origins, most of them have been subject to many changes. While time and place have also altered religious traditions, the Nativity narrative, in both its literal and metaphorical interpretation, has remained largely unaltered – like the Jewish Passover. The two central Christmas themes of *renewal* and *inversion*, discussed in the Introduction, along with the motifs associated with them (Jesus both divine and human, the virgin birth, Jesus as the Word incarnate, Jesus' identification with light and salvation, his humble birth in royal David's city and the coming of the wise men), all persist. They are articulated in the popular carols in Chapter III, as well as in the early hymns and anthems found in Chapter II, and again in the poems and hymns of the seventeenth and eighteenth centuries. They continue to be expressed down to the present: *Silent Night* (Austrian, 1818), *Once in Royal David's City* (English 1848), *We Three Kings of Orient Are* (American, 1857), and *O Little Town of Bethlehem* (American, 1868). There are even modern macaronic carols such as *The Snow Lay on the Ground* (Anglo-Irish, late nineteenth century) with its Latin refrain 'Venite Adoramus'.

The singing of Christmas carols and hymns has been a Christmas tradition, both in and out of church, since the Middle Ages. By the eighteenth century, the late hours and insolent behaviour of many carollers led writers like Henry Bourne to deplore the practice. Carolling regained respectability in the Victorian period. Today, Christmas hymns and carols drawn from many periods and places are part of our Christmas celebrations. Sung Christmas services from St Peter's Rome, from King's College Chapel in Cambridge, and from many other places are broadcast around the world. Despite the endless stream of Christmas recordings resonating through stores and shopping malls, the season's religious music still has a wide appeal.

Poets have also continued to celebrate the Nativity, though with less religious intensity than in the age of Milton, Donne and Crashaw. For some modern writers Christmas

has become less of a communal festival and more of a personal anniversary, a time of individual and family memories; a pause before the turning of the year which reminds us of
bereavement and unfulfilled hopes as well as of achievement and joy. Tennyson's *In
Memoriam*[22] gives voice to such a mood:

> The time draws near the birth of Christ;
> The moon is hid, the night is still;
> A single church below the hill
> Is pealing, folding in the mist
>
> A single peal of bells below,
> That wakens this hour of rest
> A single murmur in the breast,
> That these are not the bells I know
>
> Like stangers' voices here they sound,
> In lands where not a memory strays.
> Nor landmark breathes of other days,
> But all is new unhallowed ground.
>
> Tonight ungathered let us leave
> This laurel, let this holly stand:
> We live within the strangers' land,
> And strangely falls our Christmas-Eve.

In *My Sister's Sleep*,[23] Gabriel Rossetti recalls a sister's death on Christmas Eve.

> She fell asleep on Christmas Eve.
> At length the long-ungranted shade
> Of weary eyelids overweighed
> The pain naught else might relieve.
>
> Our mother, who had leaned all day
> Over the bed from chime to chime,
> Then raised herself for the first time
> And as she sat down, did pray.
>
> Her little work table was spread
> With work to finish. For the glare
> Made by her candle, she had care
> To work some distance from the bed
>
> Without, there was a cold moon up
> Of winter radiance sheer and thin;

The hollow halo it was in
Was like an icy crystal cup

Through the small room, with subtle sound
Of flame, by vents the fireshine drove
And reddened. In its dim alcove
The mirror shed a clearness round

I had been sitting up some nights,
And my tired mind felt weak and blank:
Like a sharp strengthening wine it drank
The stillness and the broken lights

Twelve struck. That sound, by dwindling years
Heard in each hour, crept off, and then
The ruffled silence spread again.
Like water that a pebble stirs.

Our mother rose from where she sat:
Her needles, as she laid them down,
Met lightly, and her silken gown
Settled: no other noise than that,

'Glory unto the Newly Born!'
So, as said angels, she did say;
Because we were in Christmas Day,
Though it still be long till morn.

Despite the growth of religious scepticism, twentieth-century poets continue to express traditional Christmas themes. Lisette Reese retold a *Christmas Folk-song*:[24]

The little Jesus came to town:
The wind blew up, the wind blew down,
Out in the street the wind was bold:
Now who would house him from the cold?

Then opened wide a stable door,
Fair were the rushes on the floor;
The ox put forth a horned head;
'Come, little Lord, here make Thy bed.'

T.S. Eliot wrote a poem about the wise men, Carl Sanburg about the Christ-child 'straight and wise', and Langston Hughes' *The Christmas Story* proclaims anew that 'Christ is born in all His Glory'.

CHAPTER VI

The Emergence of the Modern Christmas: A Composite 'Diary' of Christmas Observance, 1550–1850

In *The Making of the Modern Christmas*, J.M. Golby and A.W. Purdue remark that for two hundred years people have looked back with nostalgia to the time when Christmas was celebrated in the old fashion way, when actually it is impossible to find a time when this traditional Christmas ever existed. In their opinion, 'the Christmas we know and observe today is very much the creation of the Victorians in Britain and the United States'.[1] Nineteenth-century authors, such as Washington Irving, Charles Dickens and others, 're-invented' Christmas. They conjured up a Christmas past which bore little resemblance to the historical holiday. Many recent writers, take the same position. Penne L. Restad believes Americans paid little attention to Christmas before 1820, but that by the 1880s it had become the primary American holiday – 'a pastiche of customs and rituals from the past,' combined with newly introduced customs, such as Santa Claus and Christmas trees.[2] Several of the anthropologists contributing to *Unwrapping Christmas*, while accepting this thesis, place more emphasis on the influence of the Disney oriented culture of contemporary America.

There is no denying that Santa Claus with his reindeer is a nineteenth-century creation, and Rudolf of the red nose a twentieth-century embellishment; or that, although the Christmas tree may have a long history in Germany, its popularity elsewhere is less than two centuries old. It is also true that our Christmas-card picture of yuletide festivities in 'Merrie Olde England' may be derived more from Victorian fantasy than from historical evidence. Nonetheless, many of the Christmas traditions which modern writers attribute to the 'Victorians' have a much more venerable genealogy. For example, while the Victorians made a conscious effort to encourage the revival of Christmas carols and even fabricated a few, such as 'Good King Wencelaus,' most of the carols they popularised dated from earlier times, and among country people had never been totally forgotten. An article in the English *Notes and Queries* for December 29, 1855 states that carollers in Cornwall still sing such 'absurd' old folk songs as the *Holy Well*, *As Shepherds Watch Their Flocks by Night* and *Joy to the World*. In another comment in the same number of *Notes and Queries* another writer comments that one of the Christmas favourites when he was young was the 'schoolboy chant' that began:

> The first day of Christmas my true love sent to me
> A partridge in a pear tree ...

As was shown in Chapter III, St Nicholas' association with gifts for children goes back centuries. The same is true of many other Christmas customs. Even scholarly reference works sometimes underestimate their antiquity. The *Oxford English Dictionary* dates the earliest known reference to *minced pies* as 1607, but in his *Five Hundred Points of Good Husbandrie* (1557) Thomas Tusser lists shred or minced pies as appropriate Christmas fare.[3] The *Oxford English Dictionary* gives 1667 as the earliest known use of the greeting *Merry Christmas*, yet in December 1539, John Hussee closed a letter to Lord Lisle by wishing him 'long life and much honour, and many merry Christmases'.[4]

All traditions have a beginning, and most of them undergo frequent alterations both in form and interpretation. To a degree it is *plus ça change, plus c'est la même chose*; yet the contrary is often true too. The same tradition can come to have a meaning quite different from its original one. As was just noted, the Christmas tree, especially its use in people's homes is a relatively recent custom in England, but the use of evergreen decorations at Christmas goes back at least to the Middle Ages, probably to pre-Christian times. In his survey of London, written four hundred years ago, John Stow commented that according to late medieval chronicles of London:[5]

Against the feast of Christmas everyone's house, as also the parish churches, were decked with holm [holly], ivy, bays and whatsoever of the season of the year afforded to be green. The conduits and standards in the streets were likewise garnished; amongst what I read, in the year 1444 ... towards morning on Candlemas day, at the Leadenhall in Cornhill, a standard [wooden frame] of a tree being set up in the midst of the pavement, fast in the ground, nailed full of holm and ivy, for disport of Christmas to the people, was torn up and cast down [by a severe storm].

The selections in Chapter VI offer the reader an opportunity to sample a potpourri of personal observations about Christmas drawn from the three centuries stretching from 1550 to 1850. With the introduction of printing, the growth of literacy and the increasing availability of writing materials, more and more people began to write letters, keep diaries and some to publish their writings in journals, newspapers and books. Although almost all of the authors found in this chapter belonged to the middle or upper classes, they represent a fairly wide distribution of religious and ethnic groups. Some modern historians seem to believe that people either celebrated Christmas as a serious religious holy day, or they turned it into a totally secular and obstreperous holiday. For many of the people quoted below, Christmas appears to have been a little of both. Certainly many people celebrated it as a *feast* – both as 'an elaborate meal often accompanied by a ceremony or entertainment', and as 'a periodic religious observance' (*Merriam Webster Dictionary*). As with many other religious holidays (Jewish, Moslem and others as well as Christian) special dishes were associated with Christmas. As noted above, mince pie is an English example which dates back at least to the sixteenth century. In Saxony a special Christmas fruit loaf, *Stollen*, was customary by the fifteenth century.

LONDON, 1551: A TEENAGE KING CELEBRATES THE CHRISTMAS SEASON
The Chronicle and Political Papers of King Edward VI[6]

Edward VI became king in 1547, when he was only ten. He was fourteen when he wrote the following notes in his journal. According to the editor, Edward wrote in 'a bold, clean and beautiful Italianate hand'.

[Dec.] 24   I began to keep holy this Christmas and continued to Twelfth Night ...

[Jan 3, 1552] The challenge that was made last month was fulfilled, the challengers were:

The Earl of Warwick	Sir Harry Neville
Sir Harry Sidney	Sir Harry Gale

[Next is a list of eighteen defendants in the tournament.]

These eighteen in all, ran six courses a piece at tilt against the challengers, and (in the end) accomplished their course right well, and so departed again.

The Emperor's ambassador moved me severely that my sister Mary might have mass, which, with no little reasoning, was denied him.

The foresaid challengers came in to the tourney, and the foresaid defendants entered in after[ward] with two more with them ... and fought right well, and so the challenge was accomplished. The same night was a play; after a talk between one that was called RICHES and the other YOUTH, whether [which] of them was better, some pretty reasoning, there came in six champions of either side [their names listed].

All these fought two to two at barriers in the hall, then came in two appareled like Almains; the earl of Ormonde and Jacques Granado [esquire of the stable], and two in like friars; but the Almains would not suffer them to pass till they had fought ... After this followed two masques, one of men, another of women, then a banquet of 120 dishes. This was the end of Christmas.

Although the feudal pageantry of Edward's Christmas celebration was medieval, the spirit of the times was changing. One wonders how enthusiastically Edward watched the jousting courtiers, who in real life were engaged in a deathly struggle to control him and his policies. Educated as a Protestant, the young king took his responsibilities very seriously. As he relates, he refused to let his older sister, and heir apparent, Mary, attend mass. Did he sense that his RICHES and YOUTH would soon leave him? He had less than two years to live. On his death Catholic Mary became queen.

LONDON, 1552[7]
Charles Wriothesley, *Chronicle of England during the reign of the Tudors*

On Christmas day in the afternone, when my Lord Mayor and Aldermen rode to Pawles, all the children of Christ's Hospitall stood in aray, from St Lawrence Lane in Cheap, toward Pawles, all in one livery of gowns of russet and red caps, both men children and the maydens with kerchiefs on their heades, all the masters of the the hospitall beginninge first, next them the phisicians, and the surgeons, with bandes about theyr neckes of white and green satten, and between every xx children, one woman keeper, which children were in number xvii score.

CHRISTMAS IN THE COUNTRY[8]
Thomas Tusser, *Five Hundred Pointes of Good Husbandrie*

Chapter 29
Christmas Husbandrie Fare

Good husband and huswife now cheefly be glad,
things handsom to have, as ought to be had;
They both doo provide against Christmas doo come,
to welcome good neighbour, good cheere to have some.
Good bread and good drinke, a good fier in the hall,
brawn[meat], pudding and souse[picked pork] and good mustard
    withall.
Beefe, mutton, and porke, shred pies of the best,
pig, veale, goose and capon, and turkey well drest;
Cheese, apples and nuts, joly Carols to heare,
as then in the countrie is counterd good cheare.

What cost to good husband is any of this?
good household provision onely it is.

Of other the like, I doo leave out a menie
that costeth the husbandman never a pennie.

Chapter 30
A Christmas Caroll (fifth and last verse)

For these glad newes this feast doth bring
to God the Sonne and holy Ghost
let men give thanks, rejoice and sing,
from world to world, from cost to cost:
for all the gifts so many waies
that God doth send,
let us in Christ give God the praies
till life shall end.

The carol is followed by this admonition:

At Christmas be merrie and thankful with all
And feast thy poor neighbours the great and the small,
Yea, all the yeer long, to the poor let us give,
Gods blessing to follow us while we doo live.

Chapter 32
Januaries Husbandrie

When Christmas is ended, bid feasting adue,
go play the good husband, thy stock to renue.
…

LANCASHIRE, 1588-1605
CHRISTMAS SUPPLIES FOR A COUNTRY HOUSE[9]

[December, 1588] Henrie Baker wch broughte a signete [cynet or young swan] from Mr Boulde ij s: foure pottes of honey v s. iiij d: towe coppley of rabates xv d., eight dowsone of eggs xvj d. Henrie Baker wch broughte a fatte doe from Mr Boulde v s.; towe lynkes [pitchforks] ij s.; Mr Brounlaye mane wch brought half a fatte calfe from his Mr, xij d. … geven to a mane wch brought a doe from Lyme iiij s.; towe piggs ij s. … geven to the plaeres of Preston v s.; to towe pieperes [pipers, musicians] viij d.; to onne wch did bigge [beg] for the prisoners in the Marchalsie [jail] ij s.

The accounts for December 1590 are similar but include more game birds, among them:

four graye plovers, three woodcokes and two parteredges, fyffe snypes, six dowson larkes.

The accounts for most Decembers have similar entries, with some variations, such as the mention of herring and codfish in 1695. The 1601 list includes:

Spyce against Christemas, a quarter of a pound of analseed, ij onze pepp; halfe a pound of curwens ... onne pound prunes and ... maze and cloves.

The 1605 list includes similar items:

Spyce for the howse use: one pound of great raysons, one pound of corwayns; half a pound of annelles [anise seeds]; saveron, sugar and cloves.

VIRGINIA, 1608
CAPTAIN JOHN SMITH CELEBRATES CHRISTMAS[10]

The next night being lodged at Kecoughan 6 or 7 daies, the extreame wind, raine, frost and snowe, caused us to keepe Christmas amongst the Salvages, where we were never more merrie, nor fedde on more plentie of good oysters, fish, flesh, wild foule, and good breade, nor never had better fires in England then in the drie warme smokie houses of Kecoughan.

PLYMOUTH BAY COLONY, 1621
William Bradford, *History of the Plymouth Plantation*[11]

The day called Christmas Day the Govr cal'd them out to worke (as was usual) but the moste of this new company excused themselves, and said that it went against their consciences to work on that day. So the Govr told them that if they made it a matter of conscience he would spare them till they were better informed. So he led away the rest of them; but when they came home at noon from their work he found them in the street at play openly, some pitching the bar, and some at stoolball and such like sports. So he went to them and took away their impliments and told them it was against his conscience that they should play and others work.

A DUTCHMAN IN LONDON 1662-63[12]

On 11th Jan. [January 1, 1662 by the Julian calendar still used in England until 1752] we went to Lincoln's College and saw the triumph of the 'Prince de la Grange'

Nota. At the beginning of the King's reign one of the students is chosen by the professors of the college whose turn it is to act as a prince, who has an open court for his college for thirteen days from Christmas to Twelfth Night: during this time the professors and governors have nothing to say, while he who holds court like a king, appoints all kinds of high and low officers, and has an expensively dressed retinue. The prince this year was a Sir Lard, the son of a mighty rich man from the Principality of Wales, who has 140 ploughs working on his own land ...

The other students contribute somewhat towards this, but not very much. This prince, pretending that his baggage had not yet arrived, sends his chancellor as an ambassador to the King [Charles II] with a letter requesting two of his maces, which are sent to him and are carried at all times behind his halberdiers beforre him and his council. He has to entertain the King with many important persons and his entire college at a royal banquet, upholding his dignity as the King himself, addressing him as his brother. He always remains covered, while everybody attends to him bareheaded. He wears a different dress every day; the robes which he wore for the King's visit cost him 350 pounds. All told he is an expensive but short lived king.

On the 2nd January [1663] we went bear baiting ...

On the 4th, Christmas day [1662] old style, we went to church in St Paul's and heard music and sermon; in the afternoon we heard the service below St Paul's and then went to see the heads on the steaks near and at the Tower.

Among the heads Shellink viewed were those of the regicide judges who had condemned Charles I to death in 1648. Most of them had been tried and executed after the Restoration. A few escaped, among them Goffe and Whalley, who fled to Connecticut. Both have a street in New Haven named in their honour.

SAMUEL PEPYS ATTENDS A CATHOLIC MASS IN ST JAMES' PALACE, CHRISTMAS EVE, 1667[13]

[Dec, 24] Up, and in the morning to the office, and at noon with my clerks to dinner, and then to the office again, busy at the office till six at night, then by coach to St James', it being about six at night; my design being to see the ceremonies, this night being the eve of Christmas, at the Queen's chapel. But it being not begun I to Westminster Hall, and there staid and talked, and then to the Swan, and there drank and talked, and did banter a little Frank, and so to Whitehall; and sent my coach round, I through the Park to chapel, where I got in almost to the rail, and with a great deal of patience staid from noine at night to two in the morning, in a very great crowd; and there expected, but found nothing extraordinary, there being nothing but a high mass. The Queen was there and some ladies. But Lord! what an odd thing it was for me to be in a crowd of people, here a footman, there a beggar, here a fine lady, there a poor zealous papist, and here a Protestant, two or three together, come to see the show. I was afeared of my pocket beeing picked very much ...

Their music very good indeed, but their service I confess to frivolous, that there can be no zeal go along with it, and I do find by them themselves that they do run over their beads with one hand, and point and play and talk and make signs with the other in the midst of their masse. But all things very rich and beautiful; and I see the papists have the wit, most of them, to bring cushions to kneel on, which I wanted, and was mightily troubled to kneel. All being done, and I am sorry for my coming, missing what I expected; which was, to have a child born and dressed there, and a great of do; but we broke up, and nothing like it done: and there I left people receiving the sacrament: and the Queen gone, and the ladies; only my Lady Castelmayne, who looked prettily in her nightclothes, and so took my coach, which waited, and away to Covent Garden, to set two gentlemen and a lady, who came thither to see also, and did make mighty mirth in their talk of this religion. And so I stopped, having set them down and drank some burnt wine at the Rose Tavern door, while the constables came, and two or three Bellmen went by.

[25th]. It brings a fine, light, moonshine morning, and so home round the city, and stopped and dropped money at five or six places, where I was willinger to do, it being Christmas day, and so home, and there find my wife in bed, and Jane and the maids making pyes, and so to bed, and slept wel, and rose about nine and to church; and so home. Wyfe and girl and I alone at dinner – a good dinner, and all the afternoon at home, my wife reading to me 'The History of the Drummer of Mr Mompesson', which is a strange story of spies, and worth reading indeed. In the evening comes Mr Pelling, and sat and supped with us; and very good company, he reciting to us many good copies of verses of Dr Wilde, who writ 'Iter Boreale', and so to bed.

Charles II was married to Queen Catherine of Braganza from Portugal. As queen she was permitted to have Catholic services in the palace, although they were not allowed elsewhere, except in the embassies of Catholic countries.

CHRISTMAS AT SEA, 1675
From the diary of a naval chaplain, the Revd Henry Teonge[14]

At 4 in the morning our trumpeters all doe flatt [*blow*] their trumpetts, and begin at our Captain's cabin and thence to all the officers and gentlemen's cabins; playing a levite (*reveille*) at each doore, and bidding good morrow, wishing a merry Christmas. After they go to their station, viz. on the poope, and sound three levitts in honor of the morning. At 10 we goe to prayers and sermon; text Zach, ix, 9. Our Capitaine had all officers and gentlemen, to dinner with him, where wee had excellent good fayre: a ribb of beife, plumb-puddings, mince pies etc., and plenty of good wines of severall sorts; dranke healths to the King, to our wives and friends; and ended the day with much civill myrth ...

On Twelfth Night

Wee had a great kake made in which was put a beane for the King, apease for the queen, a cloave for the knave, a forked stick for the coockold, a rag for the slutt. The kake was cut in severall pieces in the great cabin, and all putt into a napkin, out of which everyone took a piece, as out of a lottery; then each piece is broken to see what is in it, which caused much laughter, to see our lieutenant prove the coockold and more to see us tumble one over the other in the cabin, by reason of the ruff weather.

BRITTANY, 1675
Letters of Madame de Sévigné to her Daughter and Friends[15]

Letter 482, to Mme de Grignan
Aux Rochers, Christmas Day [1675]

This is the day, my child, in which I have given my pen liberty to write what it pleases, it chooses to begin by the joy I feel at having returned rested and in peace from Vitré, after two tedious days of talk and ceremony, listening to all the idle news that is more suited for Paris; I had the satisfaction, however, to find fault with some of it, particularly the ball M. de Malo gave for the [leaders of the] states. Madame de Tarente laughed heartily to see me so heated and full of reasons for my disapproval. But I really prefer to be in these woods … rather than at Vitré with the air of a fine lady. The good Princess went to her religious assembly: I heard them all singing their hearts out. As I had never heard such tones, I felt real pleasure in attending mass after it; I have not for a long time been so much pleased with being a good Catholic. I dined with the minister: my son argued like a demon. I went to vespers to thwart him; now I understand a little about the sacred obstinacy of martyrdom. My son is gone to Rennes to see the governor. Last night we performed our devotions in our beautiful chapel. …

I conclude with wishing you a merry festival, and assuring you, that I love you with an affection which will probably accompany me *in articulo mortis* [till death].

AN EPIPHANY PROCESSION IN NEW FRANCE, 1680
THREE INDIAN CHIEFS VISIT THE INFANT JESUS
From an account by a Jesuit missionary[16]

All our savages, but especially the hurons, profess to have a special esteem for the all-endearing mystery of the birth of our Lord Jesus Christ. I have

seen some notable proofs of this given by these latter; they themselves have entreated the father, long before the feast day, to make arrangements so as to celebrate it in the most solemn manner possible. They sent their children to seek for what could be used in constructing a grotto, in which they were to make a representation of the mystery; and I took pleasure in hearing a little girl who, having brought with much care a beautiful sort of grass, said that she had done it in the thought and hope that the infant Jesus might be laid upon that grass. Our good Christians made some more serious preparations, for they all confessed; and those to whom permission was given to receive communion, did so very devoutly, at the midnight mass. The grotto, which was well fitted to inspire devotion, was incessantly visited; and it rendered a very pleasing although rather protracted Service ... As a climax to their devotion, they asked that the infant Jesus should do them the favor of visiting them, by being carried through their village ... The matter was conceded to them, and carried out on the Day of the epiphany in a manner that seems to me worthy of being recorded. For my part, I was much touched by it.

They desired, then, in execution of their design, to imitate what in other ages had been done by the three great stranger Captains, who came to confess and adore Jesus Christ in the Manger, and afterward went to preach him in their own country. All the hurons, Christians, and non-Christians, divided themselves into three companies, according to the different nations that constitute their village; and, after choosing their Chiefs, one for each nation, they furnished them with porcelain, of which they were to make an offering to the infant Jesus. Every one adorned himself as handsomely as he could. The three Captains each had a scepter in his hand, to which he fastened the offering, and wore a gaudy head-dress in guise of a crown. Each company took up a different position. The signal for marching having been given them at the sound of a trumpet, they heeded the sound as that of a voice inviting them to go to see and adore the Infant God new-born. Just as the 1st company took up their march – conducted by a star fastened to a large standard of the Color of Sky-blue, and having at the [head] their Captain, before whom was carried his banner – the 2nd company, seeing the first marching, demanded of them [aloud] the object of their journey; and on learning it, they joined themselves to them, having in like manner their chief at their head with his banner. The 3rd company, more advanced on the Road, did as the second; and, one after another, they continued their march, and entered our church, the star remaining at the entrance. The 3 chiefs, having first prostrated themselves, and laid their Crowns and scepters at the feet of the

infant Jesus in the Cradle, offered their Congratulations and presents to their savior. As they did so, they made a public protestation of the submission and obedience that they desired to render him; solicited faith for those who possessed it not, and the protection for all of their nation and for all that land; and, in conclusion, entreated him to approve that they should bring him into their village, of which they desired he should be master. I was engaged in carrying the little statue of the infant, which inspired great devotion; I took it from the grotto, and from the cradle, and carried it on a fine linen cloth. Every one seemed touched, and pressed forward in the crowd, to get nearer the holy Child. Our hurons left the church in the same order in which they had come. I came after them, carrying the little statue, preceded by two frenchmen bearing a large standard, on which was represented the infant Jesus with his holy mother. All the algonquins – and especially the Christians, who had been invited to assist in the pious function – followed, and accompanied the infant Jesus. They marched, then, in that order toward the village, and went into a Cabin of our hurons, where they had prepared Jesus a lodging, as appropriate as they could make it. There they offered thanksgivings and prayers, in accordance with their devotion; and the divine child was conducted back to the church and replaced in the grotto. The Christian algonquins were afterward invited by the Christian hurons to a feast.

NEW YORK, 1679-80
Journal of a Voyage to New York, by Jasper Dawkins and Peter Sluyter[17]

4th Thursday [January]

It was now Christmas, according to the old style. It has frozen hard during the night. We went to church to hear Do. Niewnhuise preach, but more to give no offense to the people, than either on his or our own account.

Dawkins and Sluter had come to New York in search of a place for a colony for religious refugees. They were anxious to please their hosts. The entry seems to indicate that the Dutch Calvinists in what had been New Amsterdam, unlike the New England Puritans, celebrated Christmas as a church holy day.

CHRISTMAS IN YORKSHIRE, ENGLAND, 1682
Memoirs of Sir John Reresby[18]

[Dec. 24] I kept Christmas at Thriberge, which it was formerly the custome to observe with great mirth and ceremony, but was much lessened, few keeping the custom of it in thos parts at that time but myselfe when I was at Thriberge. The manner of it for this year was thus:

Sunday, being Christmas Eve, I invited all the poorer sort of my tenents of Deneby and Hoton, being nineteen in number; on Christmas Day the poorer sort of Thriberge, Brinsford and Mexbrough, being twenty-six; on St Stephen's Day all the farmers and better sort of tenents of Deneby, Hoton, and Mexbrough, being in number forty-five.

Dec. 30 On the 30 of December there were invited to dine with me eighteen gentlemen and their wives from severall parts of the neighbourhood.

Jan. 1 There were sixteen more invited of gentlemen.

3 January the 3rd, twenty others.

4 Twelve of the neighbouring clergie.

6 Seven gentlemen and tradesmen of Rotherham and other places.

There laid at my hous of thes severall days, Sir Jarvaise Cutler; Anthony Francland, Esq.; Jasper Blythman, Esq., justice of the peace; Mr Turner; Captain King, an officer from Yorke; Mr Rigden, merchant of Yorke, and his wife, a handsome woman; Mrs Blythman and her daughter; Mr Belton, an ingenious clergieman, butt too much a good fellow; the cornet and quarter-master to my troop, with others. For musick I had two violins and a base from Doncaster that wore my livery, that plaid well for the country; two bagpipes for the common people; a trompeter and a drummer. The expence of liquor, both wine and others, was considerable, as well as of provisions, and my guests appeared well satisfyed. I dined two days from home this Christmas, one day at Sir Gervase Cutlers, another at my Lord Straffords. Though such remarks as thes may seem frivolous to others, yet to posterity of one's own family (for whom this worke is chiefly designed) they may appear otherwise, that sort of curiosity being as well pleased with enquiry into less things sometimes as greater.

Reresby remarks above that few keep the season as they used to, a lament often heard, then as now, at Christmas. It is impossible to tell whether Reresby's yule time hospitality was typical of men in his position. Such generous hospitality must have been unusual but certainly not unique. Addison attributes similar behaviour to his fictitious Tory squire, Sir Roger de Coverly.

SIR ROGER DE COVERLY'S CHRISTMAS, 1711
From The Spectator, no. 269 (by Joseph Addison)[19]

He [Sir Roger] fell into an account of the diversions which had passed in his house during the holidays; for Sir Roger, after the laudable custom of his ancestors, always keeps open house at Christmas. I learned from him that he had killed eight fat hogs for the season, that he had dealt about his chines [butchered pork] very liberally among his neigbours, and that in particular he had sent a string of hog's-puddings with a pack of cards to every poor family in the parish. 'I have often thought,' says Sir Roger, 'it happens very well that Christmas should fall out in the middle of the winter. It is the most dead uncomfortable time of the year, when the poor people would suffer very much from their poverty and cold, if they had not good cheer, warm fires, and Christmas gambols to support them. I love to rejoice their poor hearts at this season, and to see the whole village merry in my great hall. I allow a double quantity of malt to my small-beer, and set it a-running for twelve days to everyone that calls for it. I have always a piece of cold beef and a mince pie upon the table, and am wonderfully pleased to see my tenants pass away a whole evening in playing their innocent tricks and smutting one another [blackening their faces] …'

I was very much delighted with the reflection of my old friend, which carried so much goodness in it. He then launched into the praise of the late act of Parliament for securing the Church of England [aimed at excluding Protestant Dissenters from holding office], and told me with great satisfaction that he believed it already began to take effect, for that a rigid dissenter, who chanced to dine at his house on Christmas Day, had been observed to eat very plentifully of his plum porridge.

RECOLLECTIONS OF A GERMAN CHRISTMAS
Letters of Lisette, Elizabeth Charlotte, Princess Palatine and Duchess of Orleans[20]

Marly [France], 11 January, 1711, to Sophie [Electress of Hanover and mother of the future George I of England]

... I remember that in Hanover Christmas was always celebrated for three days, I am sure the box trees have been decorated with candles for your grandchildren. How I should have loved to see it. Here they have no idea of it at all. I wanted to introduce it but Monsieur [her husband, the duke of Orleans] said, '*Vous voulez nous donner de vos modes allemandes pour nous fair la dépense, je vous baise la main.*' I love seeing children enjoying themselves, but my son's children enjoy absolutely nothing. I never saw such children in all my days.

According to the article on 'Jeux, Fêtes, Spectacles', in *La Vie Populaire en France au Moyen Age à Nos Jours*,[21] the Christmas tree was introduced into France in 1837 by Princess Helen of Mecklenburg, when she came to Paris as the bride of the duke of Orleans. In Germany, the Christmas tree, as a domestic decoration, dates back at least to the sixteenth century. Princess Charlotte's letter implies that a tree (although of box not fir) was a regular part of Christmas at the elector's court in Hanover by the late seventeenth century. An incident in Goethe's *Sorrows of Young Werther*, published in 1770, clearly implies that Christmas trees and the exchange of presents were customary in German households by that time. When Werther visits Charlotte a few days before Christmas he finds her busy arranging Christmas presents for her brothers and sisters. During their conversation he recalls the excitement of opening a door and seeing a Christmas tree, 'decorated with fruit and candy and lighted with wax candles'.[22]

CHRISTMAS AND BOXING DAY (DECEMBER 26) IN LONDON, 1731[23]

Comments by a traveler, who, looking out of his window:
Saw the meek and resigned appearance of a crowd outside the church doors: they were the poor of the parish assembled to receive the charita-

ble doles and alms of the season. As soon as the distribution was over their meekness disappeared and they took to fighting over their shares. After the fighting they all trooped off to the public house, whence they were carried or led, an hour or two afterwards.

The next day was Boxing Day, when everybody comes for his Christmas box; from the assistant to the tradesman. The clerk – even the parish clerk was not too proud, the bellman, the watch, the constable, the beadle, the dustman – they all came in one long train.

WESTOVER, VIRGINIA, 1739 AND 1740
Another Secret Diary of William Boyd of Westover[24]

December 25, 1739   I rose about 6, read Hebrew and Greek. I prayed and had tea. I danced. The weather was cold and clear, the wind southwest but blowing fiercely. I went not to church but cleaned my self. After church came John Stith and his wife, all the Andersons, and Mr Pinkard with John Stith's son and daughter to dinner, and I ate boiled turkey and oysters. After dinner everyone went away but John Stith and his wife. I supped and prayed.

December 25, 1740   I rose about 6, read Hebrew and Greek. I prayed and had coffee. I danced, The weather very cold and cloudy, the wind north and threatened more snow. Nobody went to church except my son because of the cold. I put myself in order. After church came two play fellows for my son, young Stith and Hardyman. I ate roast turkey. After dinner we talked and I danced. I talked with my people and prayed.

A PRESBYTERIAN DOCTOR OBSERVES CHRISTMAS, BURY, LANCASHIRE, 1740-43
The Diary of Richard Kay, 1716-51[25]

[Dec. 1740]   This Day being Christmas Day I've been at Bury Chappel and have heard a sermon preached by Mr Dawson from Rixington from John 4, 11, after dinner we distributed a considerable quantity of Bread and Lin Cloth to poor People: our neighbouring Tenants as usual supp'd with us. Lord, as thou loved us in sending thine only begotten son Jesus Christ into the world, that we might live through him, so may we all love one another.

The entry for Christmas 1741 and 1742 are much the same, but in 1743 Kay attended an Anglican church, St James', in Manchester to see the royal family.

... Where Bishop of Hereford read prayers, and the Bishop of Salisbury preached from 1 Tim. 1, 15; His Majesty, the Duke and Princesses Amandis and Caroline received the sacrament from the Bishop of London. We came not in the chappel during that time but the Royal family pass'd by us thro' the wide galery to and from the sacrament; we then dined with Lord Wiloughby in Suffolk street: heard Mr Foster preach the Evening lecture at the Old Jewry from Rom. 2. 11. Lord let all my Opportunities of every Kind be both for my present and future Improvement and Advantage.

CHRISTMAS EVE, 1741, BETHLEHEM, PENNSYLVANIA[26]

From *A History of Bethlehem, Pennsylvania 1741-1892*, by Joseph Mortimer Levering. Although this history is not a contemporary source, the following account of Count Zinzindorf's visit to the Moravian settlers is based on a contemporary description.

The first extant record after the mention of his [Count Zinzendorf's] arrival brings to view an interesting Christmas Eve scene. They were assembled in the little log house at the close of a Sunday, December 24 N[ew] S[tyle] [January 5, 1742 Old Style] to observe the vigils of Christmas on the same day on which their brethren in the far-off Fatherland were similarly engaged. Besides other services of the day, they celebrated the Holy Communion ... Then, with the Christmas theme uppermost, their devotions were protracted until after nine o'clock. It was a novel and unique occasion, which awakened peculiar emotions ... It stirred the quick fancy of the Count ... Acting on impulse, he rose and led the way into the part of the building in which the cattle were kept, while he began to sing the words of a German Epiphany hymn.

Jesu rufe mich	Jesus call Thou me
Von der Welt, dass ich	From the world to flee
Zu dir eile	To Thee hasting
Nicht verweile	Without resting
Jesu rufe mich	Jesus call Thou me
Nicht Jerusalem	Not Jerusalem
Sondern Bethlehem	Rather Bethlehem
Hat bescheret	Gave us that which
Was uns naehret;	Maketh life rich
Nicht Jerusalem.	Not Jerusalem.

Moved by the words of the hymn [*Nicht Jerusalem, sondern Bethlehem*], and the inspiration of the occasion, the assembled company chose Bethlehem as the name of their new settlement.

ADVENT MUSIC, DUBLIN, 1745 AND 1750
Autobiography and Correspondence of Mrs Delany[27]

21 December, 1745   Last Monday the Dean [her husband] and I went to the rehearsal of the Messiah, for relief of poor debtors: it was very well performed, and I much delighted. You know how much I delight in music, and that piece is very charming: but I had not the courage to go to the performance of night, the weather was so excessively bad and I thought it would be hazardous to come out of so great a crowd so far, that is my kind guardian thought so for me.

December 18, 1750 to Bernard Granville Esq. [in London]   I think I have lately been as guilty of laziness about writing as you can be, but though it may have appeared laziness, truly I have been the contrary. Four days in the week I am engaged in painting. I am now copying a large Madonna and Child after Guido, for our chapel. I believe it is an original, but it has been much damaged ...

I was at the rehearsal and performance of the Messiah, and though the *voices* and *hands* were wanting to do it justice, it was tolerably performed, and gave great pleasure – 'tis heavenly. Morell conducted it, and I expected would have *spoiled* it, but was agreeably surprised to find the contrary; he came off with great applause. I thought it would be impossible for his wild fancy and fingers to have kept within bounds; but Handel's music inspires and *awed him*.

Handel's *Messiah* had its first public performance in Dublin in April 1742, but within a few years it became associated primarily with Advent and Christmas. Performances of the oratoria for the benefit of charity became a tradition in Dublin and soon afterwards in London.

A SWEDISH VISITOR SPENDS CHRISTMAS IN PHILADELPHIA, 1749
Peter Kalm's *Travels in North America*[28]

January the 5th, 1750 (Christmas Day, 1749, Old Style)   To-day Christmas Day was celebrated in the city, but not with such reverence as it is in old

Sweden. On the evening before, the bells of the English Church rang for a long time to announce the approaching Yuletide. In the morning guns were fired off in various parts of the town. People went to church, much in the same manner as on ordinary Sundays, both before and after dinner [in Sweden Christmas services were held at five or six in the morning]. This took place only in the English, Swedish and German churches. The Quakers did not regard this day any more remarkable than other days. Stores were open, and anyone might sell or purchase what he wanted. But servants had a three-day vacation period. Nowhere was Christmas celebrated with more solemnity than in the Roman Church. Three sermons were preached there, and that which contributed most to the splendor of the ceremony was the beautiful music heard to-day. It was this music which attracted so many people. It must be emphasized that of all the churches in Philadelphia only the Swedish and the Catholic possessed organs. There formerly been one in the English temple, but it later become useless, and there had not yet been any measures taken to procure a new one. The organ in the Swedish church had also through improper care become worthless. Consequently an organ was to be heard only in the papal place of worship. The officiating priest was a Jesuit, who also played the violin, and he had collected a few others who played the same instrument. So there was good instrumental music, singing from the organ-gallery besides.

People of all faiths gathered here, not only for the high mass but particularly the vespers. Pews and altar were decorated with branches of mountain laurel, whose leaves are green in winter time and resemble the lauro-cerasus (cherry laurel). At morning service the clergyman stood in front of the altar; but in the afternoon he was in the gallery playing and singing.

There was no more baking of bread for the Christmas festival than for other days; and no Christmas porridge on Christmas Eve [in Sweden the Christmas season lasted three weeks with many special breads and other festive dishes]. One did not seem to know what it meant to wish anyone a merry Christmas. However [after I had written this] I heard several members of the English Church wish one another a happy Christmas holiday. In the English church a sermon was preached in the morning; but after dinner only a prayer meeting was held, and on the day after Christmas again, only a prayer meeting. But, as I have already noted, the Quakers paid not the slightest attention to Christmas; carpentry work, blacksmithing and other trades are plied on this day as on other days. If Christmas Day falls on a Wednesday or Saturday, which are market days, the Quakers will bring all kinds of food into the market as usual; but no others will, and only Quakers will buy anything of them on such a day. Others make provision so that purchases will prove unnecessary until the first market day after Christmas. The same custom is observed at New Year's. At first the Presbyterians did not care much for celebrating Christmas, but when they saw most of their members going to the English church on that day, they also started to have services.

JAMES BOSWELL'S CHRISTMAS ROMANCE, 1762

James Boswell (1740-1795), the famous biographer of Samuel Johnson, came to London from Scotland in 1762. Soon after his arrival he met an attractive actress named Louisa Lewis.[29]

Friday 24 December. I waited on Louisa. Says she, 'I have been very unhappy since you were here. I have been thinking of what I said to you. I find that such a connection would make me miserable.' 'I hope, Madam, I am not disagreeable to you.' 'No, Sir, you are not, if it was the first duke in England I spoke to, I should say just the same thing.' 'But pray, Madam, what is your objection?' 'Really. Sir, I have many disagreeable apprehensions. It may be known. Circumstances might be very troublesome. I beg of you, Sir, consider of it. Your own good sense will agree with me. Instead of visiting me as you do now, you would find a discontented, unhappy creature.' I was quite confused. I did not know what to say. At last I agreed to think of it and see her on Sunday. I came home and dined in dejection ...

Saturday 25 December. The night before I did not rest well. I was really violently in love with Louisa. I thought she did not care for me. I thought that if I did not gain her affections, I would appear despicable to myself. This day I was in a better frame, being Christmas day, which has always inspired me with the most agreeable of feelings. I went to St Paul's Church and in that magnificent temple fervently adored the GOD of goodness and mercy, and heard a sermon by the Bishop of Oxford on the publishing of glad tidings of great joy. I then went to Child's, where little was passing. ...

I then sat a while at Coutt's, and then at McFarlane's, and then to Davies's. Johnson was gone to Oxford. I was introduced to Mr Dodsley, a good, decent, conversible man. Mr Goldsmith, a curious, odd, pedantic fellow with some genius. It was quite a literary dinner. I had seen no warm vituals for four days, and therefore played a very bold knife and fork; It is inconceivable how hearty I eat and how comfortable I felt myself after it. We talked entirely in the way of Geniuses.

We talked of poetry. Said Goldsmith, 'The miscellaneous poetry of this age is nothing like that of the last; it is very poor. Why there now, Mr Dodsley, is your Collection?' [Robert Dodsley, publisher of *Collection of Poems by Several Hands*]

Dodsley: 'I think that equal to those made by Dryden and Pope.'

Goldsmith: 'To consider, Sir, as villages, yours may be as good; but no edifices equal to the Ode on St Cecilia's Day, Absalom and Achitophel, or the Rape of the Lock,' ...

We had more many more topics which I don't remember.

Sunday 26 December. I went to Whitehall Chapel and heard service. I took a whim to go through all the churches and chapels in London, taking one each Sunday.

At one I went to Louisa's. I told her my passion in the warmest terms. I told her that my happiness absolutely depended upon her. She said she was running the greatest risk, 'Then', said I, 'Madam, you will show the greatest generosity to a most sincere lover.' She said we should take time to consider of it, and then we should better determine how to act. We agreed that the time should be a week, and that if I remained of the same opinion, she would make me blessed. There is no telling how easy it made my mind to be convinced that she did not despise me, but on the contrary had a tender heart and wished to make me easy and happy ...

Louisa granted the ardent Boswell the 'happiness' he so much desired. Unhappily it proved of short duration. Before the end of January Boswell had contracted a venereal disease. When he accused Louisa of deceiving him, she admitted that she had been infected, but insisted that she had been well for many months. He was furious. Having concluded the affair he wrote in his journal:

Thus ended my intrique with the fair Louisa, which I flattered myself so much with, and from which I expected at least a winter's copulation. It is indeed very hard. I cannot say, like young fellows who get themselves clapped in a bawdy-house, that I will take better care again. For I really did take care. However, since I am fairly trapped, let me make the best of it. I have not got in from imprudence. It is merely a chance of war

JOHN ADAMS SPENDS CHRISTMAS AT HOME, 1765
(*the year of the Stamp Act*)[30]

December 25, 1765. Christmas   At Home. Thinking, reading, searching, concerning Taxation without Consent, concerning the great Pause and

Rest in Business. By the Laws of England Justice flows, with an uninter-
rupted Stream: In that Musick the Law knows neither Rests nor Pauses.
Nothing but Violence, Invasion or Rebellion can obstruct the River or
untune the Instrument ...

Went not to Christmas. Dined at Home. Drank Tea at Grandfather
Quinceys. The old Gentleman, inquisitive about the Hearing before the
Governor and Council ... The old Lady as merry and chatty as ever, with
her Stories out of the News Papers, of a Woman longing to throw beef
Stakes in a Mans Face and giving him a Pipe [cask] of Madeira for
humoring her, and of the Doctor who could tell by a Persons Face all the
Disorders he or she suffered or would suffer.

Spent the Evening at Home, with my Partner and no other Company ...

December 26th Thursday. At Home by the Fireside viewing with
Pleasure, the falling Snow and the Prospect of a large one.

A WAR-TIME CHRISTMAS
ACCOUNT OF THE BATTLE OF TRENTON, 1776

From the 'Diary of an Officer on Washington's Staff'. The authorship of this account is
not certain, but historians generally agree that it is based on the recollections of an eye-
witness.[31]

December 23 Orders have been issued to cook rations for three days.
Washington has just given the countersign, 'Victory or Death'. He has
written a letter to General Caldwalder at Bristol, which he has entrusted
to me to copy. He intends to cross the river, make a ten-mile march to
Trenton and attack Rall just before daybreak. Ewing is to cross and seize
the bridge crossing the Assunpink [on the road leading south to Border-
town]. Putnam and Caldwalder are to cross and make a feint of attacking
Donop at Border-town so that he cannot hasten to Rall's assistance.

December 24 A scout just in sayes that the Hessians have a picket on
the Pennington road half a mile out from Trenton, and another at
Dicenson's house on the river road.

December 25 Christmas morning. They make a great deal of Christmas in Germany, and no doubt the Hessians will drink a great deal of
beer and have a dance tonight. They will be sleepy tomorrow morning.
Washington will set the tune for them about daybreak. The rations are
cooked. New flints and ammunition have been distributed. Colonel
Glover's fishermen from Marblehead, Massachusetts, are to manage the

boats just as they did in the retreat from Long Island.

Christmas, 6 p.m. The regiments have had their evening parade, but instead of returning to their quarters are marching toward the ferry. The wind is northeast and beats in the faces of the men. It will be a terrible night for the soldiers who have no shoes. Some of them have tied old rags about their feet; others are barefoot, but I have not heard a man complain. They are ready to suffer any hardship and die rather than give up their liberty. I have copied the order for marching. Both divisions are to go from the ferry to Bear Tavern, two miles. They will separate there; Washington will accompany Greene's division with a part of the artillery down the Penningtom road. Sullivan and the rest of the artillery will take the river road.

December 26, 3 a.m. I am waiting in the ferry house. The troops are all over, and the boats have gone back for the artillery. We are three hours behind the set time. Glover's men have had a hard time to force the boats through the floating ice with snow drifting in their faces. I have never seen Washington so determined as he is now. He stands on the bank of the river, wrapped in his cloak, superintending the landing of his troops. He is calm and collected, but very determined. The storm is changing to sleet and cuts like a knife. The last cannon is being landed, and we are ready to mount our horses.

December 26, noon It was nearly four o'clock when we started. The two divisions divided at Bear Tavern. At Birmingham, three and a half miles south of the tavern, a man came with a message from General Sullivan that the storm was wetting the muskets and rendering them unfit for service.

'Tell General Sullivan', said Washington, 'to use the bayonet. I am resolved to take Trenton.'

It was broad daylight when we came to a house where a man was chopping wood. He was very much surprised when he saw us.

'Can you tell me where the Hessian picket is?' Washington asked.

The man hesitated, but I said, 'You need not be frightened, it is General Washington who asks you the question.'

His face brightened, and he pointed toward the house of Mr Howell.

It was just eight o'clock. Looking down the road I saw a Hessian running out from the house. He yelled in Dutch [*Deutsch*, German] and swung his arms. Three or four others came out with their guns. Two of them fired at us, but the bullets whistled over our heads. Some of General Stephen's men rushed forward and captured two. The others took to their heels, running toward Mr Calhoun's house, where the picket guard was stationed, about twenty men under Captain Altenbrockum. They came running out of the house, some of them fired at us, others ran toward the village.

The next moment we heard drums beat and a bugle sound, and then from the west came the boom of a cannon. George Washington's face lighted up instantly, for he knew it was one of Sullivan's guns.

We could see great commotion down toward the meeting house, men running here and there, officers swinging their swords, artillerymen harnessing their horses. Captain Forrest unlimbered his guns. Washington gave the order to advance, and we rushed on to the junction of King and Queen streets. Forrest wheeled six of his cannon into position to sweep both streets. The riflemen under Colonel Hand and Cott's and Lawson's battalions went upon the run through the fields on the left to gain possession of the Princeton Road. The Hessians were just ready to open fire with two of their cannon when Captain [William] Washington and Lieutenant [James] Monroe with their men rushed forward and captured them.

We saw Rall coming riding up the street from his headquarters, which were at Stacy Pott's house. We could hear him shouting in Dutch, 'My brave soldiers, advance!'

His men were frightened and confused, for our men were firing upon them from fences and houses and they were falling fast. Instead of advancing they ran into an apple orchard, the officers tried to rally them, but our men kept advancing and picking off the officers. It was not long before Rall tumbled from his horse and his soldiers threw down their guns and gave themselves as prisoners.

While this was taking place on the Pennington road, Colonel John Stark from New Hamshire, in the advance on the river road, was driving Knyphausen's men pell mell through the town. Sullivan sent a portion of his troops under St Clair to seize the bridges and cut off the retreat of the Hessians toward Bordentown. Sullivan's men shot the artillery horses and captured two cannon attached to Knyphausen's regiment.

December 26, 3 p.m.   I have been talking with Rall's adjutant, Lieutenant Piel. He says that Rall sat down to a grand dinner at the Trenton Tavern Christmas Day, that he drank a great deal of wine and sat up nearly all night playing cards. He had been in bed but a short time when the battle began and was sound asleep. Piel shook him but found it hard work to wake him up. Supposing he was wide awake, Piel went out to help rally the men, but Rall not appearing, he went back and found him in his nightshirt.

'What's the matter?' Rall asked. Piel informed him that a battle was going on. That seemed to bring him to his senses. He dressed himself, rushed out, and mounted his horse to be mortally wounded a few minutes later.

We have taken nearly one thousand prisoners, six cannon, more than a thousand muskets, twelve drums, and four colors. About forty Hessian were killed or wounded. Our loss is only two killed and three wounded. Two of the latter are Captain [William] Washington and Lieutenant [James] Monroe, who rushed forward very bravely to seize the cannon.

I have been with General Washington and Greene to see Rall. He will not live through the night. He asked that his men be kindly treated. Washington promised that he would see they were well cared for.

THE MAYOR OF CORK'S CHRISTMAS DINNER, 1790[32]

A few days before the time, the Chief Magistrate of Cork, Richard Harris, esq. issued near 200 cards inviting company to dine with him on Christmas Day. The guests till then entertained at the Mayorality House were of the first fashion: but this time of a different description, the distressed house and room keepers. The invitation cards were given to the different clergymen of all persuasions in the city to distribute among the indigent of several parishes. The tables were laid out with a profusion of every thing comfortable; the Mayor and a number of gentlemen attended the table, carving and helping the lame and blind etc. with an uncommon degree of humanity and charity. After the company had eaten a plentiful supply of Victual and taken a reasonable quantity of drink, they were severally supplied with a large amount of what remained, and a sixpenny loaf each.

OLD STYLE CHRISTMAS HOSPITALITY, ENGLAND, 1801
News item in the Weekly Dispatch, 17 January 1802[33]

The Earl of Moira is spending Christmas at Donnington [Berkshire], in the true style of old English hospitality. The poor of the village are fed every morning at his doors, while the unfortunate of highest rank, whom anarchy and confusion drove from their country and estates, are entertained by him within.

The unfortunate of highest rank were probably refugees from the French revolution.

CHRISTMAS WITH THE LEWIS AND CLARK EXPEDITION[34]

Christmas, Wednesday 25th December 1805   At day light this morning we we[re] awoke by the discharge of the fire arm[s] of all our party & a Selute, Shouts and a Song which the whole party joined in under our windows, after which they retired to their rooms and were chearfull all the morning. After breakfast we divided our Tobacco which amounted to 12 carrots one half of which we gave to the men of the party who use tobacco, and to those who doe not use it we make a present of a hanker-chief. The Indians leave us in the evening al the party Snugly fixed in their huts. I recved a present of Capt. L. of a fleece hosrie [hosiery] Shirt Draws and Socks, a pr. Mockersons of Whitehorse a Small Indian basket of Guthrich, two Dozen white weazils tails of the Indian woman, & some black root of the Indians before their departure. Drewyer informs me he saw a Snake pass accross the path to day. The day proved Showery wet and disagreeable. we would have Spent this day the nativity of Christ in feasting, had we any thing to raise our Sperits or even gratify our appetites, our Diner concisted of pore Elk so much Spoiled that we eate it thro' mear necessity, some Spoiled pounded fish and a fiew roots.

WASHINGTON IRVING'S IMAGE OF AN ENGLISH CHRISTMAS
From Washington Irving's Sketch Book, 1818[35]

Of all the old festivals that of Christmas wakens the strongest and most heartfelt associations. There is a tone of solemn and sacred feeling that blends with our conviviality, and lifts the spirit to a state of hallowed and elevated enjoyment. The services of the church about this season are extremely tender and inspiring. They dwell on the beautiful story of the origin of our faith, and the pastoral scenes that accompanied its announcement ...

There is something in the very season of the year that gives a charm to the festivity of Christmas. At other times we derive a great portion of our pleasures from the beauties of nature ... But in the depths of winter, when nature lies despoiled of every charm, and wrapped in her shroud of sheeted snow, we turn for our gratifications to moral sources ...

The English from the great prevalence of rural habit throughout every class of society, have always been fond of those festivals and holidays which agreeably interrupt the stillness of country life; and they were, in former days, particularly observant of the religious and social rites of Christmas. It is inspiring to read even the dry details which some antiquaries have given of the quaint humors, the burlesque pageants, the complete abandonment to mirth and good-fellowship, with which this festival was celebrated. It seemed to throw open every door and unlock every heart. It brought peasant and peer together, and blended all ranks in one warn generous flow of kindness. The old halls of castles and manor houses resounded with the harp and the Christmas carol, and their ample boards groaned under the weight of hospitality. Even the poorest cottage welcomed the festive season with decoration of bay and holly – the cheerful fire glanced its rays through the lattice, inviting the passengers to raise the latch, and join the gossip knot huddled around the hearth, beguiling the long evening with legendary jokes and oft-told Christmas tales.

Irving here is certainly romanticising. It is unlikely that many castles or manor houses ever entertained so lavishly. Furthermore, as modern social historians have explained to us, the largesse of the fortunate to the lower classes was a form of insurance against disorder. Nevertheless Irving's picture had some basis in fact. Sir John Reresby did hold such a Christmas at Thriberge; Parson Woodforde regularly invited the poor old men of his parish to Christmas dinner, and the earl of Moira practised 'the true style of old English hospitality' only a few years before Irving's visit to England.[36]

Shorn, however, as it is, of its ancient and festive honors, Christmas is still a period of delightful excitement in England. It is gratifying to see that home feeling completely aroused which holds so powerful a place in every English bosom. The preparations making on every side for the social board that is again to unite friends and kindred; the presents of good cheer passing and repassing, those tokens of regard, and quickeners of kind feelings; the evergreens distributed about houses and churches, emblems of peace and gladness; all these have the most pleasing effect in producing fond associations and kindling benevolent sympathies. Even the sound of the Waits (carol singers soliciting money), rude as may be their minstrelsy, breaks upon the midwatches of a winter night with the effect of perfect harmony. As I have been awakened by them in that still and solemn hour 'when deep sleep falleth upon man,' I have listened with a hushed delight, and, connecting them with the sacred and joyous occasion, have almost fancied them into another celestial choir, announcing peace and good will to mankind …

MENDELSOHN IN ROME, DECEMBER 1830[37]
December 18, 1830

Dear Professor Zelter!

May this letter bring you best wishes for your birthday, for Christmas and for the New Year at the same time. You know that my thoughts are always with you, and so are my hopes for your cheer and happiness. I will say no more at this time; at the close of such an eventful and solemn year one is almost afraid to write a letter which will take weeks to reach its destination, when so many things can have changed in the meantime! I prefer to send you some music which cannot change before it gets into your hands; will you please give it a kind welcome. It is a chorale which I composed in Venice …

Besides this I have completed an Ave Maria, a Lutheran chorale for eight parts, a capella, one psalm, 'Non nobis, Domine', a German chorale, 'O Haupt voll Blut und Wunden' for choir and orchestra, and finally an overture for orchestra. In your last letter you seemed to be anxious lest, following my predilection for one of the old masters, I might devote myself too much to church music and be led into imitation. Such, however, is certainly not the case; for I believe that nowhere can one so swiftly outgrow the belief in the mere name as here, nor, on the other hand, feel a deeper reverence and esteem for what has been accomplished. What we know and revere is strange and unknown here; one almost admits that things must be that way. And then one finds immortal monuments which have come to life after centuries, without the possibility of discovering the names of their creators. So that nothing is valid except what has sprung from the deepest faith of the innermost soul. And though the aesthetes and scholars struggle to prove why this is beautiful and that less so, by means of purely external qualities like epochs, style, and whatever else their pigeon holes may be called, I believe that that is the only immutable criterion for architecture, painting, music and everything else. If the object alone has not inspired creation, it will never speak from 'heart to heart', and imitation is then nothing but the most superficial product of the most alien thoughts. Naturally, nobody can forbid me to enjoy the inheritance left by the great masters nor to continue to work at it, because not everybody has to begin at the beginning. But then it must be continued creation according to one's ability, and not a lifeless repetition of what is already there. And nowhere is it more wonderfully clear than in Rome that every genuinely personal and sincere work will find its appropriate place, however long it may take. And that is the thread I cling to through the maze of rich museums, galleries, and other beauties ...

The Cardinals are now in conclave, the ceremonies have come to a close, and I have listened daily to the Papal Choir. There again it struck me particularly how extraordinary it is here. They did not sing particularly well, the compositions were poor, the congregation was not devout, and yet the whole effect was heavenly. This was due to the fact that they were singing in the central nave of St Peter's; the sounds are reflected from above and from every corner, they mingle, die away, and produce the most wonderful music. One chord melts into the other, and what no musician would dare, St Peter's Church achieves. Here again it is the same as with everything else in this place; they may do as they like, build the most execrable houses, plant gardens in the worst taste, perform mediocre music; nature and the past are so rich that everything becomes beautiful and admirable ... When I see the young musicians wandering around here and complaining that there is nothing for them to gain musically, and that they had expected something quite different, and however their litany continues, I always want to rub their noses on the capital of a column, for that is where they will find music ...

So I am enjoying the most wonderful combination of gaiety and seriousness, such as can be found only in Rome. Remember me affectionately to your family. Farewell and be as happy as I wish you to be.

Your devoted
Felix.

CHRISTMAS IN MEXICO, 1839 AND 1840

From *The Letters of Fanny Calderón de la Barca*, first published in Boston in 1843. Frances Erskine Inglis, born in Edinburgh in 1804, was married to Angelo Calderón de la Barca, first

Spanish ambassador to the Republic of Mexico. She and her husband departed from New York for Mexico on October 27, 1839. They arrived in Puebla, Mexico on December 24.[38]

We dined about five. It was Christmas Eve! Christmas Eve in Puebla! Who'd have said it once? The handsomest building is the cathedral, and the best looking part of the city is the plaza, which seems generally the case. Various citizens who came to welcome Calderón accompanied us, but we could not enter the cathedral till midnight – and as we were to leave Puebla of the Angels at four in the morning, Calderón would not let me go to midnight mass, which I much wished. In fact I had a great desire to see *something*, and proposed going to the theatre, where there is to be a *nacimiento*, a representation in figures of various events connected with the Birth of Christ, such as the Annunciation, the Holy Family, the Arrival of the Wise Men of the East, etc. – but it was said after deliberation that it would not do. In short I could arrange nothing, and had to sit listening to the polite conversation of several dozen Spaniards and Mexicans who had come to congratulate Calderón on his arrival ... Finding that people were all too stupid to do anything and tired of polite conversation, I went to bed.

Wednesday, Christmas Eve, 1839

It is now about three o'clock, but I was awakened an hour ago by the sound of hymns with which they were ushering in Christmas morning. I went to the window, and saw, by the faint light, bands of women or girls dressed in white, singing in chorus through the streets ...

Thursday, December 26th, 1839

[Last night] I thought of Christmas in Merrie England, and of our family gatherings in the olden time, and, as if I had not travelled in the body,

began travelling in my mind, away to far different and distant, and long-gone-by scenes; fell asleep at length with my thoughts in Scotland; and wakened in Mexico! ...

Friday, December 25th, 1840
San Fernando, Mexico

Christmas Day! One year this evening since we made our entry into Mexico.

What a different aspect everything has assumed to us in one year! Then every object was new, every face that of a stranger. Now we are surrounded by familiar sights and sounds, and above all friendly faces. But, though novelty which has its charms and also its *disagreements* have gone, nothing in Mexico ever appears commonplace. Everything is on a large scale, and everything is picturesque. Then there is so much interest attached to its old buildings, so much to see – even though there are no *sights* and no show places, unless we are to put in that class the Mineria, museum, cathedral, university, and botanical garden, usually visited by travellers – that, at whatever period we may leave it, I feel convinced we shall regret some point of interest that we have left unvisited.

Some days ago coloured cards printed in gift letters were sent around inviting all the senator's friends to the [annual Christmas] mass, in this form:

> Jose Basilio Guerra requests that you will honour him with your presence and that of your family, in the solemn function of Kalends and Mass, which annually makes a humble remembrance of the Birth of the Saviour, which festivity will take place on the morning of the 24th of this month, at nine o'clock in the Parish Church of the Sagrario of the Holy Cathedral.
>
> Mexico, December 1840

By nine we were all assembled in the choir: Don Basilio in his uniform, dark blue and gold; we in mantillas. The church looked very splendid, and, as usual on these occasions, no *leperos* were admitted; therefore the crowd was very elegant and select. The affair went off brilliantly. Four or five of the girls, and several of the married women, have superb voices; and not one of those who sang in the chorus had a bad voice ...

The orchestra was really good, and led by a first-rate musician. I was thankful when my part of the entertainment was over and I could give my undivided attention to the others. The celebration lasted four hours, but there was rather a long sermon. You will shortly receive a detailed account of the whole, which will be published in the Mexican annual called *The Ladies Guide*.

In the evening we went to the house of the Marquesa de Vivanco to spend Christmas Eve. On this night relations and intimate friends of each family gather in the house of the *head of the clan* – a real gathering, and in the present case to the number of fifty or sixty persons.

This is the last night of what is called the Posadas, a curious mixture of religion and amusement, but extremely pretty. The meaning is this: At the time that the decree went forth from Caesar Augustus that 'all the world should be taxed', the Virgin and Joseph, having come out of Galilee to Judea to be inscribed for the taxation, found Bethlehem so full of people who had arrived from all parts of the world that they wandered about for nine days without finding admittance in any house or tavern, and on the ninth day took shelter in a manger where the Saviour was born. For eight days this wandering of the Holy Family to the different *posadas* [inns] is represented, and seems more intended for an amusement to the children than anything serious.

We went to the *marquesa*'s at eight o'clock, and about nine the ceremony commenced. A lighted taper was put in the hand of each lady and a procession was formed, two by two, which marched all through the house – the corridors and walls of which were all decorated with evergreens and lamps, the whole party singing the litanies. Kate walked with the dowager marquesa, and a group of little children dressed as angels joined the procession. They wore little robes of silver or gold lame, plumes of white feathers, and a profusion of fine diamonds and pearls – in *bandeaux*, brooches and necklaces – white gauze wings and white satin shoes embroidered in gold.

As the last procession drew up before a door, and a shower of fireworks was sent flying over our heads – I suppose to represent the descent of the angels for a group of ladies appeared to represent the shepherds who watched their flocks by night upon the plains of Bethlehem. Then voices, supposed to be those of Mary and Joseph, struck up a hymn in which they begged for admittance, saying the night was cold and dark, that the wind blew hard, and they prayed for a night's shelter. A chorus of voices within refused admittance. Again those without entreated shelter, and at length declared that she at the door, who thus wandered in the night and had not where to lay her head, was the Queen of Heaven! At this time the doors were thrown wide open, and the Holy Family entered singing.

The scene within was very pretty: a *nacimiento*. Platforms, going all round the room, were covered with moss, on which were disposed groups of wax figures, generally representing passages from parts of the New Testament, though sometimes they begin with Adam and Eve in paradise. There was the Annunciation – the Salutation of Mary to Elizabeth – the Wise Men of the East – the Shepherds – the Flight onto Egypt. There were green trees and fruit trees, and little fountains that cast up fairy columns of water, and flocks of sheep, and a little cradle in which to lay the Infant Christ. One of the angels held a waxen baby in her arms. The whole was lighted very brilliantly, and ornamented with flowers and garlands. A padre took the baby from the angel, and placed it in the cradle, and the *Posada* was completed.

We then returned to the drawing room – angels, shepherds, and all – and danced till supper time. The supper was a show for sweetmeats and cakes.

Today, with the exception of there being service in all the churches, Christmas is not kept in a remarkable way.

From the Dutch celebration of St Nicholas in New Amsterdam came the American Santa Claus. Several early nineteenth-century descriptions of St Nicholas (or 'Claus) suggest the jolly rotund figure we know so well, but the primary source of the modern Santa is the well known poem Clement Clarke Moore wrote for his children in 1822, which begins:

'Twas the night before Christmas, when all through the house.
Not a creature was stirring, not even a mouse.

A copy of Moore's poem appeared in a newspaper the next year. Soon Santa Claus had become an indispensable part of the American Christmas. During the middle decades of the nineteenth century the popularity of Christmas trees spread from Germany to England and France and became a regular part of Christmas celebrations in the United States. Louise Alcott includes a tree in the Christmas Scene in *Little Women*. Christmas trees are found in the accounts of Christmas in New Orleans (1859) and Montevallo (1867) found below in Chapter VII, page 202 and 212. The next selection by Hanelin Garland, describes a mid-western American Christmas in the 1870s.

MY FIRST CHRISTMAS TREE[39]

I will begin by saying that we never had a Christmas tree in our house in a Wisconsin coulée; indeed, my father never saw one in a family circle till he saw that which I set up for my own children last year. But we celebrated Christmas in those days, always, and I cannot remember a time when we did not hang up our stockings for 'Sandy Claws' to fill. As I look back upon those days it seems as if the snows were always deep, the night skies crystal clear, the stars especially lustrous with frosty sparkles of blue and yellow fire – and probably this was so, for we lived in a northern land where winter was usually stern and always long.

I recall one Christmas when 'Sandy' brought me a sled, and a horse that stood on rollers – a wonderful tin horse which I very shortly split in two in order to see what his insides were. Father traded a cord of wood for the sled, and the horse cost twenty cents – but they made the day wonderful.

Another notable Christmas Day, as I stood in our front yard, mid-leg deep in snow, a neighbor drove by closely muffled in furs, while behind his seat his son, a lad of twelve or fifteen, stood beside a barrel of apples, and as he passed he hurled a glorious big red one at me. It missed me, but bored a deep round hole in the soft snow. I thrill yet with the remembered joy of burrowing for that delicious bomb. Nothing will ever smell quite as good as that Wine Sap or Northern Spy or whatever it was. It was a wayward impulse on the part of the boy in the sleigh, but it warms my heart after more than forty years.

We had no chimney in our home, but the stocking-hanging was a ceremony nevertheless. My parents, and especially my mother, entered into it in with the best of humor. They always put up their own stockings or permitted us to do it for them – and they always laughed next morning when they found potatoes or ears of corn in them. I can see now that my mother's laugh had a tear in it, for she loved pretty things and seldom got any during the years we lived in the coulée.

When I was ten years old we moved to Mitchell County, an Iowa prairie land, and there we prospered in such wise that our stockings always held toys of some sort, and even my mother's stocking occasionally sagged with a simple piece of jewelry or a new comb or brush. But the thought of a family tree remained the luxury of millionaire city-dwellers; indeed it was not till my fifteenth or sixteenth year that our Sunday school rose to the extravagance of a tree, and it is of this wondrous festival that I write.

The land about us was only partly cultivated at this time, and our district schoolhouse, a bare little box, was set bleakly on the prairie; but the Burr Oak schoolhouse was not only larger but it stood beneath great oaks as well and possessed the charm of a forest background through which a stream ran silently. It was our chief social center. There of a Sunday a regular preacher held 'Divine service' with Sunday school as a sequence.

At night – usually on Friday nights – the young people let in 'ly-ceums', as we called them, to debate great questions or to 'speak pieces' and read essays; and here it was that I saw my first Christmas Tree.

I walked to that tree across four miles of moonlit snow. Snow? No, it was a floor of diamonds, a magical world, so beautiful that my heart still aches with the wonder of it and with the regret that it has all gone – gone with the keen eyes and bounding pulses of the boy.

Our home at this time was a small frame house on the prairie almost directly west of the Burr Oak grove, and as it was too cold to take the horse out my brother and I, with our tall boots, our visored caps and our long woolen mufflers, started forth afoot defiant of the cold. We left the gate on the trot, bound for a sight of the glittering unknown. The snow was deep and we moved side by side in the grooves made by the hoofs of the horses, setting our feet in the shine left by the broad shoes of the wood sleighs whose going had smoothed the way for us.

Our breaths rose like smoke in the still air. It must have been ten below zero, but that did not trouble us in those days, and at last we came in sight of the lights, in the sound of the singing, the laughter, the bells of the feast.

It was a poor little building without tower or bell and its low walls had but three windows on a side, and yet it seemed very imposing to me that night as I crossed the threshold and faced the strange people who packed it to the door. I say 'strange people', for though I had seen most of them many times they all seemed somehow alien to me that night. I was an irregular attendant at Sunday school and did not expect a present, therefore I stood against the wall and gazed with open-eyed marveling at the shining pine which stood where the pulpit was wont to be. I was made to feel the more embarrassed by reason of the remark of a boy who accused me of having forgotten to comb my hair.

This was not true, but the cap I wore always matted my hair down over my brow, and then, when I lifted it off invariably disarranged it completely. Nevertheless I felt guilty – and hot. I don't suppose my hair was artistically barbered that night – I rather guess Mother had used the shears – and I can believe that I looked the half-wild colt that I was; but there was no call for that youth to direct attention to my unavoidable shagginess.

I don't think the tree had many candles, and I don't remember it glittered with golden apples. But it was loaded with presents, and the girls coming and going clothed in bright garments made me forget my own looks – I think they made me forget to remove my overcoat, which was a sodden thing of poor cut and worse quality. I think I must have stood there agape for nearly two hours listening to the songs, noting every motion of Adoniram Burtch and Asa Walker as they directed the ceremonies and prepared the way for the great event – that is to say, for the coming of Santa Claus himself.

A furious jingling of bells, a loud voice outside, the lifting of a window, the nearer clash of bells, and the dear old Saint appeared (in the person of Stephen Bartle) clothed in a red robe, a belt of sleigh bells, and a long white beard. The children cried out, 'Oh!' The girls tittered and shrieked with excitement, and the boys laughed and clapped their hands. Then 'Sandy' made a little speech about being glad to see us all, but as he had many other places to visit, and as there were a great many presents to distribute, he guessed he'd have to ask some pretty girls to help him. So he called upon Betty Burtch and Hattie Knapp, – and I for one admired his taste, for they were the most popular maids of the school.

They came up blushing, and a little bewildered by the blaze of publicity thus blown upon them. But their native dignity asserted itself, and the distribution of the presents began. I have a notion now that the fruit upon the tree was mostly bags of popcorn and 'corny copias' of candy, but as my brother and I stood there that night and saw everybody, even the rowdiest boy, getting something we felt aggrieved and rebellious. We forgot that we had come from afar – we only knew that we were being left out.

But suddenly, in the midst of our gloom, my brother's name was called, and a lovely girl with a gentle smile handed him a bag of popcorn. My heart glowed with gratitude. Somebody had thought of us; and when she came to me, saying sweetly, 'Here's something for you', I had not words to thank her. This happened nearly forty years ago, but her smile, her outstretched hand, her sympathetic eyes are vividly before me as I write. She was sorry for the shock-headed boy who stood against the wall, and her pity made the little box of candy a casket of pearls. The fact that I swallowed the jewels on the road home does not take from the reality of my adoration.

At last I had to take my final glimpse of that wondrous tree, and I well remember the walk home. My brother and I traveled in wordless companionship. The moon was sinking toward the west, and the snow crust gleamed with a million fairy lamps. The sentinel watchdogs barked from lonely farmhouses, and the wolves answered from the ridges. Now and then sleighs passed us with lovers sitting two and two, and the bells on their horses had the remote music of romance to us whose boots drummed like clogs of wood upon the icy road.

Our house was dark as we approached and entered it, but how deliciously warm it seemed after the pitiless wind! I confess we made straight for the cupboard for a mince pie, a doughnut and a bowl of milk!

As I write this there stands in my library, a thick-branched, beautifully tapering fir tree covered with the gold and purple apples of Hesperides, together with crystal ice points, green and red and yellow candles, clusters of gilded grapes, wreaths of metallic frost, and glittering angels swinging in ecstasy; but I doubt if my children will ever know the keen pleasure (that is almost pain) which came to my brother and to me in those Christmas days when an orange was not a breakfast fruit, but a casket of incense and of spice, a message from the sunlands of the South.

That was our compensation – we brought to our Christmastime a keen appetite and empty hands. And the lesson of it all is, if we are seeking a lesson, that it is better to give to those who want than to those whom 'we ought to do something because they did something for us last year.'

In twentieth-century America, Santa Claus, Christmas trees and the widespread commercialisation of the season seem to have overwhelmed earlier Christmas traditions; and the modern American version of the season appears to be spreading around the world. At the same time, older Christmas customs persist. The celebration of the season in almost any community combines ancient ceremonies with recent innovations, local pecularities with universal customs.

A MEXICAN POSADA IN THE 1950s[40]

In December nine religious dramas, called *posadas*, re-enact the search made by Mary and Joseph for lodging before the birth of Christ. Christmas posadas are private parties in Mexico City and in many mestizo villages in the Valley of Mexico but in Tecospa they are religious fiestas celebrated by the entire community at the church.

My wife and I gave a posada for Tecospa on December 20, 1952. We arrived at the church bringing cookies, candy, peanuts, candles, fireworks, piñatas, and fruit. Our most elaborate piñata was a large white elephant with gold foil tusks which the Indians placed on a pedestal near the altar. As the church services began, women and children knelt in a circle in front of the images of Mary and Joseph, who wore tiny Stetson hats. Each year the godparents of these images give them a set of new clothes.

Don Amado Perez, the church prayermaker, led the rosary in the can-

dlelit church. Two women prayermakers said the responses. When the prayers and songs ended the women and children received candles for the procession led by two boys carrying images of Mary and Joseph.

Fireworks heralded the advent of the procession which lasted about half an hour before returning to the church. At the church door women sang traditional songs appealing for lodging which was refused by those inside the church. Then the church doors opened and the worshippers rushed inside where they said the last prayers of the evening.

While my wife passed out the traditional baskets of goodies to the worshippers after the church service, a group of Indian women sang this ditty to her:

Andale, Claudita, no te dilates
Con las canastas de cachuates
Yo no quiero ni oro ni plata

Lo que quiero es romper la piñata

Hurry, Claudia, don't delay
With the baskets of peanuts
I don't want gold or silver
All I want is to break the piñata

Nearly all the men and boys of the town joined the circle of hopefuls who wanted to try breaking the piñatas. The mayor acted as master of ceremonies and chose those who might swing sticks at the piñatas. The men broke the last piñata at midnight.

Before we left, church officials asked my student assistant to take a picture of my wife and me with the image of the Virgin Mary so they could hang the photograph in the church as a memento of the miracle the Virgin had performed in bringing us to Tecospa to give the posada.

On Christmas Eve the posada lasts until dawn. The birth ceremony begins at 3 a.m. when curtains covering the nativity scene are opened. The godmother of the crèche picks up the image of he Christ Child and sings lullabies to him while candles are handed out for the procession. When the procession returns to the church each person kneels to kiss the image as the godmother holds it beside the nativity scene. Children dressed as shepherds offer it gifts: girls give cookies and candies, boys give toys.

CHAPTER VII

Christmas in the Southern United States

In 1807 the English poet, Robert Southey, predicted that the rapid growth of cities would destroy local Christmas traditions. Since 1800 the revolution in mass communications, along with urbanisation, has created an almost world-wide syncretic Christmas. Yet, as Daniel Miller observes, 'It seems that at whatever date and region we encounter the festival it has accreted to itself a wealth of local rites and customs.'[1] Furthermore, specific groups, such as churches, clubs and individual families preserve their own peculiar manner of marking the holiday. The next chapter, 'An Irish Perspective', and the present chapter, 'Christmas in the Southern United States', illustrate some of the ways in which regions retain their own distinctive Christmas customs. Although their history has been very different, both Ireland and the American South possess a strong sense of cultural identity.[2]

This chapter will 'drop in' on various Christmas celebrations in different parts of the Southern United States over the last three centuries. These accounts offer a glimpse of how the first settlers to New Orleans celebrated Christmas, how the season was enjoyed in the slave cabins of the South as well as in the wealthy homes of plantation owners, how the Holiday season was marked during the civil war, and how Christmas is celebrated today by two specific groups of people whose circumstances have isolated them from partaking in the modern homogenised Christmas: the fishermen/trappers of the remotest bayous and the inmates of a maximum security prison.

It may be that the first writings in the American South concerning Christmas do not appear in any book but may be writings carved in rock in West Virginia in the ancient script of the monks who are believed to have followed in the footsteps of St Brendan the Navigator. Centuries before Columbus made his voyage St Brendan in *Navigatio* recounts his journeys across the Atlantic. The petroglyphs in West Virginia, carved on a recessed portion of a rock face, become illuminated by the rising sun on the winter solstice. The carvings tell the story of the Nativity and depict a radiant sun.[3]

The traditions that now define Christmas in the South have their roots in the practices of the much later settlers who made their homes in the region; those practices are as diverse as the people who brought them. As Harnett Kane observes:

While Puritan New England shunned ceremonial Christmas, the southerners nurtured it and kept it ever before them. But as there are many Souths, so there have been many Southern Christmases – festivals as different from one another as Maryland is from Georgia, and Tennessee or Alabama from South Carolina and Florida.[4]

The first immigrants to the New World brought with them the hopes and dreams afforded by a fresh start, a new unexplored country awaited them on which they could forge a new tradition and culture. Yet, the adventurers, awed by the new environment, sought to anchor their new world with the culture, traditions and behaviour they had practised in the old. For some, freedom to practise their chosen religion was the reason they had journeyed to the New World, for others, the practice of religion was a link of constancy to the land they had left behind. Christmas was celebrated in New Orleans in 1717, just months after the area was designated to be the capital of Louisiana.

NEW ORLEANS' FIRST CHRISTMAS[5]

For months a band of hardy men had laboured in the wilderness – clearing the land, hewing, digging and burning. It was rough going. The land was a quagmire filled with alligators, frogs, snakes and mosquitoes. Plagues were frequent and danger lurked behind every tree ...

It is said that a fine feast was held in the barracks that first Christmas Eve. This was a harsh country, but it teemed with good things for the table. Wild turkey was plentiful, along with duck, quail and myriads of small game birds. The waters provided amply of fish, crab, shrimp and oysters. There was venison from the forest, and vegetables and grain from Indian fields and gardens.

And best benison of all to pioneers far from the comforts of home had been the arrival, a few days before, of the *Neptune*, a square-rigged ship from France, bearing wine and brandy in her hold ...

It is said to have been a celebrated feast. The workmen ate heartily and drank and sang late. Then as midnight neared, they prepared to troop out into the raw night, making their way by the light of pine knot torches to the little improvised church of logs, mud and palmetto thatch.

It would have been a simple service, with a primitive altar and the plainest of vestments. But the legend persists that there was a crèche and tiny figures of the Holy Family. Together the workmen and the gentry

knelt and prayed and said the litany. The service over, they moved out of the church. And then, for the first time, the town echoed to *Heureux Noel, Joyeux Noel!*

By contrast, Christmas was a more somber and less primitive affair in Georgia in 1738 according to the account of William Stephens' journal entry:

A JOURNAL OF THE PROCEEDINGS IN GEORGIA, 1738, DECEMBER[6]

Sunday
Monday, Christmas Day   These two days were observed with due Reverence, and Mr Norris administered the Sacrament according to the usage of the Church.

Tuesday   This was kept as a Holiday (or rather an idle day) according to the Custom of our Mother Country; but with us it was a festival without feasting.

Some elements of the western Christmas tradition, such as the use of the Poinsettia plant, began in the southern United States. The poinsettia plant was brought to South Carolina by Joel Robert Poinsett, from whom it gets its name. Poinsett served as ambassador to Mexico where he came across the plant and discovered that he was able to cultivate it back in South Carolina. Legends associating the poinsettia with Christmas now abound. The shape of the plant and the arrangement of leaves are seen as symbols of the Star of Bethlehem which led the wise men to the Christ Child. The red colored leaves are symbolic of the blood of Christ while the white leaves represent the Virgin's purity. According to legend, the origin of the plant itself is related to a Christmas miracle. The story goes that a poor Mexican brother and sister were on their way to pay tribute to the baby Jesus on Christmas eve but had no gift to offer him. They gathered weeds and made them into a small bouquet. When they laid the bouquet of weeds at the Nativity scene in the church they were transformed into the bright red and white leaves of a poinsettia plant.

As the European colonists established themselves they imposed their culture and tradition upon the indigenous population and upon the slaves who worked their lands. In the West Indies, as well as the southern United States, Christmas became the primary holiday which slaves were permitted, indeed encouraged, to celebrate. The Christmas festivals of both medieval peasants and American slaves represented a means of keeping servile labourers content with their bondage, the spirit of the holiday encouraged mutual kindness and enjoyment. Very rarely has the story of the daily toil of the slave population been authentically told by those who lived in slavery. One of these rare exceptions is the story of Solomon Northup, an educated free man of colour, who was kidnapped in Washington in 1841 and sold into slavery. His subsequent twelve years of slavery are recorded in his memoirs, written and published after his rescue from a Louisiana plantation in 1853.

According to Northup, Christmas day was 'the happiest day in the whole year for the slave'.

TWELVE YEARS A SLAVE[7]

The only respite from the constant labour the slave has through the whole year, is during the Christmas holidays. Epps allowed us three – others allow four, five and six days, according to the measure of their generosity. It is the only time to which they look forward with any interest or pleasure. They are glad when night comes, not only because it brings them repose, but because it brings them one day nearer Christmas. It is hailed with equal delight by the old and the young; even Uncle Abram ceases to glorify Andrew Jackson and Patsey forgets her many sorrows amid the general hilarity of the holidays. It is the time of feasting, and frolicking, and fiddling – the carnival season with the children of bondage. They are the only days when they are allowed a little restricted liberty, and heartily indeed do they enjoy it.

It is the custom for one planter to give a 'Christmas supper', inviting the slaves from neighbouring plantations to join his own on the occasion: for instance, one year it was given by Epps, the next by Marshall, the next by Hawkins, and so on. Usually from three to five hundred are assembled, coming together on foot, in carts, on horseback, on mules, riding double or triple, sometimes a boy and girls, at others a girl and two boys, and at others again a boy, a girl and an old woman. Uncle Abram astride a mule, and Aunt Phebe and Patsey behind him, trotting towards Christmas supper, would be no uncommon sight on Bayou Boeuf.

Then, too, 'of all days i' the year', they array themselves in their best attire. The cotton coat has been washed clean, the stump of a tallow candle has been applied to the shoes, and if fortunate as to possess a rimless or a crownless hat, it is placed jauntily on the head. They are welcomed with equal cordiality, however, if they come bare-headed and bare-footed to the feast. As a general thing, the women wear handkerchiefs tied about their heads, but if chance has thrown their way a fiery red ribbon, or a cast-off bonnet of their mistresses' grandmother, it is sure to be worn on such occasions. Red – the deep blood red – is decidedly the favourite color among the enslaved damsels of my acquaintance. If a red ribbon does not encircle the neck, you will be certain to find the hair of their woolly heads tied up with red strings of one sort or another.

The table is spread in the open air, and loaded with varieties of meat and piles of vegetables. Bacon and corn meal at such times are dispensed with. Sometimes the cooking is performed in the kitchen on the plantation, at others in the shade of wide branching trees. In the latter case, a ditch is dug in the ground, and wood is laid in and burned until it is filled with glowing coals, over which chickens, ducks, turkey, pigs, and not infrequently the entire body of a wild ox are roasted. They are furnished also with flour, of which biscuits are made, and often with peach and other preserves, with tarts, and every manner and description of pies, except the mince, that being an article of pastry as yet unknown among them. Only the slave who has lived all the years on his scanty allowance of meal and bacon, can appreciate such suppers. White people in great numbers assemble to witness the gastronomical enjoyments.

They seat themselves at the rustic table – the males on one side, the females on the other. The two between whom there may have been an exchange of tenderness, invariably manage to sit opposite; the omnipresent Cupid disdains not to hurl his arrows into the simple hearts of slaves. Unalloyed and exulting happiness lights up the dark faces of them all. The ivory teeth, contrasting with their black complexions, exhibit

two long, white streaks the whole extent of the table. All round the bountiful board a multitude of eyes roll in ecstasy. Giggling and laughter and the clattering of cutlery and crockery succeed. Cuffee's elbow hunches his neighbour's side, impelled by an involuntary impulse of delight; Nelly shakes her finger at Sambo and laughs, she knows not why, and so the fun and merriment flow on.

When the viands have disappeared, the hungry maws of the children of toil are satisfied, then, next in the order of amusement, is the Christmas dance. My business on these gala days always was to play the violin. The African race is a music-loving one, proverbially; and many there were among my fellow-bondsmen whose organs of tune were strikingly developed, and who could thumb the banjo with dexterity; but at the expense of appearing egotistical, I must, nevertheless, declare, that I was considered the Ole Bull of Bayou Boeuf. My master often received letters, sometimes from a distance of ten miles, requesting him to send me to play at a ball or festival of the whites. He received his compensation, and usually I also returned with many picayunes jingling in my pockets – the extra contributions of those to whose delight I had administered. In this manner I became more acquainted than I otherwise would, up and down the bayou ...

[My violin] heralded my name round the country – made me friends, who, otherwise would not have noticed me – gave me an honoured seat at the yearly feast, and secured the loudest and heartiest welcome of them all at the Christmas dance. The Christmas dance! Oh, ye pleasure-seeking sons and daughters of idleness, who move with measured step, listless and snail-like, through the slow winding cotillion, if ye wish to look upon celerity, if not the 'poetry in motion' – upon genuine happiness,

rampant and unrestrained – go down to Louisiana and see the slaves dancing in the starlight of a Christmas night.

Christmas within the plantation home was considerably different from Christmas without as described by Northup. In the next extract David Strother, an artist and writer who
contributed articles to *Harper's New Monthly Magazine* under the nom de plume 'Porte
Crayon', recalls Christmas in Virginia. Strother is recalling a Christmas he spent with relations in the 1840s. Strother did not support the southern secessionists and aligned himself
with the unionists during the war rising to the rank of colonel in the Federal army.
Strother was appointed adjutant general of Virginia after the war and was instrumental in
the rebuilding of his native state. It was not until a few years before his death that he reconciled with his childhood friends whom he had fought against during the civil war.

A WINTER IN THE SOUTH[8]

Those who had spoken were from the North, and town or city-bred, and
the joys they had pictured were such as they knew of. But it was now my
turn; so I painted them a picture of an old-fashioned Christmas in our
region. I drew it lovingly and truly, with heart as well as words.

'Comrades,' I began, 'let me invite you to a country Christmas eve in
the mountains. Take a peep into the roomy whitewashed parlor, lighted
with flaming tallow-candles, and floored with a striped carpet. In the
wide-mouthed fire-place a hickory fire roars and glows like a furnace. A
black and turbaned damsel is present, whose time is occupied snuffing the
candles and sweeping up the hearth with a turkey wing. Two swarthy
elves bring in alternate armfuls of wood to keep up the blaze, always leaving the door wide open behind them. In rushes the wintry wind, flaring
the candles, and whirling the hickory-ashes over the hearth-rug; in rushes
a brace of shivering dogs, and with them "a sound of revelry" from the
kitchen across the yard: squeaking, booming, and clattering in mingled
cadence. The dogs are turned out, the wind is shut out, and with it the
merry noise of the fiddles; the candles snuffed, the hearth swept, and then
"*da capo al fine*". On the right hand sits the landed proprietor, plainly clad,
strong-featured, and bronzed; a face that can easily assume the sternness
of command, for he has smelled powder on the field of battle, and rules
his estate like a feudal lord: yet the companionship of a loving wife and a
troop of coaxing daughters has smoothed away all trace of harshness.
Opposite to him sits the comely dame, knitting a gray yarn stocking; her
demeanour nicely balanced between placidity and fidgetiness; observing
sparks on the carpet, ashes on the rug, thieves in the candles, and quietly

signaling "Cassy" on the subject. There are some good-looking, gawky boys, or would-be men, sitting around, talking about horses and guns. There is a great stone pitcher sitting by the fire, covered with a plate. This appears to be under the charge of the proprietor, and nobody knows what is in it; but when he takes the plate off to stir it, as he does occasionally, you may smell hot apple-toddy all over the room. You are disappointed at not seeing the girls, your cousins, of course. The good dame smiles – they are in *déshabillé* – not visible yet; then she leans over and whispers confidentially, "Go in the next room and surprise them." This is a sufficient hint. You open the door, and glide into the presence of half a dozen bouncing, blooming girls, gathered about a table with crocks of milk, bowls of sugar, eggs, and various et ceteras. Now for a moment you may look on and admire that exquisite, unstudied grace of movement and expression which our dear girls are careful never to exhibit in general society. But your heart thumps like a pheasant drumming. You had secretly hoped, but had hardly expected it – but there she is, her face flushed with the frolic, the comb just falling from her hair, which tumbles in luxuriant confusion upon her shoulder, her rosy tapering arms quite bare – beating, with all her might and main, the whites of two dozen eggs into a foam – Cousin Mary, with whom you have walked, and talked and ridden, and danced so often – she that is such a madcap that the old folks are outdone with her; and so shy and prudish withal that you have often been outdone herself – she that will fearlessly mount the most mettlesome steed and scream so prettily at the sight of a mouse; who sometimes bears herself so proudly that a prince would dare to woo her, then with such winning, girlish gentleness that you think she might be had for the asking.

'In short, there sits the little maiden who can tweedle you between her finger and her thumb as easily as she twirls that same egg-beater – can bind you with a thread of pink worsted, and lead you, blind and helpless, as Samson was of old. You forget you are an intruder, but are presently reminded of it by half a dozen affected little screams. Then all the sweet little coquetries, simperings, and pretenses which the engaging sex always puts on in the presence of an admirer are immediately resumed. They try to hide their handsome hands, but don't succeed; to arrange their frolicsome ringlets, but only toss them about more charmingly. You are scolded, menaced, ordered to retire (a pretty sneak would you be to go!) but you know better, and join the gleeful bevy with laughing assurance.'

'Then the egg-nog is mixed, and poured into the mighty glass bowl, and crowned with whipped cream; the great silver ladle is produced, a regiment of glasses is mustered, and numerous plates with cakes, nuts, and apples. Then the company unites, and the refreshment is paraded into the parlour.

'Then the lass with the turkey-wing and snuffers grins as if she had a ear of corn in her mouth; the swarthy elves grin as they bring in fresh wood; the shivering dogs yelp with eagerness as they rush in for the fiftieth time; the sound revelry from the kitchen comes fast and furious.

'Then the healths go round – first to absent friends, then to smiling present. The host's apple-toddy is steaming hot and potent. You are now brave enough to whisper sweet things to Cousin Mary, and she looks down and smiles and blushes most bewitchingly. "Now," cries the master, "we must have a dance! Bring in the music." "But," says the considerate matron, "the poor souls in the kitchen – it will spoil their frolic." "What!" replies the master, "because we have the misfortune to be white, shall we never forget our cares and troubles? Bring in the fiddlers! Young folks, take your partners." Yours, doubtless, is already engaged. In come the joyful musicians, grinning from ear to ear, and bowing until they sweep the floor with their greasy hats, anticipating extra drams and half-dollars for their holiday spendings,

> 'Then the dance –
> No apish polka, new from France,
> But jolly old Virginia reels –
> Put life and mettle in their heels.'

Christmas trees became popular in the south in the 1840s. These trees differed from the modern Christmas tree as they were not limited in variety, size or shape as today's conical evergreen trees are. The early Christmas trees were usually put on display by a church or club for the enjoyment of its members rather than in a private house. More affluent members of the community began displaying Christmas trees in their homes in the 1850s. One traveller to the city of New Orleans in 1858 described his awe at participating at the unveiling of the Kearney Christmas tree.

LETTER TO THE CRESCENT NEWSPAPER[9]

Crescent Newspaper
Dec. 26, 1858
New Orleans, La.

Messrs. Editors –
It was my good fortune, on Christmas Eve, to be present at one of the most delightful and joyous re-unions that in my desultory and fun-loving

life I have ever witnessed. The event was the inauguration of the 'Christmas Tree' at a friend's house, who is a prince of goodfellows, and with the affable courtesy and the amiable manners of his good lady, made all feel at home, and contributed much in carrying out every arrangement with entire satisfaction.

The tree, with all its manifold presents and ornaments, had been secretly reared under lock and key in one of the apartments, and for several days little curious and peering eyes had tried in vain to discover the hidden mysteries of that room. A beautiful myrtle of about eight feet high reared its head in an appropriate box in the center of a large stand, surrounded with steps, upon which were placed the many gifts. Ornamented with gay coloured ribbons and illuminated with hundreds of small wax candles, it presented a most delightful '*coup d'oeil*'; again, to the right and to the left were two other stands also filled with souvenirs for the young and old, for be it known that this large assemblance of over sixty souls was composed (with but few exceptions) of members of one family, headed by the dear grandmother, with her sweet smiles and bland and gentle manners, moving about among her children, grandchildren, and great-grandchildren with love and cheerfulness; and more astonishing to relate, this veritable matron has, within the past season, worked nine of the most beautiful handkerchiefs for keepsakes to some of her grandchildren and great children. Oh! What a glorious and cheerful sight to witness those dear happy faces.

A great feature of the evening was the advent of a veritable, true flesh and blood 'Santa Claus'. While the two parlours were filled with juveniles, a continued ringing of the door-bell and a great thumping at the front entrance caused quite a sensation, when the host, in tones loud and clear, demanded –

'Who comes here,
And makes such noise?
Little children do not fear,
It must be friendly –'

At this instant the intruder entered, and uttered 'Santa Claus'. What a picture for the pencil of an artist! The various expressions, some of them fear but most of unbounded surprise, for sure enough instead of the mythical patron of the Christmas Festival, who usually descends chimneys in the dead hour of the night to distribute his gifts, there stood the veritable in '*propria persona*' dressed in full costume, boots, bells and all. As soon as the older members greeted and cordially met him, the younger ones were inspired with more confidence, and then came a thousand questions, 'Where did he come from?' 'How did he get here?' He answered, 'On the wings of the hoary North wind', that he had traveled far that night to meet them and wish them all a 'Merry Christmas' and to distribute his gifts, which he carried in an immense sack on his back but; ere he distributed them, he read them a moral lecture, told them he knew the bad children who were before him as well as the good ones, and cautioned the first named to be better, or on next year he would bring for them a bunch of rods that he always kept in pickle; to the good ones he gave his kindest congratulations and begged them to continue improving.

Then followed the wild excitement of his grab-bag, each one plunging in and drawing out something pleasing. When they had emptied it, he arranged them in couples, placing himself at their head, perambulated all over the premises, all singing 'Auld Lang Syne', 'Home, sweet home', and winding up with 'Yankee Doodle', which brought them to the mysterious chamber; that in the meantime had been brilliantly illuminated and after placing them in proper positions to receive their presents, Santa Claus mysteriously and suddenly disappeared, no doubt through the chimney!

It was the merriest and most cheerful collection I have seen for a long time and will be treasured and appreciated in the pleasantest memories of all present, and by none more than

NUX

The experience which wrought the Southern States together as an entity, however briefly, was the Civil War which broke out in April 1861. The diverse cultures that made up these states suffered, to varying degrees, similar hardships during the war. The Jones family of Montevideo, Georgia offer a glimpse of what the Christmas season was like during the war years. The extracts below include two letters exchanged between Lt Charles C. Jones and his father, the Revd C.C. Jones, on December 25, 1861, when the war had been raging for less than a year; as well as an extract from the journal of Mary (Jones) Mallard, their sister and daughter on December 25, 1864, when the war had taken its toll.

THE CHILDREN OF PRIDE[10]

Lt Charles C. Jones, Jr. to Revd C.C. Jones
Camp Claghorn, Wednesday, December 25th, 1861

My dear Father,
Christmas Day! Many happy returns to you and my dear mother and precious little daughter! And long before the coming of another anniversary may these storm clouds which now hover about us have been succeeded

by the pure light of love, of peace, and of righteousness! This is my hope, but whether it will be realized within the time specified, and by whom, is known only to Him who disposes all things in infinite wisdom and according to His own great pleasure. Of the ultimate success of our cause I have no doubt; but I am persuaded that the struggle will be not without privation and (it may be) great personal danger and perhaps death to many whose immediate keeping is committed the defense of all who we hold dear in life and sacred in death.

The enemy with a force of five vessels is now within a few miles of us, threatening the Skidaway battery, an earthwork mounting several guns. Night before last our company bivouacked on Skidaway Island in supporting distance of the battery, without shelter and to a great extent without food, having moved from our camp at very short notice. A slight skirmish took place that afternoon between a portion of Commodore Tattnall's fleet lying under the guns of the battery and the enemy's vessels, in which several shots were fired but neither man nor vessel injured on either side. Yesterday, we returned to our camp. Today, heavy firing heard to seaward, and this afternoon the vessels of the enemy again in the neighborhood of the Skidaway battery. An attack is expected upon the Skidaway battery tomorrow, and we are in expectation of orders to move in the morning. There may be nothing in the present demonstration of the enemy; but everything appears to indicate a contemplated effort to possess themselves of Skidaway Island, which will enable them effectually to cut off our inland navigation, and would afford additional facilities in the event any direct operations upon Savannah.

Our bivouac night before last was the first real taste of soldier's life. Our caps were all frosted in the morning, and the canteens of the men sleeping around the fires had ice on them. It was quite cold, but clear, bracing; and no evil effects have been experienced by either men or horses.

George goes home tomorrow in the morning to see his mother and family, and I send these hurried lines with him ... I much regret to see that the Lincolnites are reported prepared to surrender Mason and Slidell in obedience to the demands of the British government, although I must say I fully expected the result ... It is late, and I must bid you all good night. My warmest love to self, dear Father, and to my dear mother, with tenderest kisses for my precious little daughter. May a good God continue to bless you all at home!

As ever,
Your affectionate son,
Charles C. Jones, Jr.

Revd C.C. Jones to Lt Charles C. Jones, Jr
Montevideo, Wednesday, December 25th, 1861

My dear Son,

With the shadow of God's judgment and displeasure still resting over our beloved country, and no ray of absolute light breaking from any quarter, I do not know that we can greet each other with a 'Merry Christmas'. But the Apostle bids us 'Rejoice in God always', and this is the privilege of His people. Hoping we are such, we can rejoice that He reigns, that His ways are just and true, that His judgments are right, that we can commit ourselves and all that concerns us into His merciful care, and so rest upon Him to keep and sustain and bless us. We can rejoice in His mercies to our country in her struggles thus far, in His mercies to us and ours, and even see His tender mercies mingling in the cup of His severe afflictions put to our lips this year. We can greet each other with a 'Happy Christmas in our ever blessed God and Saviour.' What a vanity is all the earth without the present favour of God and the hope of glory with Him hereafter!

Our waking eyes have been saluted with the light of as brilliant a sun and as beautiful a day as ever the world saw. Your dear little one put her hands together and said her prayers as the sun rose; and soon after, the servants came with their 'Merry Christmas', and our venerable old man wishing us and all ours 'peace all the days of our life, without difficulty or trial in the way; the Blessed Jesus was the Lord and Master, in whom was all power and grace, and He was and would be to us the only Giver of all peace'. Next followed your sister's two sweet children, rejoicing in their stockings stored with all manner of things pleasing their eyes and their ears and their tastes ...

The Liberty Troop have a meeting today of all the families and friends of the troopers, and a contribution dinner, as no one can go home on Christmas to his family. Shall not go on account of the cold, and think none from our house will.

Mr Barnard is really dead, and his funeral takes place tomorrow at 12 M. The measles have appeared in the troop, and a considerable number have never had them. Your brother is well, but has too much sickness to attend to. Hope it may not last. The firing today, I learn, was south. Mother, Sister, and Robert and Brother send much love. Little ones quite well. Respects to Captain Claghorn.

Your affectionate father,
C.C. Jones

The civil war did not come to an end as the correspondents had prayed and by the Christmas of 1864 the scene described by their sister and daughter, Mary S. Mallard, depicts the trials of living in occupation.

Mrs Mary S. Mallard in her Journal
Montevideo, Sunday, December 25, 1864

With great gratitude we hailed the light this morning, having passed the night. And no enemy has come nigh our persons or our dwelling; although there are appearances of horse tracks, which we have observed before, and believe they are often around at night to try to detect any gentlemen ('rebels', as they call them) coming here. We were much alarmed towards morning by Sue's calling to have the house opened; Prophet had come bringing Kate some beef and meal.

At breakfast two Yankees rode around the lot, but seeing nothing to take went away; and we were not further interrupted.

George and June came back, saying the ox-wagon had been cut to pieces and the oxen killed. They were carried to Ogeechee, where George saw Mr Mallard and says he preached to the Yankees.

Monday, December 26, Saw no one all day. Towards evening we ventured out with the poor little children, and as we were returning saw one at a distance.

Tuesday, December 27, No enemy today, Bless the Lord for this mercy!

Wednesday, December 28, Another day without the appearance of the Yankees. Could we but know we should be spared one day we would breathe freely, but we are in constant apprehension and terror. Everyone that comes has some plea for insult or robbery. Was there ever a civilised land given up for such a length of time to lawless pillage and brutal inhumanities?

Thursday, December 29, Free from intrusion until afternoon, when three Yankees and one Negro came up. Lucy ran into the house and locked the door after her, which seemed to provoke them. Three came to the door, and after knocking violently several times one broke open the door. Mother and Kate went down as soon as they could, and when he saw them he cursed awfully. They insisted upon coming in, and asked for that 'damned wench' that had locked the door, threatening to 'shoot her damn brains out', using the Saviour's name in awful blasphemy.

Nothing seemed to keep them from going over the house but Mother's telling them the officers had advised the locking of the doors, and the men had no right to enter the house, under General Sherman's orders. She told them the situation of her family, and her daughter. One went into the parlour and pantry and into one or two other rooms; and one went into the room we are compelled to cook in, and crouched like a beast over the fire. He was black and filthy as a chimney sweep. Indeed, such is the horrible odour they leave in the house we can scarcely endure it.

The cook, seeing the party, locked herself in the cooking room; but they thundered at the door in such a manner I had to call to her to open it, which when she did I could scarce keep from smiling at the metamorphosis. From being a young girl she had assumed the attitude and appearance of a sick old woman, with a blanket thrown over her head and shoulders, and scarcely able to move. Their devices are various and amusing. Gilbert keeps a sling under his coat and slips his arm into it as soon as they appear; Charles walks with a stick and limps dreadfully; Niger a few days since kept them from stealing everything they wanted in his house by covering up in bed and saying he had '*yellow fever*'; Mary Ann kept them from taking the wardrobe of her deceased daughter by calling out: 'Them dead people clothes!'

Although circumstances were similarly grim at the Confederate White House during the last Christmas of the Civil War, Christmas was still celebrated in style as described by the Confederate's First Lady, Varina Jefferson Davis. The occupants of the Confederate White House used their ingenuity to provide a traditional Christmas for the children of a nearby orphanage.

CHRISTMAS IN THE CONFEDERATE WHITE HOUSE[11]
Written especially for the Sunday World Magazine *by Mrs Jefferson Davis*

... Rice, flour, molasses and tiny pieces of meat, most of them sent to the President's wife anonymously to be distributed to the poor, had all to be weighed and issued, and the playtime of the family began, but like a clap of thunder out of a clear sky came the information that the orphans at the Episcopalian home had been promised a Christmas tree and toys, candy and cakes must be provided, as well as one pretty prize for the most orderly girl among the orphans. The kind-hearted confectioner was interviewed by our committee of managers, and he promised a certain amount of his simpler kinds of candy, which he sold easily a dollar and a half a pound, but he drew the line at cornucopias to hold it, or sugared fruits to hang on the tree, and all the other vestiges of Christmas creations which had lain on his hands for years. The ladies dispersed in anxious squads of toy-hunters, and each one turned over the store of her children's treasures for a contribution to the orphans' tree, my little ones rushed over the great house looking up their treasure eyeless dolls, three-legged horses, tops with the upper peg

broken off, rubber tops, monkeys with all the squeak gone silent and all the ruck of children's toys that gather in a nursery closet.

Makeshift toys for the orphans

Some small feathered chickens and parrots which nodded their heads in obedience to a weight beneath them were furnished with new tail feathers, lambs minus much of their wool were supplied with a cotton wool substitute, rag dolls were plumped out and recovered with clean cloth, and the young ladies painted their fat faces in bright colours and furnished them with beads for eyes.

But the tug of war was how to get something with which to decorate the orphans' tree. Our man servant, Robert Brown, was much interested and offered to make the prize toy. He contemplated a 'sure enough house, with four rooms'. His part in the domestic service was delegated to another and he gave himself over in silence and solitude to the labours of the architect.

My sister painted mantel shelves, door panels, pictures and frames for the walls, and finished with black grates in which there blazed a roaring fire, which was pronounced marvelously realistic. We all made furniture of twigs and pasteboard, and my mother made pillows, mattresses, sheets and pillow cases for the two little bedrooms.

Christmas Eve a number of young people were invited to come and string apples and popcorn for the trees; a neighbour very deft in domestic arts had tiny candle moulds made and furnished all the candles for the tree. However the puzzle and triumph of all was the construction of a large number of cornucopias. At last someone suggested a conical block of wood, about which the drawing paper could be wound and pasted. In a little book shop a number of small, highly coloured pictures cut out and ready to apply were unearthed, and our old confectioner friend, Mr Piazzi, consented, with a broad smile, to give 'all the love verses the young people wanted to roll with the candy'.

A Christmas Eve party

About twenty young men and girls gathered around small tables in one of the drawing rooms of the mansion and the cornucopias were begun. The men wrapped the squares of candy, first reading the 'sentiments' printed upon them, such as 'Roses are red, violets blue, sugar's sweet and so are you', 'If you love me as I love you, no knife can cut our love in two.' The fresh young faces, wreathed in smiles, nodded attention to the reading, while with their small deft hands they ginned the cornucopias and pasted on the pictures. Where were the silk tops to come from? Trunks of old things were turned out and snippings of silk and even wool of bright colors were found to close the tops, and some of the young people twisted sewing silk into cords with which to draw the bags up. The beauty of those home-made things astonished us all, for they looked quite 'custom-made', but when the 'sure enough house' was revealed to our longing gaze the young people clapped their approbation, while Robert, whose sense of dignity did not permit him to smile, stood the impersonation of successful artist and bowed his thanks for our approval. Then the coveted eggnog was passed around in tiny glass cups and pronounced good. Crisp home-made ginger snaps and snowy lady cake completed the refreshments of Christmas Eve. The children allowed to sit up and be noisy in their way as an indulgence took a sip of eggnog out of my cup, and the eldest boy confided to his father: 'Now I just know this is Christmas.' In most of the houses in Richmond these same scenes were enacted, certainly in every one of the homes of the managers of the Episcopalian Orphanage. A bowl of eggnog was sent to the servants, and a part of everything they coveted of the dainties.

At last quiet settled on the household and the older members of the family began to stuff stockings with molasses candy, red apples, an orange, small whips plaited by the family with high-coloured crackers, worsted reins knitted at home, paper dolls, teetotums made of large horn bottoms and a match which could spin indefinitely, balls of worsted rags wound hard and covered with old kid gloves, a pair of pretty woolen gloves for each, either cut of cloth and embroidered on the back or knitted by some deft hand out of home-spun wool. For the President there were a pair of chamois-skin riding gauntlets exquisitely embroidered on the back with his monogram in red and white silk, made, as the giver wrote, under the guns of Fortress Monroe late at night for fear of discovery. There was a hemstitched linen handkerchief, with a little sketch in indelible ink in one corner; the children had written him little letters, their grandmother having held their hands, the burthen of which compositions was how they loved their dear father.

... On Christmas morning the children awoke early and came in to see their toys. They were followed by the negro women, who one after another 'caught' us by wishing us a Merry Christmas before we could say it to them, which gave them a right to a gift. Of course, there was a present for every one, small though it might be, and one who had been born and brought up at our plantation was vocal in her admiration of a gay handkerchief. As she left the room she ejaculated: 'Lord knows mistress knows our insides; she jest got the very thing I wanted.'

Mrs Davis's strange presents

... After breakfast, at which all the family, great and small, were present, came the walk to St Paul's Church. We did not use our carriage on Christmas or, if possible to avoid it, on Sunday. The saintly Dr Minnegerode preached a sermon on Christian love, the introit was sung by a beautiful young society woman and the angels might have joyfully listened. Our chef did wonders with the turkey and roast beef, and drove the children quite out of their propriety by a spun sugar hen, life-size, on a nest full of blanc mange eggs. The mince pie and plum pudding made them feel, as one of the gentlemen laughingly remarked, 'like their jackets were buttoned', a strong description of repletion which I have never forgotten. They waited with great impatience and evident dyspeptic symptoms for the crowning amusement of the day, 'the children's tree'. My eldest boy, a chubby little fellow of seven, came to me several times to whisper: 'Do you think I ought to give the orphans my I.D. studs?' When told no, he beamed with the delight of an approving conscience. All throughout the afternoon first one little head and then another popped in at the door to ask: 'Isn't it 8 o'clock yet?' burning with impatience to see the 'children's tree'.

David helped Santa Claus

When at last we reached the basement of St Paul's Church the tree burst upon their view like the realisation of Aladdin's subterranean orchard, and they were awed by its grandeur.

The orphans sat mute with astonishment until the opening hymn and prayer and the last amen had been said, and then they at a signal warily and slowly gathered around the tree to receive from a lovely young girl their allotted present. The different gradations from joy to ecstasy which illuminated their faces was 'worth two years of peaceful life' to see. The President became so enthusiastic that he undertook to help in the distribution, but worked such wild confusion giving everything asked for into their outstretched hands, that we called a halt, so he contented himself with unwinding one or two tots from a network of strung popcorn in

which they had become entangled and taking off all apples he could when unobserved, and presenting them to the smaller children. When at last the house was given to the 'honour girl' she moved her lips without emitting a sound, but held it close to her breast and went off in a corner to look and be glad without witnesses ...

Officers in a starvation dance

The night closed with a 'starvation' party, where there were no refreshments, at a neighbouring house. The rooms lighted as well as practicable, some one willing to play dance music on the piano and plenty of young men and girls comprised the entertainment. Sam Weller's soirée, consisting of boiled mutton and capers, would have been a royal feast in the Confederacy. The officers, who rode into town with their long cavalry boots pulled well up over their knees, but splashed up their waists, put up their horses and rushed to the places where their dress uniform suits had been left for safekeeping. They very soon emerged, however, in full toggery and entered into the pleasures of their dance with the bright-eyed girls, who many of them were fragile as fairies, but worked like peasants for their home and country. These young people are grey-haired now, but the lessons of self-denial, industry and frugality in which they became past mistresses then, have made of them the most dignified, self-reliant and tender women I have ever known – all honour to them.

So, in the interchange of the courtesies and charities of life, to which we could not add its comforts and pleasures, passed the last Christmas in the Confederate mansion.

Varina Jefferson Davis

After the war, the celebration of Christmas again became a grand affair. Below is an extract describing a Christmas visit to Montevallo, Alabama in 1867 at which the author observes a Christmas Tree.

SOCIAL LIFE AFTER THE WAR – CHRISTMAS[12]

On Christmas Eve there was a general gathering of both old and young to the Female Institute where the young ladies of the school had arranged a Gift Tree upon which presents were placed, not only for the school children, but for many of the citizens ...

Christmas night by special invitation we repaired to the Methodist Church where we witnessed one of the most beautiful sights it has ever

been our lot to enjoy. Just inside the altar, raised upon a large stand, was a holly tree filled with glistening leaves and bunches of red berries, the top reached the ceiling of the church. Hundreds of various coloured tapers threw a clear brilliant light over the tree while a double row of tapers illuminated the stand upon which the tree was placed. The altar was beautifully decorated with wreaths of evergreens and lit up with tapers. On the branches of the tree was hung every conceivable variety of article from a small ornamented portemonie to large pieces of silver plate. It was a sight *grande, magnifique*. Our observations were interrupted by the entrance of the Sunday School procession. Immediately the organ was opened and the children sang, with spirit and understanding, a glorious Christmas anthem after which a short but expressive prayer was uttered by the minister. Then commenced the excitement of the distribution of the presents and ... no child was forgotten. But each went home well satisfied with his share of the spoils of their never-to-be-forgotten Christmas Tree. Several prizes were received for good

lessons, good behavior and punctual attendance. What an encouragement was this exhibition of love and good will to the noble cause of
Sabbath Schools.

The traditional images of Christmas with snow-covered trees and carol-singers warmly
wrapped against the cold are rarely seen in the Southern United States. Tropical breezes
from the Gulf of Mexico can blow warmly even in December. Ironically these tempera-
tures probably more closely match the conditions on the night of the Nativity than the
snow covered images on Christmas cards.

Louisiana is unique among the Southern States in that its earliest and primary cultural
influence is French. Christmas eve in nineteenth-century New Orleans was a noisy day,
with groups of youths marching through the streets, blowing horns, and making music to
the background of ringing church bells. For most Creole families the celebration of
Christmas began with midnight mass at St Louis Cathedral. Following mass, families
returned home for the *reveillon*, a late night meal which often lasted until morning. The
meal usually consisted of eggs, daube glacé, grillades and many fancy desserts served with
dark chicory coffee. Upriver of the city of New Orleans another tradition is preserved to
this day; the lighting of the *Feux-de-Joie*, fires of joy. These bonfires are lit along the levees
on the banks of the Mississippi river on Christmas eve. The reasons given for the lighting
of the bonfires are varied but include: to guide *Papa Noel* on his Christmas eve journey
along the fog-shrouded banks of the river; to carry on the tradition of spreading peace and
goodwill to far off villages through the symbol of fire; or perhaps to guide the way for the
Holy Family on the eve of the Nativity.

The following story includes many elements of a New Orleans Christmas. It was published in the *Daily Picayune* newspaper on December 25, 1892 and tells the story of a man
outcast from society who reverses his role on a Christmas eve in the 'old days'.

CLOPIN-CLOPANT [13]

It was Christmas eve, the merry, maddening Christmas eve of New Orleans, in those old days when all above Canal street, from the rue
Tchoupitoulas to the woods, lay the broad indigo fields of opulent
planters, and the boys went sailing in pirogues in Carondelet street, and
the dreamy, old-fashioned *faubourg*, with its gay marchands in the rue
Royale, and its grand promenade in the boulevard Esplanade, thought
more of defending its old fortifications along the rue Rampart than building levees to protect the riverfront, or advertising the superior commercial situation of the city in the great markets of the world.

But it was Christmas eve, and the glow of the tropics rested with
lingering witchery upon the old-fashioned gardens, hidden behind the
high brick walls, over which the golden clusters of oranges hung
temptingly; the shadows of the quaint courtyards, with gorgeous gera-
niums blooming in potted jars, seemed to reflect the incipient light that

shown [*sic*] from the Christmas skies. Anyone who loitered along the old *carré* that evening would have been impressed with the undertone of happiness that prevaded all like the awakening notes to a joyous overture. For all day long the *belles demoiselles* loitered among the roses and jasmines of the courtyards, twining bouquets and planning for the *reveillon* which every Creole home from that day to this holds on Christmas eve.

And the moon rose on the great birth-night glorious everywhere beneath God's heaven, because of the message it brings, but especially beautiful in this southern latitude, where the skies echo in starlit greetings the tidings that angels brought to Bethlehem. The pent-up joyousness of the week broke forth in the old *faubourg*; the streets were filled with a surging fun-loving people, who laughed and smiled and greeted one another over and over again, shaking hands as though they had not met in years, and all because of the Christmas joy that filled their hearts to overflowing, and which must find vent one way or another; the boys shouted themselves hoarse; the ubiquitous tin-horn kept up a continuous 'toot-toot-toot'; the echo of firecrackers and the incessant reverberations of pistol-shooting rang through the old thoroughfares; and men and women pressed eagerly forward through the dim stores, closing bargains with the old *marchands*, and marching out with arms filled with gifts that would bring to young and old one day in the year of unalloyed happiness – one day grant with vows and whispered blessings. But the mischief-making prank playing element in the community was also abroad, and, as the night progressed, the merry band of camarades headed by Raoul, the aristocratic scapegrace of the *faubourg*, gathered in the shadow of the ancient café, which stood in those days at the corner of the rues Ursulines and Chartres, and looking jestingly from the laughing barmaids to the *ancient habitués* who, keeping Christmas in their own peculiar way, had opened bottle after bottle of champagne in hilarious excitement, instinctively queried, 'What next?' It was a débonnaire crowd that followed Raoul that Christmas eve, a crowd who thought no prank too wild to play on an unsuspecting community, and whose sole aim seemed to be to get out of life all the fun that could be extracted without any thought of the consequences. Christmas night – the night that meant pathos and tenderness and angel greetings for the rest of the *faubourg* – meant for them a carnival of mischief, here, there, anywhere, just so they were not discovered, and could view the results from the distance, and laugh to their hearts' content. Already they had played tricks enough to set half the community wild before morning;

they had moved the steps from one quarter of the houses in the *faubourg*, leaving some on the outskirts of the town, others six squares or more down the street from their proper location, or exchanging the high steps of one neighbour's home for the low ones of another; as the spirit moved them. They had fastened cords on the old-fashioned door-knockers, and hiding over the way, kept up an incessant banging from door to door, till the good housewives, in sheer despair, stationed a servant within the gate shadow to discover the miscreant. Then they had slipped into the old cathedral while the ancient *suisse* was decking the altars for the midnight mass, and filled one holy water font with ink and the other with crabs, so that all the *belles demoiselles* might make black crosses on their foreheads when they took the *eau-bénie*, or scream with terror when the crabs bit their pretty, pink fingers as they piously dipped them in the *bénitier. Ma foi*! It would take too long to tell the doings of Raoul and his followers that Christmas night; and now they had gathered up all the old tin pans and bones and squeaky fiddles and horns and accordions they could find, making merry at the expense of every one they passed till they reached the old café, where their stock of mischievous plans seemed exhausted. It was not yet 12 o'clock, and the hours before dawn must be filled.

Suddenly a bright thought broke upon Raoul. '*Tiens!*' he cried: 'I have it! Let us go and *charivari* old Clopin-Clopant!'

'Hooray!' shouted the crowd. 'Tree cheer! tree cheer! Let us go charivari old Clopin-Clopant.'

And, suiting the action to the word, down the street they went, blowing their horns, playing the squeaky accordions and tapping the tin pans and shouting to all the boys they met to come and join in the fun. They were going to '*charivari* old Clopin-Clopant'.

'Zey gone make one *charivari* for old Clopin-Clopant,' said Mère Jeanne to the little German woman next door; 'mais, dat ole man go'ne come to de door of his miserab' cabane, and fling five, ten, fifteen dollar in deir face an' tell dem 'go to de dey' an' get drunk, an' let one hole man keep his Noel in peace.'

'Mais, we no want get drunk,' said Raoul, catching her words and stopping to parley, in ridicule of her broken English: 'we no want touch de ole hoodoo money dat de dev' help Clopin-Clopant for make come out like that from *feu-follet* when de night make dark in de *marais*. We go'ne take dat ole *croque-miton* to de "Café de Joie" and make him drink one good cocktail with gentleman, and not with witch, on Christmas night.'

'Yes,' roared the crowd, 'we go'ne take Clopin-Clopant to de Café de Joie wiz one band music, and we go'ne make him drink cocktail like gentleman to-night.'

... He was only an ugly, crippled, old hunchback, who had come into the *faubourg* nobody knew when, and who lived, nobody knew how, in the old deserted hut which popular traditions had invested with wild and weird superstitions. There were strange stories told in those days of the little hunchback; dark, uncanny rumors floated around, both among blacks and whites, of the strange psychological and occult influence he exercised at will over the unthinking faubourg. Every night, when the moon was hid, the *feu-follet* came dancing out of the marshes, and making three turns around the rickety old cabin, entered like ghosts with tails of fire, and way off in the distance, the midnight hunter, seeking *becasine* and *gros-bee* along the bayou, could see Clopin-Clopant dancing the weird calinda with his strange, unearthly visitants; then he would set his pot to boiling, and light his candles over the heads of his intended victims, while the wind played strange music among the reeds and palmettos of the *marais* [swamp].

Somehow or other Clopin-Clopant was held directly responsible by the ignorant blacks and whites for every misfortune that happened in the *faubourg*. To the former, gradually imbued with the wild theories of fetish belief brought to New Orleans by the San Domingo negroes after the island insurrection, the old hunchback was the slave of the great Zombi, and many whispered he was the Zombi himself, who had followed them in anger from his chosen island to wreak vengeance upon them and their masters wherever they dwelt. Did anyone die in the *faubourg*; sure, the owl that lit upon the old man's chimney the night before, had brought the summons at his bidding; were the whippoor-wills to cry in the old ruins at daybreak, *ma foi*, look out for the next news from Paris; the city was sure to be given over to the blamed Americans some day; did Clopin-Clopant, contrary to his usual custom, walk in the rue Royale, alas, for *ma belle Oreole* who came within glance of his evil eye; *certes*, she would quarrel with her lover before night and die in a nunnery of a broken heart. Oh it would take too long to enu-merate the category of disasters of which Clopin-Clopant was held to be the direct author.

... And so the old cabin in the swamp and the little garden of roses that the little hunchback had painted just behind it, became in time the symbol of superstitious dread in the *faubourg*. No one dared to pass the place after nightfall; no one dared to speak to the singular old recluse;

and yet strange things happened in the old quarter at times. There were well-chosen instances of liberality coming at opportune moments from an unknown source that could only spring from a heart naturally inclined to goodness; but no one dreamed of associating these with the little hunchback. There had been strange legends too, in the days when he first came to New Orleans – stories which floated around among the intelligent portion of the community; that proud and cultured race of Creoles who scorned the superstitions of the ignorant whites and negroes, and strove to put them down as unworthy of an enlightened community. In the annual trips which the wealthy and cultured made to Paris, queer rumours had reached the *faubourg* from time to time; snatches of an old love story of a hunchbacked cripple, born to wealth and position; the apparent acquiescence to parental demands of the daughter of the noble house in which he sought alliance, her flight on the wedding eve with the younger brother of the prospective bridegroom, and how rumour had it that they had married and fled to New Orleans, and the misshapen cripple had left the gay haunts of Paris and had become a misanthropical hermit in the forests of La Bretagne. The story ran, too, of the wild life the young husband led in the old *faubourg*, and how the echoes of the sorrows of the neglected wife reached Paris and penetrated to the Brittany wilds. One day the hunchback was missing, and vague rumours floated around that stung with anguish, and, mindful of the old passion yet undimmed, he, too, had gone to New Orleans to watch in secret over the happiness of the woman he loved: and there were many Parisians returning from New Orleans, in those days, who had caught glimpses of the haunted cabin in the swamp, who openly asserted that the identity of the recluse of Bretagne was the same as that of the hunchback of the bayou St John.

But that was long ago, and the gay, laughing *faubourg* had no time to investigate the love affairs of an ugly, misshapen cripple ... and excluded from him her fairest enjoyments. *Tiens!* who ever dreamed that he had a heart, that the scoff of the rabble, the suppressed titter of the young men, and the yet more offensive horror of the maidens as he passed and, above all, the dreadful superstition which the common people had invested him, were like poisoned arrows piercing his soul ...

Perhaps some thought of the unjust sentiment of the community passed through the old hunchback's mind as he stood in his little garden that Christmas night gathering the beautiful roses that his own hands had tended, and big tears watered to freshness and beauty, and perhaps as he looked from them to the speaking stars above, his heart found an answer for the long years of loneliness and misjudgment, and he softly whispered to himself. 'She at least can read my heart and understand' ... He raised his eyes heavenwards, and pressing the beautiful bouquet of roses closest to his heart, as though the starry petals could understand its throbbings and waft them above with each breath of fragrance they inhaled, he passed from the old cabin in the swamp towards the restless *faubourg*. 'But not there,' he said, 'not there.' He felt happier than he had been in years, and hobbled along; forgetful of his infirmity, forgetful of all save the new sweet thought that had come with the Christmas roses. Suddenly, a sound broke through his reverie, a confused echo that rose into a din of ringing cowbells, horns, squeaking accordions, rattling bones, all combined as though pandemonium itself had broke loose. The old man drew back within the shadows of a moss-hung oak, but Raoul and his *charivari* band had already caught sight of him.

'What's that,' called Raoul, calling a halt.

'*Ma foi*! It's a ghost,' said Sylvestre shrinking back.

'*Parbleu*,' said Raoul, springing forward, 'it's old Clopin-Clopant himself and, *mon Dieu*! He is going to pay his respects to his lady-love with a bouquet on Christmas night!'

That was a bright thought – a veritable inspiration. The boys caught it up. 'Taking flowers to his lady-love!' 'At 1 o'clock in the morning!' 'Eh, Clopin-Clopant? you sly, old dev'l!' 'Who bin tink you got one lady-love?' 'Ah! Clopin-Clopant; he don't keep so still for nothing.' 'Come, Monsieur Clopin, out with the name of the *belle demoiselle* who takes your hoodoo roses on Christmas night!'

'Yes, yes!' cried the crowd; 'you got for tell her name, *mon Dieu*. We no go'ne let you off like dat. You got for tell where you go'ne keep your *reveillon*, and who go'ne take your hoodoo roses.'

'Hoodoo roses!' cried Raoul; 'Clopin-Clopant go'ne keep one *reveillon*! Eh, old man? and he blew his horn in the hunchback's ear. It was the signal. Such a din as broke upon the air! Such cries of 'Clopin-Clopant; we go'ne help him keep his *reveillon* on Christmas night!'

But the old hunchback did not answer. He only pressed his roses closer to his heart, as though the tender touch of his hands could ward off their cruel words. But Raoul is again at his side, singing gay snatches of the flower song in Faust –

> '*Faites lui mes aveux,*
> *Portez mes veux*
> *Dites-lui qu'elle est belle*'

'*Non, Non,*' said Sylvestre singing in a rich voice and trying to pluck the flowers-

> *Reviens à son âme, le secret de ma flamme,*
> *Que mon coeur, nuit et jour, languit d'amour*

'Ha! ha! ha!' they roared; 'old Clopin-Clopant dying of love!'

'Come, Monsieur Clopin,' said Raoul, 'you will keep your *reveillon* with gentlemen to-night, and drink a cocktail with us at the Café de Joie. And, parbleu, you shall give me those roses, too. Tiens, they will look better in my sweetheart's hair than in your witch's curls', and he strove to snatch the flowers from the hunchback's hand.

'Stand back!' cried the old man, fixing his dark, piercing eyes on the unruly leader of the band. 'Touch one of these roses if you dare! If you wish to see my lady-love, follow me.'

'Ha! ha! that's what we mean to do,' they cried, 'and you shall have music on the way', and the horns began playing again.

'If you wish to see where my lady-love lies', said the old man, as the whitened walls of the old cemetery rose in full view. 'Do you wish to know where I shall keep my *reveillon* to-night? There!' said he, pointing down the walls glistening like snow in the moonlight. 'And now, *messieurs*, do you wish to bear me company? Will you care to give me music on the way?'

The crowd shrunk back abashed: the horns and accordions stopped; the old hunchback gave the band a withering look of contempt, and passed within the gates. '*Mon Dieu!*' said Raoul, 'who would have ever thought old Clopin-Clopant had a romance in his life?'

'Come boys!' said Sylvestre, 'we can find better pastime than ridiculing an old man's sorrows on Christmas night.' And the crowd moved on. But not Raoul: some strange, indescribable feeling impelled him to follow the hunchback, and he slowly, stealthily kept pace behind him down the graveled walk: he saw the old hunchback stop at an ancient oven-shaped tomb; he saw him kneel and place the beautiful roses – a Christmas message from the living to the dead – upon it, and Raoul drew back in amazement – it was the grave of his own mother. A thousand thoughts came surging through the young man's brain; the old, forgotten legends of the *faubourg*, the quaint love-story that floated from distant France, all came back in that hour, and acquired a truth – a significance Raoul could as yet but vaguely define. What reason had this old hunchback to kneel at the grave this Christmas night? Why should he caress those Christmas roses, calling upon the name that Raoul had venerated and loved in the days gone by, and repeating over and over again that while the *faubourg* laughed and made merry, he had come to keep his *reveillon* alone with the beautiful and forgotten dead.

'Not forgotten,' said Raoul to himself, 'nay, not forgotten,' and shrunk back in the shadowy aisle determined to learn the romance of the hunchback's life on to-morrow, when the weird old man, plucking a single rose from the fragrant mass, placed tenderly in his bosom and went on once more into the starry night. His musings have been sweet, why should he have the message of this holiday marred by returning to the old cabin with its hidden memories. And he loitered on unmolested down the riverbank for the streets are almost deserted now. The Christmas joy and merriment is at its height in the homes of the *carré*, and the old story that has swayed the world for 1,900 years seems wooing him back to love and forgiveness, and he wonders if it were indeed meant for all, or if its echoes were only the lingering refrain of an epic fragment. And ever and anon his thoughts wander from the story to the river spinning along at a rapid, tumbling pace, the waves dancing one above another in glee, and every moment seeming to threaten the shore. Then Clopin-Clopant heard a slight gurgling sound, he paused to listen, and groping carefully along, he saw a fine long crevice through which the water was forcing its way. A ton or more of earth had settled into the boiling edge and the bank was caving at a fearful pace. By morning –

The old man looked at the *faubourg* that all unconscious laughed and danced and sang while the waters too had prepared for a *reveillon* on Christmas night. For a moment he thought of giving the alarm; but, bah! who would believe old Clopin-Clopant, the slave of the Zombi, the wizard of the *marais*? Then a fearful thought crossed his mind – what did he owe to these people who had heaped nothing but scorn and indignities upon him; let the waters come upon them! And then, like the touch of an angel's breath, there swept over him the fragrance of the roses hidden in his bosom. For her sake! – And all night the stars kept vigil while the little old hunchback knelt near the caving bank filling the crevice with earth dug with his own hands and pieces of drift-wood and broken twigs. And all night long he whispered to his heart, 'She at least will understand,' and with the thought came pity and love and forgiveness and 'peace and goodwill to all men'. The night that bears the heaven-born tidings to all had brought to him a new and better meaning.

And morning found Clopin-Clopant at his self-appointed post, tired, benumbed, sunk down into the crevice and keeping the water back by the force of his own body. Some market men passing saw him, and dragging the poor little hunchback out, gave the alarm. And while the people gathered and the governor and intendant sent volunteers steadily to work on the caving bank, the old man, unnoticed and forgotten, stole quietly back to the cabin in the swamp, still pressing his Christmas rose to his bosom, and whispering, 'She understands.'

Ah! He felt his loneliness, but for once, he had misjudged the *faubourg* who knew better than any other people how to be generous and reward a noble deed nobly wrought. The sun is high in the Christmas heavens; the danger to the city is passed, the bank is safe, and Clopin-Clopant is the hero's name on every lip. From one end of the city to the other the people have all turned out, carrying boughs of holly and mistletoe, and headed by Monsieur le Gouverneur and the intendant, once the most rollicking leader in the *faubourg*, but now one of its most staid and useful citizens, they wend their way to the cabin on the bayou St John.

The old man sees the demonstration from afar. Alas! he fears, and bolts his doors securely. But the governor commands him, in the name of the king, to open the portal and come forth. And Clopin-Clopant obeys tremblingly, and falling upon his knees says: '*Monsieur*, have pity. I am not the Zombi! I have never harmed any one in my life. I am only a miserable old man, who wants to die in peace. I am not the Zombi.'

'*Tiens!*' cried the governor indignantly, 'we want a hundred Zombies like you in New Orleans. Rise, monsieur, and receive from your fellow citizens the reward of your noble service. Monsieur l'Intendant, do your duty.'

The official stepped forward, holding in his hand the set of resolution which the people had prepared in honour of the little hunchback. For a moment he reads in a loud, pompous voice, and then his eyes rest on the misshapen mass before him – the ugly frame that concealed such a noble heart – and the paper falls from the intendant's hands.

'Colas!' he cried, 'my brother, forgive the past. You were worthier of her than I,' and forgetful of the crowd that pressed eagerly around, he knelt at the hunchback's feet.

'Nay! nay!' said the old man; 'she loved you not me! No one whom she loved could be unworthy.' And Raoul, seeing his father clasped in old Clopin-Clopant's arms, needed no explanation of the scene of the night before.

It was Monsieur le Gouverneur who spoke first.

'Come, Monsieur Colas, you must eat your Christmas dinner with me.'

'No,' said the little hunchback. 'I am an old man now, the saddest days of my life were spent in this cabin, the happiest hour has come to me here, the brightness of this Christmas will light me to the grave. Here let me stay to-day with my brother, my memories and my flowers. Let this Christmas hour be sacred,' and he motioned them away.

But the people filled the cabin with mistletoe and holly and left old Clopin-Clopant there in the Christmas glow feeling that after all, it was neither the holly nor the mistletoe that makes the beauty of the old, old Christmas but love, and love makes Christmas all the year.

While many elements particular to the South still persist today, they exist side-by-side with the commercialised rendition of how Christmas should be celebrated. The final two selections in this chapter visit two specific groups who, isolated from the commercial world, each celebrate Christmas in a unique manner that complements the message of the Nativity.

CHRISTMAS IN MARCH [14]

Twenty miles south of Houma, Louisiana, in Terrebonne Parish, is located the little fishing and trapping settlement of Bayou du Large. About twenty-four families make up this quaint settlement – of the purest Scotch and English blood, as their fair skins, blue eyes and blond hair will testify. Four generations of these hardy Nordics have lived in this sequestered spot on the peaceful banks of Bayou du Large. Where they came from, nobody knows, not even themselves. One theory is that they have moved down from the hills of Kentucky and Tennessee, possibly joining Lafitte's pirate band at Barataria and eventually settling further inland. This theory is further strengthened by the fact that these fair-headed Bayou people speak a drawl alien to Louisiana. It is certain that on their arrival they were entirely without knowledge of the methods of fishing that now forms one of the chief means of their livelihood.

These people draw their living from Nature. In the winter they set their traps for muskrats along the bayou, in the swamps and out on the prairies. In the summer they strike for the coast and trawl for shrimp in the Gulf of Mexico. For the little while they are at home they plow the soil and raise potatoes and beans on small back-yard farms.

The muskrat season opens in November and closes in February. During those months the men work their traps. A few of them stay close by home, moving up and down bayous and nearby swamps. But most of them fill their cabin boats with gasoline and strike out for points fifty and sixty miles distant. These take their wives and children along. For this four-month period they live in their house-boats and the women and children help with the work, setting traps and collecting the catch. For this reason only a part of the some three hundred inhabitants are at home for the twenty-fifth of December.

In order that they, and particularly their children, might not be deprived of the celebration of the Christmas season, these simple, sturdy pioneers hit on the plan of observing Christmas at the close of the trapping season – on their return to the home settlement. Thus they established the unique custom of celebrating Christmas in March, taking the sensible view that it is the spirit of the occasion that makes the Yuletide important!

A '90S NATIVITY[15]

If you want to know how much faith it took for the early Christians to accept the virgin birth as told in the Nativity story, consider how you would feel about a messiah born on a bus in New Orleans to an ex-con just a few days out of the maximum security wing.

That's the Christmas story as dramatised this holiday season by a group of inmates at the Louisiana Correctional Institute for Women in St Gabriel. The play was staged for inmates, their children, prison staff and a small number of visitors last week.

The basic elements of the St Gabriel story are the same as they were in Bethlehem two millennia ago: A God full of love decides to send his son to save the world from itself. Mary is a woman of faith whose friends have a difficult time believing she's virgin. ('I'm telling you, I have not had sex,' she says during one scene in the middle of a volleyball game in the compound. 'Yeah?' a fellow inmate chides her, 'since when?') Joseph is a blue-collar worker who is justifiably concerned that his fiancée has turned up pregnant.

But, inside the freshly painted, bright white cinderblock walls of the prison gym, this telling of the Nativity is up-to-date and decidedly urban: instead of shepherds hearing about Jesus' birth from a chorus of heavenly host, a trio of winos gets the blessed news while tending a garbage-can fire. The three wise women are not starwatchers from the Far East, but Mary's nearby relatives and friends. And the inn isn't exactly full – Mary and Joseph are shunned from the Tulane University hospital and Touro Infirmary because they don't have health insurance.

Along the way, there's ample humor – some unique to life in prison, some universal – New Testament readings and plenty of music provided by a seventeen-voice, crimson-robed choir delivering spirited renditions of holiday classics such as 'Joy to the World' and 'Oh Come, Oh Come, Emanuel'.

CHAPTER VIII

An Irish Perspective

Short crisp days and long cold nights mark December in Ireland. Christmas candles in the window of every home dot the dark countryside with beacons of light. Nowadays, the 'candles' are often flickering electric light bulbs atop plastic stands, nevertheless the tradition to place a candle in the window to light the way for Joseph and Mary on Christmas eve is maintained. Light, after all, is a most powerful symbol in the darkness of mid-winter in Ireland. Long before Christianity, the inhabitants of ancient Ireland captured the low rays of light on the morning of the winter solstice to flood light into the tomb of their god, Dagda, on the very day that their mortal world experienced the longest night of the winter.[1]

This chapter contains a selection of extracts which were all written in Ireland and all have some link to the Nativity or the Christmas season. Diverse as they initially appear, they share themes which all contribute to our modern Christmas.

Light is the primary image that recurs. In his eleventh-century 'Chronological Poem' Gilla Coemáin addresses Jesus as 'Sun over every field' while Daithí Ó Bruadair, writing in the seventeenth century, describes the Nativity as 'a leap like sun through glass'. The Christmas eve altar visited by Peig Sayers was 'ablaze' with light, and the stable in Kate Ahern's Christmas eve parable was 'one blaze of light'. The sparkle in Eibhlís de Barra's memories of Christmas come from the lemonade and 'razza', and to a little girl in the inner city of Dublin the new star shining brightly up in the sky was fundamental to the Christmas story.

Ireland has a long tradition of story-telling and most of the extracts in this chapter were intended for oral recitation, Gilla Coemáin 'sang' his chronology; the internal rhyme and assonance of Daithí Ó Bruadair's *Adoramus Te, Christe* needs to be heard not read; Peig Sayers, Kate Ahern and Eibhlís de Barra were all storytellers in their communities, their tales committed to writing only for the sake of posterity. *It Was a Beautiful Star* is a transcript from a recital.

Most of our writers or storytellers weave the Christmas story into their own terms of reference. Gilla Coemáin intermingles the feats of great pagan warriors of Ireland among the biblical milestones. Peig's story about the Flight into Egypt seems to be set in a village in Ireland rather than the Middle East. Kate Ahern's story transforms a stable in a local parish and the little Dublin storyteller has no problem imagining the Nativity in terms of her everyday life.

Ireland's transition to Christianity did not eradicate the pagan beliefs completely, rather the two blended together; even today superstition plays a role in Irish Christian beliefs. The sense of good and evil is very acute and overcomes even the authority figures of the established Church. This can be seen clearly in *The Light of Heaven*. The difference between the 'good people' and the 'bad people' in *It Was a Beautiful Star* speaks for itself.

Prior to the christianisation of Ireland in the latter half of the first millennium AD, the ancient traditions of Ireland were preserved by the *filí* (druid-poets). These custodians of the tribal-history – keepers of tales of battles, genealogy, territory, tribal and dynastic inter-relationships – held considerable legal and spiritual influence on society. Theirs was an oral tradition and subtle changes could be wrought on the history depending on the circumstance surrounding the telling. As Christianity spread, literacy in Latin and later in Irish also spread among the poet class.

Irish Christianisation was a slow process and, in many circumstances, greeted with great scepticism by the people, who struggled to understand the concept of a God who they could not judge by the strength of his residence, the valour of his sons or the beauty of his daughters. This difficulty is portrayed in the poem 'The Questions of Ethne Alba' as translated by James Carney.[2]

THE QUESTIONS OF ETHNE ALBA
Anonymous

Who is God
And where is God,
Of whom is God,
And where His dwelling?

Has He sons and daughters,
Gold and silver, this God of yours?

Is He ever-living?
Is He beautiful,
was His son
fostered by many?

Are His daughters
Dear and beautiful
To the men of the world?

Is He in heaven
Or on the earth?
In the sea,
In the rivers,
In the mountains,
In the valleys?

Speak to us
Tidings of Him:
How will He be seen,
How is He loved,
How is He found?

Is it in youth
Or is it in old age
He is found?

The new church absorbed much of the pagan culture, maintaining the pagan feasts of
Bealtaine, Samhan and Lughnasa, albeit under the guise of a saint's feast day. Pre-Christian
Ireland had not had a centralised system of rule and the church mirrored this organisation,
establishing itself primarily as a monastic church. It was at these ecclesiastical centres that the
ancient traditions of the *filí* met with the biblical teaching and genealogical knowledge of the

monastic scholars. Each seat of learning influenced the other. For the first time, the ancient secular histories were recorded using the vernacular, transcribed by monks who often added a Christian element or conclusion to the story. Reciprocally, the annals recorded by the monks, instead of being purely religious records, draw on the sagas, dynasties and verse of the secular world to enliven events. It is from documents such as the Book of Invasions, the Book of Leinster and the Book of Ballymote that the early history of Ireland is gleaned.

In 1072, the cleric Gilla Coemáin undertook the task of chronicling key events 'from the world's beginning' up to the year of his writing. This chronological poem is preserved in the twelfth-century Book of Leinster. His verse demonstrates the interweaving of the Irish secular tradition and Christianity. Gilla Coemáin's chronology pivots on the Nativity to which he returns regularly as a time base amid references to Biblical, Celtic, Trojan and Persian sagas.

Gilla Coemáin's 'Chronological Poem', written in 1072, was translated and edited by Whitley Stokes and published in *The Tripartite Life of Patrick* in 1887.[3] Extracts of that version are reproduced here.

GILLA COEMÁIN'S CHRONOLOGICAL POEM
(1072)

Gilla Coemáin sang:

1 All the annals down from the yellow topped world's beginning I will set forth here as the latest time.

2 Fifty-six years – pure deed – a thousand and six-hundred years I reckon – for it is knowledge without disgrace – to the Flood from the world's beginning.

3 Two hundreds (and) noble ninety two from the Flood to Abraham. From Abraham nine hundred – no weariness – and forty-two to David.

4 From David to the Captivity – no lie – seventy-three (and) four hundreds. From the Captivity to Christ – fair His fame – nine, five hundreds (and) eighty.

5 Three thousand years – no lie – fifty-two years and nine hundred to Mary's Son's birth there in the east down from the world's beginning.

6 Seventy-two – pure course – but it is in addition to a thousand years, from Christ's nativity to (this) fair year, seven days' space (to) January.

7 Four and twenty, true for me, and five thousand years to this year – it is a great renown – since the fair-faced world was formed.

8 Two hundred years to the victory, to the confusion of Nimrod's famous tower from the Flood – save ten years, it is certain for thee if thou regulates it.

9 Sixty-two – noble the might – from the Confusion of the Tower to Ninus' reign: twenty-one years thence to Abraham, to the father.

10 Sixty years, without any grief, from Abraham to Partholón, when he seized the fair Island three hundred years after the Deluge.

11 From Abraham's birth – that is known to me – to the passage of the Red Sea, five hundred and two years exactly when Egypt's host was drowned.

12 At that time, verses say, Conann's Tower was destroyed in the west and Srú went eastward on a journey, out of Egypt to Scythia.

13 That was in the middle of Ascades' reign, the passage of the strong Red Sea. Two hundred years after him (was the) end of Lampades' reign.

14 In Lampades' reign, conspicuous renown, Vesoges brought the host, and a most numerous host came after him out of Scythia.

15 At that time, then (was) the beginning of the might of the Burnt Paps: at that time –how melodious is the order! – the Fir Bolg inhabited Ireland.

16 Eighty years afterwards Tutanes was the king of the Earth: it is in his time that the Gael set up in the east, in the (Macotic) Marshes.

17 At that time, though I say it, the battle of Mag Tared was fought. It is at that time, without a lie, Trojan Troy was destroyed.

18 Thenias was the name of the king who lived at the same time as David: then did the king go into clay, at the time of the dour Darcellus.

19 Darcellus was prince of the lands when Solomon proceeded (to build) his temple. In the middle of the reign of the fair man came the Gael into Ireland.

20 Astyages (was) abbott without guile, when Jerusalem was ruined: last prince of the Medes – well he was praised – reigning along with Nabcodnosor.

21 Darcellus (and) Solomon of the spears were at the same time as Mél's sons. Five hundred save twenty (years) after them (were) Nabcodon (and) Astyages.

22 Sirna, king of Tara of the Towers, reigning along with Nabcodon: Then was fought – cause of valour – the battle of the heavy Bog of Trógaide.

23 Three hundred and thirty years thence to the beginning of Ugaine's reign. (was the) end of the Persian's kingdom – wise fame – the beginning of Philip's son's reign.

24 Three hundred and sixty goodly years from Alexander's lofty reign, and from Ugaine's reign – until Mary's good Son was born.

25 Forty-seven years from Christ's Nativity was Conchobar's death. Thirty-two from thence to the bloody death of Conaire.

26 Fifty-seven years (and) a fair hundred from the death of musical Conaire in the Bruden – cruel his fame – till Tuathal Tochtmar fell.

27 Thirty-two years thereafter, after the slaying of the prince Tuathal to the death of Conn the fair Hundred battled on the hill in Tuathamar.

28 Thirty-seven after hard Conn to the battle red-maned Mucerims, wherein fell – great their valour –Art, Cain, Cormac, and Eogan.

29 Fifty-seven years, without pain, from the battle of Muccrima of the nobles till Find fell by them, though it was treachery, by the spear-points of Urgrin's three sons.

30 Forty-five fair years after find's death out of Almu to the valiant rout of Dub Commar by battle-valiant Collas.

31 Five years from thence to the destruction of Emain Macha, and thirty-four, be ye sure, to Muridach Tírech's death.

32 From the death of Murideach of Meath, at Duball of the brown old trees (there were) fifty years save a year to the fall of Niall the Nine-hostaged.

33 A score of years and seven since Niall was parted from his strength till Patrick came, crown of Bregia, to help the children of Míl's sons.

34 Fifty-eight years, be thou sure, from that to Patrick's obit. From Patrick's death, bright fulfillment, Brigit's death was thirty years.

...

57 Seventy-two and a thousand (years) from Christ's Nativity, if thou computest to this year, though I say it, in which fell hard-mouthed Diarmait.

58 O Christ, O Sun over every field! Take pity on my soul in my body! Let not Thy deliverance be slender to me; through me Thy annals will be famous.

Gaelic poets continued to have considerable influence in Irish society as it underwent colonisation. Not only were they the keepers of the ancient tradition, but also the law makers and in many cases strategists in planning counter-measures against the conquering forces. By the late fifteenth century the monasteries in Gaelic Ireland had more or less become a part of secular society. Like the poets, the clerics operated as an extension of the Gaelic chieftains' households. Christian asceticism and monastic piety were preserved by the Observant Friars, small bands of pious men who strived to keep the Irish church in line with European Christianity. In the seventeenth century it was the friars, as custodians of the religion, who were influential in spurring the counter-reformation zeal of the Catholic Anglo-Norman families known as the 'Old English'.

As well as facing the onslaught of new religion and laws the Irish also had to face a foreign language. The transition in Irish literature from the Irish to the English language

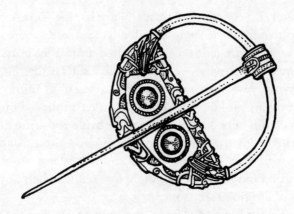

was a slow process and lasted from the seventeenth to the nineteenth century when Anglo-Irish writers emerged in their own right.

The poet, Daithí Ó Bruadair, persisted in using the classical style of strict meters and internal rhyme and assonance. His poem 'Adoramus Te, Christe'⁴ which, as translated by Thomas Kinsella, describes the Nativity and incarnation as 'a leap like sun through glass' upholds the classical style.

ADORAMUS TE, CHRISTE
Daibhí Ó Bruadair c.1625-98

Ghost of our blood, I worship You,
Hero on Heaven's rampart,
Who left for love a mighty Father
– by Mary's grace – to save us.
You made a leap like sun through glass
to abolish Adam's evil
and saved with a cross Man and his tribe
at Eastertime from Hell.

Harbour-candle that lulls to rest
the quarrel of deadly dangers,
the poor man's soul, I beg of You,
save, and restrain Satan.
Your broken side is all my fault,
and the tracks of the three nails,
but do not shut your calm bright eye
upon me – make me welcome.

We regard Your nurse the more, God's son,
that she was of David's line:
a virgin with milk, to prove the Law,
with a mother's looks and grace,
bright, noble and fair to nurture You,
Child, in a holy nook.
Pure like her never grew in womb
nor will till the end of time.

The English gentry, who participated in the plantation of Ireland by accepting tracts of land, established their stately residences in the wilderness of the Irish countryside. Despite their location, these Planters were determined to maintain the decorum and culture found in the English country homes. These families led a life quite isolated from the native population, socialising only with their peers from the neighbouring Big House. Such was the case with Aubrey de Vere who was born in 1788 in Curragh-Chase, Co. Limerick. In *Recollections of Aubrey de Vere*[5] he recalls a humorous incident from a Christmas spent with friends at Adare, Co. Limerick. The lifestyle and incident described in this recollection underline the gulf which existed between the English Planters and their Irish neighbours.

'CHRISTMAS HOLIDAYS'
Sir Aubrey de Vere, 1788-1846

Our home life pursued the even tenor of its way. We, the three elder brothers, worked at our classics in the morning, and in the afternoon took a long walk or a long ride, for each of us boasted a horse, though we seldom rode together; and in the evening there was often music, especially when Lord Monteagle was with us, for he and his sister, my mother, had been used to play duets from Mozart in their youth, he on the flute, and she on the pianoforte, and they continued the habit in advanced life. At Christmas we used to visit Adare Manor. It was a gay as well as a friendly and hospitable house; after dinner we had private theatricals, games of all sorts, dances, and, in the daytime, pleasant wanderings beside the beautiful Maigue, which mirrored, in waters that even when swiftest seldom lost their transparency, as stately a row of elms, ninety feet high, as England herself can boast, and the venerable remains of a castle which belonged to the Kildares – though islanded, as it were, in a territory almost all the rest of which belonged to the Desmond branch of the same Geraldine race. Adare, then as now a singularly pretty village, had for centuries been a walled town. It had seen many battles, and had been more than once burned down; but it was famous chiefly for the number of monastic institutions, still represented by the ruins of a Franciscan convent, as well as by one of the Trinitarian and one of the Augustinian order, the churches of which have been restored, and are now used, one for Catholic and the other for Protestant worship. The Knights Templars once possessed a house at Adare; but its site cannot now be discovered.

Among our Christmas holidays at Adare there is one which I am not likely to forget. About eight miles from the village rises a hill eight hundred feet in elevation, with a singularly graceful outline, named 'Knockfierna', or the 'Hill of the Fairies', because in popular belief it abounded in the 'Good People', then universally believed in by the gaelic race in Ireland. We set off to climb it one day soon after breakfast – we, meaning my two elder brothers and I, and the son of our host, Lord Adare, afterwards well-known as Earl of Dunraven, the author of two valuable works, 'Memorials of Adare' and an excellent book on Irish antiquities. Two other members of the exploring party were our tutor and a friend of Adare's several years older than he. It was hard walking, especially after the ascent of the hill began; we had to climb many walls and ditches, and to force our way through many a narrow lane. We had brought no luncheon with us, and before we reached the summit the winter sun had sunk considerably.

We walked about the hill top for some time admiring the view, a very fine one, though, like many Irish views, somewhat dreary, from the comparative absence of trees, the amount of moorland intersected by winding streams, and the number of ruins, many of them modern. All at once we discovered that we were faint with hunger, so much fatigued without refreshment that we could hardly make our way home. Halfway down the hill stood a farmhouse. The farmer was most courteous, but, alas! there was not a morsel of food in his house. What he had, he gave, and that was cider, for which, like the Irish peasant of that day, he would take no payment. Each of us drank only one cider glass of it, and we took our departure, cheered, but by no means invigorated. After a lapse of some ten minutes one of us became so sleepy that he could hardly walk, and his nearest companion neighbour at once gave him an arm. A little later the same complaint was made by another of us, and the same friendly aid was forced upon him. But in a few minutes more not only were we unable to walk, but we were unable to stand, the only exception being to two among us who were no longer boys – our tutor and Adare's friend.

Never shall I forget their astonishment first, and afterwards their vexation. They were in some degree in charge of us, and the responsibility seemed to rest upon them. The Christmas evening was closing around us;

there was no help near, and apparently no reason why our sleep should not last till sunrise. They argued, they expostulated, they pushed us, they pulled us; but all would not do. I was the last to give way, and my latest recollection was that my second brother had just succeeded in climbing on top of the wooden gate, but they could not lift his leg over it, and lay upon his face along it. Our tutor stamped up and down the road indulging in his favourite ejaculation 'Gracious patience! Gracious patience!' to which my brother replied, with his last gleam of wakeful intelligence, 'There is one very amiable trait about you, Mr Johnstone, you are never tried of toasting absent friends.' The next moment he rolled over and slept beside us in the mud. The cider had affected our brains because our stomachs were empty. In about a quarter of an hour the trance was dissolved almost as suddenly as it fell on us; and we walked forward mirthfully, reaching home just in time to hear the dressing bell ring. Only one light shone through the mullioned windows of the manor-house; and I remember Adare's remark as we drew near: 'Beside that light my little sister sits weeping. She is sure that I am dead.' At dinner we told the story of our adventures, and it excited much laughter. Lord Dunraven 'moralised the tale'. 'You see, young gentlemen, each of you undertook to support and guide his neighbour, though not one of you could take care of himself. That is the way of Ireland. You will help your neighbour best by taking care each of himself.' His advice was like that of another old Irish gentleman, a relative of mine, whose 'good-night' to his grandchildren often ended with this counsel, 'Take good care of yourself, child; and your friends will love you all the better.'

The remote areas in west of Ireland were the last areas to feel the advance of Anglicisation and Gaeltachts (Irish speaking communities) still survive in pockets of the west today. During the course of the nineteenth century Irish speakers dropped from about 4 million to less than three quarters of a million,[6] a decline which was accelerated by the government enforcing the mandatory use of English. The Gaeltacht areas unwittingly acted as the guardians of a culture and language that was all but lost to the rest of the island. The Irish language is a wonderfully descriptive medium drawing on everyday life to conjure up vivid images.

At the end of the nineteenth century, as the English language wave advanced, Peig Sayers was growing up in the parish of Dunquin, a parish at the extreme tip of the Dingle peninsula which is still a Gaeltacht today. Eking out an existence from the wild Atlantic and the rocky mountainside of the Dingle peninsula and the Blasket Islands proved to be harsh life. Despite the hardships, Peig lived to the age of 85 and after, much prompting, agreed to recount the story of her life. In so doing, Peig made a significant contribution to preserving the traditions of rural Ireland as well as eloquently demonstrating the beauty of the Irish language. In 1974 Bryan MacMahon translated Peig's tale into English,[7] opening it up to a wider audience yet ensuring, even in translation, that the spirit and musical flow of the Irish language was preserved.

When Peig was thirteen her father put her 'in service' with a family living in the town of Dingle. Peig helped out with the household chores and cared for the children. The Curran family owned a store in the centre of the town and their premises was at the hub of the town's activities. Peig recounts her first Christmas in Dingle. The townspeople spoke English and refer to Peig by the English version of her name, Margaret. This extract relates the events of Christmas Eve including: the hustle and bustle of the town; the decorating of the house; the story of the Slaughter of the Innocents (told from an Irish perspective) the visit to the crib; and poetry at the fireside.

'CHRISTMASTIDE'
Peig Sayers (1873-1953)

By this time Christmas was not far away and this is the time of the greatest hustle and bustle for townspeople. On the Saturday before Christmas the street was black with people: they were like harvest midges moving in and out through each other, collecting 'commands' as they went from house to house and a good number of men with hats on the side of their heads as a result of their having a jorum taken. I thought there wasn't so many people in the world as were gathered into the house at that hour of the day! The taproom was a solid mass of people; in the middle of the floor stood a great long table with forms on either side of it and the

people were so crushed together that a tiny wren wouldn't have found room among them.

...

Christmas Eve fell on a Tuesday and everyone was busy preparing for it. Seáinín came in the door carrying a bundle of ivy and holly.

'Give me a hand, Margaret', he said, 'till I fasten this to the window.'

'I know nothing about it', I said, 'because I never saw it done.'

'You'll see it now, girl, and when it'll be fixed up it will be simply beautiful.'

Anna and Eibhlín were busy making paper flowers of every colour; according as they had a flower finished Seáinín would tuck it in among the ivy.

'Bring me the candle now,' he told me.

I got a great red candle and a candlestick; this he set on the window-sill.

'Make the tea, you,' he told me, 'while I'm fixing up the rest of it.'

I hung the kettle over the fire and while I was waiting for it to boil I fixed the table in the middle of the kitchen. Seáinín told me to get a blue candle, to light it and place it on the table. While I had it lighting I laid the table with delf for the tea. Then Nell got up, and bringing with her three kinds of bread, she sliced it on the bread board. There was plenty jam and butter on the table too and when the lights were lighting and the kitchen was decorated I thought I was in the Kingdom of Heaven because I had never seen such a lovely sight. Nell poured out the tea and everyone sat down to the table; they were all pleasant and cheerful, especially Nell. Every single move her family made, filled her with joy.

I was watching them very closely as I drank my tea. Thoughts ran into my mind: I was thinking of my poor mother at that time. I knew the kind of night she had, a near-sighted, lonely, unfortunate woman without light or joy for I was the one comfort she had in this life. I was far away from her now and couldn't raise her spirits nor offer her a scrap of happiness.

'The way of the world is strange', I told myself. 'Look at Nell and the comfort she draws from her family and there are some poor mothers who never get the slightest scrap of satisfaction out of life.'

In spite of all the pleasure around me tears came to my eyes. Seáinín noticed me. 'Margaret is lonesome', he said.

He came over to me from the other side of the table and began to give me soft talk so as to take my mind off my loneliness.

'Seáinín', I told him, 'I'm not a bit lonely in the way you imagine, but I was thinking of my mother. Go back and drink your tea.' Then I began eating just like he was.

When we had supper eaten and all the things were set aside Séamas came in with a bottle of wine and a class in his hand. 'would ye like punch?' he asked us.

'We would, Daddy', the children said. 'This is Christmas Eve!'.

'I don't care for wine at all, Darlin',' Nan said, 'I prefer a little drop of whiskey.'

Back he went and returned with a jugful of whiskey.

'Here, take your pick of them', he said.

Nell made a small drop of wine-negus that was suitable for the family and she gave me a fine jorum of it too.

'Won't you have a drop yourself, Missus?' I asked her.

'I won't, child', she said, 'I never let a spoonful of the drink pass my lips nor would I give it to these children but for respect for the Night that's there.'

'Would you be afraid you'd get drunk?' I asked for curiosity was picking me.

'Not that, child, but it has always been said: 'Taste the food and you'll get fond of it.' I don't think there was every a person who was sipping and tipping at drink but got a mind for it in the latter end.'

Séamaisín and Eibhlín were over at the window-sill examining the small lovely pictures that Seáinín had placed here and there. Eibhlín took one of them in her hand and went over to where Nan was.

'Nan', she said, 'look at the nice little Lamb with his feet tied.'

'Aye', said Nan, 'that's the Blessed Infant whom we all adore tonight.'

'Why does He take the shape of a lamb?' the child wanted to know.

'Sit down there quietly,' Nan said, 'and I'll tell you.' They all sat down.

'At that time a king of high rank named Herod ruled the district where Mary and the Infant were living. He heard about the child Jesus and made up his mind to put to death every male child under the age of three months. He ordered his bodyguard and his soldiers to guard the great city of Bethlehem and not to allow anyone in or out without first finding out all about their business. Immediately the order was received, sentries and guards were posted at every street, at every street corner and on every road and highway. Mary had a close friend named Bríghde and when she heard the news she went to Mary who, when she saw her coming, gave her a warm welcome. 'Mary', Bríghde told her, 'this is no time for talking; it's time to do a good deed.' 'What's the news now, Bríghde?' Mary asked. 'You surely must have heard the dreadful command that Herod has issued? I've come to see if I can think of any plan that will help you to save little Jesus from the strait He's in.' 'God will help us, Bríghde.' Mary answered. 'Get ready so,' said Bríghde, 'and make no delay. Before daylight in the morning I will dress myself in *oin-seach's* rags and head for such and such a street. Maybe those on guard will follow me; if they do, face southward for the road that leads from the city and perhaps you'll succeed in crossing the bridge of the Great River before anyone challenges you. Goodbye now, I'll be off about my business.'

'When Joseph came in, Mary told him the whole story from start to finish. The following morning, as it was brightening for day a terrible uproar could be heard outside. A foolish woman was decked out in straw and around her waist was a belt studded with lights and on her head was a ring with twelve candles lighting upon it. She made her way to the point most convenient for Mary to escape. She had a kind of flute that made an odd sound: as she played the flute the guards were startled and when they raised their heads they saw the witless woman all lighted up. They went towards her, but she kept moving away before them like a gust of wind. As soon as Mary got the guards out of the way she set about making her way out of the city. Things went well until she came to the bridge across the Great River and there were two soldiers of the guard: they stood right before her on the crown of the road.

'Where are you off to so early, decent woman?' one of them asked.

'I've been a week in the city', Mary answered, 'and my home is a good distance away. That's why I'm on the road so early.'

'What's that load you have on your back?' a soldier asked again.

'A little lamb I got to rear as a pet.'

'Maybe this is an excuse,' said the other soldier seizing her and dragging the mantle off her. All he saw was a lamb, its four legs tied with a light cord.

'See now; she's right', said the other soldier. 'It's a great shame for us to delay her.'

'Mary was walking on and on until she was free from danger; she sat down in a little corner under a green clump of bushes and lifted Jesus off her back. When she was rested she replaced Him on her back and some time later reached her destination. She now had the Infant safe; a few days afterwards there was appalling desolation and terror because of the slaughter of the little children of the city. The only sound to be heard was the sorrowful crying of the mothers whose children were being put to death by Herod the destroyer. When the dreadful scourge was over Bríghde went out to where Mary was and the pair of woman were overjoyed at meeting each other again. They went on their knees and earnestly thanked God for having saved them. Mary could bestow no greater honour on Bríghde than to present her with a feastday. She did so in these words:

'Your day will come before my day, Bríghde, until the end of the world.'

'It has been thus ever since and Bríghde's Day comes before Mary's Day and, since there were candles in the plan that Bríghde thought of, candles are blessed in every church throughout the world; 'Candlemas Day' it's called.'

'How I love the tiny Lamb!' Eibhlín said.

That love remained in the girl's heart ever afterwards for she offered herself up to the Merciful Lamb and became a nun.

I myself told Nell that Séamaisín, Eibhlín and myself would go to the chapel to see the crib. 'Don't stay there long!' she said.

I caught the children by the hands and off we went. The night was dark but indeed you could pick out the tiniest object on the pavement by the light of all the candles in the windows. When we entered the chapel, praise be to God! It was a beautiful sight with lamps lighting and the altar decorated with a mass of candles all ablaze. The crib was at the side of the altar and if you were the dullest person who ever lived it would remind you of the Kingdom of Heaven. The nuns were playing sweet hymns and my heart was filled with joy and pleasure as I listened to music the likes of which I had never heard before.

I scrutinised everything around me so that I didn't find the time passing. I got a start when I heard the thump of Séamaisín's head hitting the altar rail; the poor little man was falling asleep.

'Let's go home, darling', I said, 'you're sleepy.'

It was ten o'clock when we arrived home.

'Sit down here now,' Nell said, 'I have boiled milk and sweet cake for ye.'

She didn't put me in a place where I'd feel humbled and I had my share as well as the rest. Before we were ready Seáinín and his father came in after having been out for a stroll.

'*Sha*, let's go down on our knees in the name of God and say the rosary', Nan said.

When we finished: 'Off to sleep with ye now, my little clan', Séamas said.

There was no need for him to say it a second time. They went upstairs to bed. I remained on with Nell and Séamas in the kitchen until twelve o'clock and we had a great deal of chat and pleasant company. I recited 'The Welcome of the Child Jesus', for them. This is how I began it:

> Seventeen hundred thousand welcomes, nine and twenty times and more
> To the Son of the God of Glory, whom the Virgin Mary bore
> Who to her glorious womb descended, in His essence, God and man
> For upon the Eve of Christmas, the King of Kings his reign began
>
> And on the eighth day thereafter, Circumcision Feast its name
> In the Temple of the Triune, His precious blood when shed became
> Clearest portent for the faithful that for Him the future chill
> Held a bitter grievous passion, and a cross on Calvary's Hill
>
> Hail to Thee, Most Glorious Virgin, Queen of Heaven without a taint
> Who, entering life as white as angel was baptised as pure as saint
> Never, never sin committed, neither knew its track nor trace
> From whose womb emerged in triumph, Christ who saved the human race
>
> Hail, once more the glorious Virgin, maiden powerful, mild and good
> Beating her two palms together as her tears were turned to blood
> As the heavens darkened o'er her, and the sun refused to shine
> God's Son on the cross spread-eagled who had ne'er committed crime
>
> The Son of God the Glory is my treasure beyond all
> And my heart and restless spirit make no marvel at His call
> For 'twas he in crucifixion on the rood his blood had shed-
> The poisoned lance it pierced His heartstrings and the Crown of Thorns His Head
>
> Then the rabble black as midnight bore Christ to His burial place
> Not a board to clothe His body nor cloak of silk to shield His face
> And the smooth flesh of the Saviour was laid low in yellow clay
> And the mighty stone upended to await the Judgement Day
>
> He shall hold the same appearance till the heavens are rent in twain
> Till the sepulchres are opened and the dead shall rise again

Till the trumpet-blast is sounded at the dawnlight's primal ray-
From the Hill the King will listen on that awful Judgement Day

Christians of this troubled world make your peace with God above
Cry your sins in full contrition, beat your breasts in sorrowed love.
Scorn to sell your bright Redeemer for the gleaming gold or
      wealth that dies
For this life is but a plaything when compared with Paradise.

When the poem was ended Séamas put his hand into his pocket and
handed me a half-crown.

'Here!' he said, 'a little Christmas box for you.'

I took it; needless to say I was pleased.

'You'll have to teach me that hymn, Margaret', he said.

'I will and welcome, Master', I told him and I meant what I said.

'Bedtime now in God's name!' Nell said. 'We'll be getting up early in
the morning for Mass.'

Then we went to bed.

Storytelling, as demonstrated by Peig Sayers, was a part of life among the Irish until the
advent of radio and television usurped visits to a neighbour's house to partake of music,
dancing, stories and song as an evening's entertainment. These stories, passed down from
generation to generation at the fireside, covered a variety of genres, some were from the
ancient heroic sagas of Ireland, others were biblical stories, and others were folk tales
common throughout Europe but given an Irish flavour.

In 1967 Kevin Danaher, observing that the tradition of storytelling was dying out,
decided to record the stories he had heard in his childhood and published them in a book
entitled *Folk Tales of the Irish Countryside*.[8] When he was growing up in the parish of
Athea, Co. Limerick, Kevin Danaher's neighbour, Mrs Kate Ahern, was never short of a
story. Mrs Ahern was renowned for her piety and charity and her stories often reflected
her values. Her story *The Light of Heaven* is a parable which plays on the long held Irish
belief that one should be charitable to the poor no matter what. Who is to know that it
is not an incarnation of God or a saint sent to test us?

For extra emphasis, the story is set on Christmas eve to highlight its association with
Mary and Joseph searching for shelter in Bethlehem.

'THE LIGHT OF HEAVEN'
Kate Ahern

There was a poor woman going the road one time, and she had two children along with her and no sign of a husband. And the only way of living
she had was the charity of the people. And, faith and sure, it was very

seldom that the poor would be refused a bite or a sup or a place to sleep at any farmer's door, or at the labourer's cottage, either. When a poor person asked for alms in the name of God, I tell you it would be hard-hearted person that would refuse it.

But there was a certain parish priest and he was a very strict and hard man. And he thought that this woman was leading a bad life, and he spoke against her, telling his parishioners not to have anything to do with her. And the curate of the parish tried to put in a good word for the poor woman, but the old man wouldn't listen to him. And it came about that the poor woman and her children were passing through that parish on Christmas Eve, and the weather was perishing cold and showers of snow flying in the wind. And she couldn't put up with it, and she knocked at a farmer's door. And the woman of the house began to cry; she had pity for the woman, but what about the parish priest – hadn't he put a ban on her? But her husband, a big rough kind of a man, stood up and let a swear out of him. 'By this and by that,' says he, 'parish priest or no parish priest, it will never be said that a poor woman and her children were turned from my door on the very night that that other poor Woman was refused lodging in Bethlehem. Let you come in, poor woman', says he, 'and sit to the fire and eat a bite, yourself and them creatures, and I'll go and shake a bed down for you in the loft of the stable where you'll have plenty hay to keep you warm.'

They all went to sleep and out in the night the woman of the house called her husband. 'Get up quick', says she, 'for the stable is on fire. And I don't know if it was the right thing we did to let her in at all.' Out he ran, and the stable was one blaze of light. And he ran into it to save the horse, but there was no fire, only the poor woman and the two children lying dead on the hay, and a great light shining out of them. Off with the farmer to the priest's house and brought the parish priest and the curate back with him to see the wonder. And they all went into the stable, the farmer and his wife, the servant boy and the servant girl and the two priests. And faith if they did, the minute they were inside the door the great light quenched and the place was pitch dark. They felt their way out into the yard, and the minute they were outside the light came on again.

'It must be one of us', says the curate, 'that is making the light quench, for it is a heavenly light, and one of us must be a sinner.' And he sent them in one by one, the farmer and his wife and the two servants, and they all knelt down and said a prayer for the dead, and the light stayed shining. And the curate went in, and the light stayed shining. But the minute the old priest put his leg over the threshold the light quenched.

'It is I am the sinner', says he, 'and my sin was that I was too hard on this poor woman.' And the very next Sunday he preached a sermon and told the congregation that he was at fault, and that no matter how bad appearances were that they should always be charitable to the poor, and let God make the judgement.

The tradition preserved by storytellers such as Peig Sayers and Kate Ahern was not the Irish literary tradition that the Dublin literary revivalist class of the early nineteen hundreds wanted to associate themselves with. 'That generation was painfully aware that, for more than two centuries, the Irish language had been, with few exceptions, bereft of serious intellectual content; and its members were impatient with men who believed that *caint na ndaoine*, the daily speech of the small farmers and fishermen on western seaboards, was sufficient for a literary language ...'[9] Their solution was to retrace the link to the heroic sagas of ancient Ireland.

James Joyce observed these revivalist movements, and even attended Irish language classes given by Patrick Pearse, one of the leaders of the Easter Rising in 1916, but ultimately he found himself unable to exist in Dublin and exiled himself to Europe where he wrote about the city he had abandoned. James Joyce described a Christmas celebration in his short story *The Dead* which is the final story in his book of short stories *Dubliners*. The Christmas celebration described by Joyce and enjoyed by the Dublin middle class was a world away from Christmas experienced by the poorer people who often didn't have enough money to make ends meet. Nevertheless, there were many ingenious ways of making the best of one's lot and nowhere is this more evident than in the description of Christmas in the homes of the lanes of Cork city in the 1930s, provided by Eibhlís de Barra in her book *Bless 'em All*.[10]

In spite of the poverty and in many cases unemployment people made a special effort for Christmas. Eibhlís de Barra describes the various methods by which money was saved leading up to Christmas in order that luxuries like meat, lemonade and even records for the gramophone could be bought. It was also traditional for shopkeepers to reward loyal custom with a gift of a fruit cake and candle at Christmastime. The Christmas candle was lit on Christmas eve in the window of every Irish home in order to guide the Holy family on their journey. The Christmas meal in Cork city was more likely bacon or pork than turkey, as fowl was never popular in the city. Christmas day was a family day when the extended family would gather and tell stories or listen to the gramophone.

St Stephen's day, December 26, is celebrated in Ireland as a day of sports, especially hunting and shooting. Also the tradition of 'hunting the wren' continues today. Groups of costumed youths go from house to house singing in return for food, drink or money. Although the exact origins of the wren-boys is in debate, the scene described by Eibhlís de Barra does bear some resemblance to a Swedish tradition: 'an early morning jaunt of the so-called 'Stephen's men', companies of peasant youths, who long before daybreak ride in a kind of race from village to village and awaken the inhabitants with a folk-song called *Staffansvisa*, expecting to be treated to ale or spirits in return'.[11]

The Christmas season comes to a close on the Epiphany, which in Ireland is known as Nollaig na mBan or Women's Christmas. Woman celebrated the day with a lighter meal than on Christmas day and by cleaning the house of the holiday decorations. The season was over; it was time to begin saving for next year.

'BLESS 'EM ALL'
Eibhlís de Barra

Christmas was undoubtedly the highlight of the year for both young and old, even though it was an expensive time for already hard-pressed parents. However they never complained of bad times or scarcity of work as long as they had Christmas to look forward to. They were quite prepared to skimp and scrape so as to have a few pounds to spend for the festive season. Those at work would join a diddle-um at their place of employment. The diddle-um commenced at the beginning of January and one of the workers was selected to take over the running of it. Members would hand over one penny each to that person on the first payday of January. The next payday subscription would be two pence, and each week it increased by a penny until the final subscription of four shillings and four pence. The total subscribed over the year amounted to nearly six pounds, a considerable sum. Workers often found it hard to pay as the payments rose, yet they almost invariably persevered until the end. They drew their diddle-ums the week before Christmas and brought the money home, and that money made it possible for the mother to buy ham, roast pork, and all the other things that went with Christmas. It would also enable her to buy tarpaulin for the kitchen and about six rolls of wallpaper to decorate the house. The tarpaulin being of the cheapest kind cost only about thirty shillings and within eight to ten weeks the design would have worn off it. The wallpaper was always bought at Stevie O'Mahony's in Barrack Street.

Another method employed by workers to ensure that they had money for Christmas or indeed for any other occasion was known as the 'manage'. It differed from the diddle-um in that a set amount of money was paid in each week, two shillings or five shillings depending on one's pay. It was different also in that it usually ran over a shorter period. Ten people might agree to subscribe ten shillings a week for ten weeks, a total of five pounds weekly from the first week. Each subscriber was allotted a number between one and ten. The person who collected the money and took care of it was given the privilege of being Number One, and the remaining nine drew from two to ten out of a hat. Number One received five pounds at the end of the first week, Number Two received the same amount at the end of the second week and so it went on until Number Ten received his or her five pounds at the end of the tenth week. It was an ingenious way of providing financial assistance when most needed, because a person who might urgently need such assistance could offer to become collector and therefore be Number One. There was seldom if ever a defaulter while no collector was ever known to defraud.

In addition to the fare bought with the aid of the diddle-um or the manage, families could also look forward to a Christmas present from the local shopkeeper in appreciation of their custom. A good customer usually received a large square Killarney fruitcake wrapped in silver paper with a red band around. That was accompanied by a pound Christmas candle which was known to all as a 'pounder'. A less valued customer received a smaller Killarney cake and a candle, but the person who only called sporadically was given just a smaller cake. The difference between the presents always posed a headache for the shopkeeper who understandably did not wish to hurt the feelings of any customer. If there was a few people in the shop at any given time – and those shops were quite small –it was no easy matter for the shopkeeper to slip the larger cake and candle undetected to one customer in the presence of another not so highly esteemed, and despite the best ruses he was not always successful in avoiding disaffection and indeed the loss of some customers. Luckily for us my mother always qualified for the large cake and candle and knowing how we loved any sort of cake she would also buy a seed cake to tide us over the holidays.

As Christmas approached the children would go around the streets chanting outside the door of each house:

> Christmas is coming, the goose is getting fat
> Please put a penny in the old man's hat
> If you haven't got a penny, a ha'penny will do
> If you haven't got a ha'penny, a piece of bread will do
> If you haven't got a piece of bread may God bless you

Every night for some time before Christmas the Salvation Army Band would visit streets and entertain the people with Christmas carol music. The Salvation Army in those years had a refuge on Pope's Quay where homeless men could seek shelter for the night for just a few pence.

On Christmas Eve Mam would gather all us children and complete with pram we would set off for town. Our first stop was the Coal Quay where she bought the red-berried holly and some ivy. These were considered to bring luck and so no house wished to be without them. Then she would go into the second-hand record shop nearby to purchase some records to play on Christmas Day. Impatiently we would stand by the pram outside while she rummaged through stacks of records in search of some of her favourites. Her next stop was Paul Street where she would order me to go into Kiloh's mineral waters shop for raspberry cordial, more familiarly known as razza.

'Here's a half-crown to give the man and tell him we have a shop.' I would go in as I was told and go over to the counter and place the half-crown on it.

'A quart bottle of razza, please sir, and we have a shop.'

The man would hand me a square quart bottle at the wholesale price and for that half-crown our drinking needs for the Christmas season were secured. Mam never allowed intoxicating drink into the house. Every household in the area had razza for Christmas and even to this very day I have maintained the custom myself. Having got the razza she would then buy a good-sized piece of pork from Mackey's in the North Main Street and some bacon from O'Callaghan's just across the street. Using a long pole with a crook on the end of it the assistant would lift the piece of bacon off a hook on the ceiling. She bought it only if it was Cork-cured because she considered the up-country bacon far too salty. The pram would be filling up by this time but we still had to call to Glass's shop in Patrick Street to buy oilcloth for the kitchen table. The pattern on the oilcloth was always the same, black grapes, green grapes, rosy red apples, green apples, golden oranges and clusters of yellow bananas.

...

For some unfortunate families the hustle and bustle of shopping on Christmas Eve wouldn't yet have begun. Many a mother would have to wait for her husband to come home with the wages, while some might have to search the pubs for the husbands and bring them home. Others still in very poor circumstances might have to borrow money. They would all have to do their shopping in nearby Barrack Street. That meant that the shops there were open until all hours.

Mam would have made the Christmas pudding a day or two before Christmas. There was never a bowl to make a pudding large enough to satisfy our appetites, so having mixed all the ingredients together she would shape it with her hands and flour the pillow-slip which was to act as a superbowl. This flouring left a fine skin on the outer side of the pudding when cooked, like a baby's bottom we always said. She would then put the pudding into the pillow-slip and tie the corners of the slip so that a bockety odd-shaped specimen would not result. She would then plunge the pillow-slip, cake and all into boiling water for a few hours and the resultant skin acted as a seal thus preventing any water from getting into the pudding. When it was cooked she took it up and hung it, still in the pillow-slip, from the ceiling. Very soon the skin would be quite hard and when Mam's back was turned the boys would start tapping it with a hurley or firing darts at it to test its resistance.

After nightfall on Christmas Eve we would light the pounder Christmas candle which might be either red or white. We preferred the red one as we felt it was more traditional but it had the disadvantage of being much more inclined to drip. We then put some tinsel around the candle which stood in a jam pot and stuck a sprig of holly with red berries into it near the base. That was a sight to delight even the most sophisticated. It was then time to sit down to tea. There was, however, no question of having meat with the tea because Christmas Eve was a day of fast and abstinence and nobody disobeyed the rule.

We could do without meat, however, but not without sultana cake. Christmas to us was sultana cake. We just gorged ourselves on it. We never had a home-made Christmas cake of our own because we had only the open fire for cooking and baking a cake was not possible.

...

We children were then ushered back upstairs to bed but of course we didn't forget to hang up our stockings on the fireplace. Next morning we were up at dawn. Our living-room had been transformed since the previous night, because while we slept Mam put red-berried holly and ivy behind all the pictures and gilded some of the picture-frames so that they glowed a golden colour. The strange but welcome smell of the new oil-cloth on the freshly scrubbed timber was the first thing to attract our attention. Then there was the beautiful little coloured cardboard crib. We never had a Christmas tree, however. The mantelpiece was covered with a red plush cloth to which woollen baubles had been attached and the fireplace limed while its surround was newly painted cherry-red. But we children had eyes only for our stockings on the fireplace and what they contained. Daddy Christmas never brought us much, a small toy perhaps, an orange, an apple, a few sweets, a small paper packet of sultanas if there were any left over after making the pudding. We might get a couple of pencils, a cheap colouring book or a game of ludo. In the toe of each stocking would be a brand new golden Irish penny with the hen and clutch of chickens on one side and the harp on the other. The presents amounted to very little but we never complained because those which the children around us got were very similar to ours. Our joy knew no bounds, and we wouldn't call the queen our aunt.

Later on in the morning we would go to Mass and Holy Communion in the Lough Chapel but it was always extremely hard to concentrate. For dinner we would have bacon and a bit of pork along with plenty of floury potatoes. If money was flush there might be a piece of silverside corned beef. Of course there was always the cabbage. No house would be without cabbage for dinner any Sunday or special feast-day such as Christmas Day. We all loved pork, particularly the cracknel which was biscuit-like pieces of fat fried crisp. We would eat a *taoscán* of pork about which the older people used to say 'Tis grand; 'tis like chicken', and you wouldn't mind but they wouldn't eat chicken if they got it for nothing! We delighted in potato stuffing but bread stuffing meant absolutely noth-ing to us. The meal was rounded off with a bowl of jelly.

We never had a turkey in those days, nor indeed did any of the neigh-bours, but when some of my brothers and sisters and myself went out to work perhaps we got notions because one year we gave Mam the money to buy a turkey for us. She cooked it, but all to no avail because we refused to eat it, particularly the black meat, and so it was given to the dogs who didn't seem to have any qualms about either the meat or its colour. As for the stuffing you put into a bird we wouldn't insult our palate with it.

A similar fate befell the goose my father won playing cards one Christmas in Miss O's pub. All shopkeepers and publicans were known to their customers as Mr O, Mrs O and Miss O depending on their mar-ital status. When Mam cooked the goose nobody would eat it so the dogs in the cowluck had the Christmas goose all for themselves. Fowl meat of any sort was an anathema to the old Corkonians and only in later years have some of them taken to eating it at all.

After dinner was a time for rest and relaxation. My father would stretch himself across the double bed in the room to read the *Cork Holly Bough*, a Christmas magazine produced by the *Cork Examiner*, and it was required reading in every home for the festive season. Mam would put on the gramophone. It was not unlike an attaché case. Having placed the box of silver needles beside it she would then take the records down from the top of the glass case. Some of them were in light brown paper covers while others were in heavy cardboard covers. The twelve-inch records were mostly from the operas and the eight-inch ones were of the popular singers of the day. Each time Mam placed a record on the turntable she would have to wind up the spring of the gramophone and change the needle. Failure to change the needle was regarded as a serious omission and rightly so, because it caused the record to be scratched permanently damaged. Sometimes in the middle of an aria on a twelve-inch the gramophone would slow down with a wah-wah-wah sound. That was the signal for Mam to rush to its aid and turn the handle again to increase the speed. If the gramophone was over-wound the spring would break, and there was nothing for it then but to put it into the baby's pram and bring it down to Bachelor's Quay, where a man had a room in his house set aside for repairing of gramophones and children's prams. For renewing a spring he charged one shilling, that's five pence in today's money.

...

On Christmas night we would join our grandparents and aunts and uncles around the fire. Gran would provide more food and insist on everyone having a piece of her loin of pork out of their hand. Then she would tell us of various events that she associated with previous Christmases.

...

Before going to bed the last thing to be done was to put a few pennies – coppers we usually called them – on the mantelpiece in readiness for the wren boys next morning, St Stephen's Day.

About six o'clock in the morning loud banging on the doors of the neighbourhood announced the arrival of the wren boys, young lads from about ten years of age and upwards, and their raucous rendering of 'The wren, the wren, the kings of all birds' would result in mothers leaping out of their beds, grabbing a penny from the mantelpiece and throwing it out the window to get rid of the wren boys before they awakened their husbands and children. They were anxious not to incur the displeasure of the wren boys by refusing them money because if they did they would then be subjected to a derogatory verse reserved for such an occasion:

> Mrs O' Sullivan is a holy woman who goes to Mass on Sunday
> She prays to God for half-a-crown when she visits the pawn on
> Monday

There was one cranky old man who lived on Friar's Walk and detested the wren boys. He always rose early on St Stephen's morning to heat some pennies on a shovel in the fire and then took a fiendish delight in throwing them out the window and watching the wren boys pick them up and get their fingers burnt. The wren boys generally ceased their caterwauling about ten o'clock and then it was to share between them the money which they had collected. This share-out provided them the wherewithal to get into the special matinees for children in the Palace and the Coliseum cinemas, and usually left them enough to give their sisters who would come scrounging the admission fee off them. On entering the cinemas each child received a small paperful of sweet mixtures and this little act of generosity ensured a full house.

...

On New Year's Eve the Christmas candle was lit and a long-standing custom observed. A minute after midnight all the doors in the area were opened. The housewives emerged from their homes with a loaf of bread in their hands and with this would beat on the doors calling out at the same time 'A Happy New Year'. This ritual was performed in the firm belief that it ensured their families would have sufficient food right through the coming year. Shandon's Bells would ring out over the city and the ships in the harbour added to the din by hooting their foghorns. People also believed that if a dark-haired man was the first to cross their threshold just after the birth of the New Year luck would follow him into the house and remain there for the year, so every household endeavoured to have such a man waiting outside ready for the moment when Shandon's Bells commenced their chimes.

The feast of the Epiphany was known in Cork, and indeed in many other places, as the Poor Women's Christmas. The Christmas candle was again lit on that night. There is an old saying in Irish '*Nollaig na bhfear Nollaig mhór mhaith agus Nollaig na mBan Nollaig gan mhaith*', which translated means 'The men's Christmas [December 25] is a fine big Christmas and the Women's Christmas is no good'. This was usually understood to mean that after all the money spent on luxuries for Christmas Day there was very little left to purchase anything for the Women's Christmas. It could also have arisen from the fact that dainties which women usually preferred, tea and cakes and such like, were cheaper and less appealing to men. The older women who were partial to a drop of drink went out to the pubs and gathered not in the main bar but in the snug which was a small section specially partitioned off for the privacy of women. A hatch in the partition enabled them to purchase their drink out of the sight of prying eyes. The men would often send them a 'whacker' or a half of a half-glass of brandy in through the hatch in honour of the occasion.

The women in our house honoured the Epiphany by cleaning and scrubbing the kitchen until it gleamed like a new pin. Then a glass of water was placed on the table in readiness for Our Lord who would visit the house during the night, in remembrance of His first miracle when He turned water into wine at the wedding feast of Cana. Everybody had to be in bed before midnight, and if any of displayed any reluctance to do so we were reminded of the story concerning the man who once boasted that he was staying up to see the Lord, and was found dead in his chair by the fire the following morning. He had died, we were told, at the moment of the miracle. We duly obliged and went to bed in good time. Next morning the glass was taken outside and emptied down the shore.

Emigration has been a part of life in Ireland since the eighteenth century. Initially those who emigrated, particularly to America or Australia, never expected to see their home-land again. The evening before an emigrant departed his home parish, an 'American' wake was held in honour of the person, as Peig Sayers explained: 'It's a sad occasion when a person leaves for America; it's like a death for only one out of a thousand ever again returns to Ireland.'[12]

In more recent times air travel and greater affluence among emigrants has allowed visits home. The most popular time to make a return is Christmas. Despite the shortness of the days, the Christmas season in Ireland has become a gathering time when returning emigrants not only spend time with family still living in Ireland but also with friends and family who have returned from the other three corners of the earth for the Christmas visit. In fact, it is reported that the population of Ireland increases by 20-30 per cent at Christ-mastime.

In his humorous essay, 'On Not Going Home for Christmas',[13] John D. Sheridan cap-tures the essence of the hustle and bustle which reigns in every Irish home on Christmas eve and the plight of those who never get a chance to 'come home for Christmas'.

'ON NOT GOING HOME FOR CHRISTMAS'
John D. Sheridan (1948)

During the first fortnight of December every newspaper carries a stock picture of sailors going ashore for their Christmas leave. It is a very sad picture. It always makes me cry. For the one big regret of my life is that I never had the privilege of going home for Christmas. I never *could* go home for Christmas: I was always there.

I was there, but nobody noticed me, and I got less and less notice as the days went by, so that by the time Christmas Eve came I might as well have been the Invisible Man.

Everyone else in the house was a member of the deputation of welcome, and every time a knock came to the door they dropped things – hammers, stitches, holly, decorations, brown paper parcels, or puddings – and rushed out into the hall. Sometimes it was only the boy with the potatoes, sometimes it was the man with the milk, and sometimes it was only me. There might be snow on my collar and a glow in my cheeks, but they never kissed me tremulously and told me that I was frozen. They told me that I ought to be ashamed of myself, that I should have used a latchkey or gone round the back.

I was only an inmate, part of the setting, one of the locals, and they made no fuss of me; they would as soon have made a fuss of the sideboard or the grandfather clock.

They weren't waiting for me – bless your heart, no. They had me all the time. They were waiting for the prodigals, for the members of the family who had achieved esteem and affection by going away, and glory by coming back again. No man is a prophet in his own house until he comes home for Christmas.

Later on in the night the sycophants began to grow anxious. They checked the clock against their watches and talked about train disasters. They rubbed the frost off the windows and looked out into the dark. They listened for taxis, and sighed resignedly after every car that went down the road without stopping. They rushed out excitedly to answer wrong knocks, and came back brokenly to wait for the right one.

And when the right knock came at last the real ceremony began. They stood back to view him from every angle. They turned him round and approved his every aspect. They embraced him with floury arms, knocked the snow off his hat, and wept on his collar. They fought for his smiles and passed wordless votes of thanks. He had honoured the home of his fathers by coming back to it, and his very presence was a guarantee of a happy Christmas.

My job was to take his coat, carry his bag upstairs, put a fresh hot-water bottle in his bed, warm my slippers for him, and thereafter efface myself as much as possible. And I had no difficulty in effacing myself, I could have worn a false beard without attracting any notice.

The conversation followed a beaten track and was geared to adulation. It wasn't easy getting away, I suppose? (Wild horses wouldn't have kept him away.) I think your getting stouter. (Had it been I they would have said 'fatter'.) You must be perished. (Does the snow no longer fall on both just and unjust?) Had you a tiresome journey? Christmas Eve is always a *dreadful* day for travelling. (It's a worse day for staying at home.) Maybe you'd like a glass of sherry? Or a little nip of whisky? Or maybe you'd rather wait until you get something to eat? (Why all the maybes? And why a 'little nip'? I get the little nips – when I get any at all, and by the look of things I'll get none to-night. I know my place, and I mustn't sit with my betters.)

Run out and put the kettle on. Get up and give your brother the chair. Move out from the fire and let him warm himself. Bring down his pyjamas and air them.

They sugared and milked his tea for him. They passed him salt and mustard. They debated whether he would rather have white bread or brown. They sat down to watch him eat, and every bite that went into his mouth was caressed by their admiring eyes. And when he was stuffed full they discovered that there was no jam on the table and beat their breasts in shame.

He would have got the purple garment had he needed it. But he didn't need it – he had it already. Prodigals who come home for Christmas are always insultingly well-dressed –this is just another slap to the lads of the village. When a prodigal is not well dressed he doesn't come home. He sends a telegram – *Unavoidably delayed at the last minute* – and sweats it out in the digs.

After his great meal the great man sat by the fire – by special invitation. They pulled the armchair round for him and put cushions at his back. They got me to take off his boots for him and put my own slippers on his great, expectant feet. Then they sat round and listened to his stories of the outside world. It was his big moment.

(They were very nice to me, too. They let me put coal on the fire.)

The deputation of welcome saw him to the couch, drew the curtains for him, patted the bed for him, lit the electric fire for him, and asked him if he had 'everything'. (He had everything but the silver, and he could have had that for the asking.)

Next morning everyone wished him 'A Happy Christmas' – everyone but myself. It wasn't that I had any grudge against him. It was simply that, had I spoken at all, I would have said 'A Happy Christmas, your Honour,' and I didn't feel equal to it.

By dinner-time he was still a very important person, and he got the first second-helping of stuffing, but he lost a little ground later in the night, and at supper-time he had to reach for the sugar. On St Stephen's Day the decline had definitely set in, and he was allowed to lace his own boots. The position deteriorated rapidly, and by nightfall he had been flatly contradicted twice and elbowed away from the fire once. We made him feel so much at home that he might never have left it.

Had I got a full week at him I might have made a new man of him, but I never got as long as that; for he always left us again before the turkey was picked clean, and in leaving he played his trump card and won the last round. The deputation packed his bag for him, fell on his neck, and cried him to the door.

There is something very pleasant about staying in one place all your life, but it has some disadvantages. It gives you mental barnacles, and it prevents those who are nearest and dearest to you from seeing you for the magnificent person you really are. And if I have sometimes felt like running away from home and joining the navy it was not because I wanted to leave home but because I wanted to come back to it again. I am too old now to sign on before the mast, and I shall never be photographed coming ashore for my Christmas leave with a turkey over my shoulder, but I should die happy if, for once, I owned the first plate to be passed along for a second helping of stuffing.

Children have been the main targets of the twentieth-century's commercialisation of Christmas. The images of Santa Claus and glitzy toys have obliterated the wonder which was associated with the visit to the crib on Christmas Eve. Yet, the Nativity is the biblical story which is most magical for children, they are all familiar with the excitement associated with the arrival of a new baby and so can relate to the birth of Jesus.

The children growing up in Dublin's Inner City in the 1950s needed as much excitement as they could get to transport them from the daily realities of life growing up among poverty and unemployment. Some lucky children got this sense of excitement from their teacher, Miss Margaret Cunningham. Miss Cunningham, who taught up to sixty children in one classroom at one time, found a unique way to keep their attention. She told the children bible stories and encouraged them to learn them and retell them so that they could be on the radio. The children vied with each other to give the best re-telling, their reward was to tell the story into a microphone of a cassette recorder. Although the children did not know it, these stories were never meant to be broadcast, the lure of the 'wireless' was simply a ploy to encourage concentration and quietness among the school children. Miss Cunningham saved these tapes and some thirty years later these stories were indeed broadcast 'on the wireless'. Father Brian D'Arcy, a familiar voice on Irish radio, recognised the powerful simplicity of these bible stories when he was introduced to the tapes. Fr D'Arcy broadcast the stories to the nation on his 'Reflection' segment on *The Ronan Collins Breakfast Show*. By popular demand, they have since been compiled on cassette.[14]

The following transcript contains the telling of the story of the birth of Jesus. It contains all the fundamental elements of the story; no room at the inn, the incarnation in a stable, the heralds of angels, the annunciation to the shepherds, and the new star shining overhead. The moral of the tale is also clear to the storyteller; not only should the children be charitable to those without shelter, but they should also welcome Christ through the sacraments on Christmas morning. Some words were unfamiliar to the children and they grapple with them, for example, the occupation of the shepherds needs explaining and the angel 'disappears' to the shepherds rather than appears.

'IT WAS A BEAUTIFUL STAR'
A Dublin Schoolchild, c.1950

Brian D'Arcy: ... the birth of Jesus is the one we all remember most vividly and was the one Miss Cunningham taught to the children most dramatically. It all began as Joseph and Mary started out on a journey ...

Child: This night Our Lady and St Joseph was going up to get registered and when they were walking down the road they were knocking at the doors – and – they said they had no room. And the good people, if they had known that it was Our Lady and St Joseph, they would have got up and let them in and the bad people looked out and said, 'Sah, they're only poor, they'd only pay a few coppers'.

And the mean kids that don't get holy communion or confession on

Christmas morning, they're just like the second fellahs, the bad fellahs that said to Our Lady 'we've no room for you'. And the mean kids what are too busy eating their sausage or playing with their toys or whatever they had for their breakfast.

They were going down the road and met this man and said, 'Have you got any room?' and he said, 'No, but there's an old stable over there that I own if youse want to go into it.' And they went over. And Our Lord came down from heaven at 12 o'clock and loads of beautiful angels. And Miss, there was these shepherds, and shepherds are fellahs that mind bulls and cows and sheeps and little lambs an' all, and they heard this beautiful music up in the sky and they were wondering what was up and an angel disappeared to them and he said 'Are youse wondering what's up?' and they said 'Yeh' and he said 'the Saviour is born and if youse want to go see him, follow that star up in the sky' and Miss, it was a beautiful star.

Notes

INTRODUCTION

1 Libanius, fourth century pagan philosopher describing the celebration of Kalends throughout the Roman Empire. Adapted from Clement Miles, *Christmas Customs and Traditions*, New York, 1976.

2 Stephen Nissenbaum, *The Battle for Christmas* (Alfred A. Knopf, N.Y., 1996)

3 Miller, Daniel, *Unwrapping Christmas*, Oxford University Press (New York, 1993).

CHAPTER I

1 *The Aprocryphal New Testament: A Collection of Apocryphal Christian literature in an English Translation*, ed., J.K. Elliott, Oxford University Press, 1993, pp. 63-64.

2 'The Epistle to Diognetus', *The Apostolic Fathers with an English Translation by Kirsopp Lake*, 2 vols, Harvard Univ. Press, 1959, II, 351, 365.

3 Origen, *Contra Celsus*, transl. with an introduction and notes by Henry Chadwick, Cambridge Univ. Press, 1953, pp. 27-29 (abridged). Celsus' *True Discourse*, although lost, is thought to have been one of the ablest attacks on Christianity. Origen wrote *Contra Celsus* between 246 ans 248 AD. Edgar J. Godspeed, *A History of Early Christian Literature*, revised and enlarged by Robert H. Grant, Univ. of Chicago Press, 1966, p. 139.

4 *The Aprocryphal New Testament*, ed. J.K. Elliott, p. 94.

5 Ibid., pp. 95-96.

6 Ibid., pp. 106-107. This selection is from the Infancy Gospel of St Thomas, not the earlier and better known Nag Hammach Gospel of Thomas.

7 Ibid., pp. 75-76.

8 Ibid., pp. 97-98.

9 *The Koran*, transl. George Sale, introd. by Robert D. Richardson Jr, Garland Publ., N.Y. and London, 1984 (facsimile made from copy in Harvard Library), pp. 38-39.

10 Ibid., pp. 249-51.

CHAPTER II

1 F. Homes Dudden, *The Life and Times of St Ambrose*, 2 vols, Clarendon Press, Oxford, 1935, I, 385-86, 388.

2 Ibid., I, 391.

3 Quoted by Kate Norgate, *Dictionary of National Biography*, 21 vols, Oxford Univ. Press, 1921-22, XIX, 650 (under Thomas à Becket). Used by permission of Oxford University Press.

4 *The Hymnal of the Protestant Episcopal Church in the United States*, 1940 ed., Church Pension Fund, N.Y., Hymns 20 and 48.

5 Ibid.

6 Clement A. Miles, *Christmas in Ritual and Tradition, Christian and Pagan*, T. Fisher Unwin, London, 1912, pp. 100-01.

7 *Episcopal Hymnal*, 1940 ed., hymn 18.

8 Quoted by Pierre de Labriolle, *History and Literature of Christianity from Tertullian to Boethius*, transl. from French by Herbert Wilson, Barnes and Noble, N.Y., 1968, p. 498.

9 Francis Weiser, *Handbook of Christian Feasts and Customs*, Harcout Brace and World, N.Y., 1958, pp. 49-50.

10 *Saint Caesarius of Arles, Sermons*, transl. by Sister Mary Magdeleine Mueller OSF, Catholic Univ. Press, Washington, pp. 7-9 (vol. III, *Fathers of the Church, a New Translation*, eds Bernard M. Peebles et al.).

11 *Scriptores Latini Hiberniae: Adaman's De Locis Sanctis*, ed. Denis Meehan, Dublin Institute for Advanced Studies, Dublin, 1958, pp. 7-10, 75-77, 79, 95, 97.

12 Clement A. Miles, *Christian Customs and Traditions*, pp. 123-25; E.K. Chambers, *The Medieval Stage*, 2 vols, Clarendon Press, Oxford, 1903, II, 11.

13 *Early English Poetry*, translated into verse by Charles W. Kennedy, Hollis and Carter, London, 1952, p. 143

14 *The Monastic Agreement of the Monks and Nuns of the English Nation*, transl. from the Latin with Introduction and Notes by Dom Thomas Symons, Oxford Univ. Press, N.Y., 1953, pp. 28-31 (abridged).

15 Gale R. Owen, *Rites and Religion of the Anglo-Saxons*, David and Charles, London, Barnes and Noble N.Y., 1981, p. 34

16 *William of Malmesbury's Chronicle of England from the earliest period to the reign of King Stephen*, ed., J.A. Giles, George Bell & Son, London, 1895, p. 183.

17 Sister Mary Vincentine Gripkey AM, *The Blessed Virgin Mary as Mediatrix in the Latin and French Legend prior to the Fourteenth Century*, Catholic Univ. Press, Washington, 1938, pp. 51-52.

18 *The Steps of Humility by Bernard, Abbot of Clairvaux*, transl. with an introd. and notes by George Bosworth Burch, Univ. of Notre Dame Press, 1963, pp. 133-39 (abridged).

19 *Saint Francis of Assisi, First and Second Life of St Francis with Selections from the Treatise on the Miracles of the Blessed Friar by Thomas of Celano*, transl. from the Latin with introduction and footnotes by Placid Hermann OFM, Franciscan Herald Press, Chicago, 1963, pp. 75-78 (abridged).

20 For a coloured photo of a painting of Francis's nativity in a stable see *Saint Francis of Assisi*, photographs by Dennis Stock, text by Lawrence Cuningham, Harper Row, San Francisco, 1981, p. 41.

CHAPTER III

1 Father Pascal Robinson, *Writings of St Francis*, London, p. 175, quoted by C.A. Miles, *Christian Customs and Traditions*, p. 39

2 *Aucassin and Nicolette and other Medieval Romances and Legends*, transl. from French by Eugene Mason, E.P. Dutton and Co., N.Y., 1910, pp. 55-62.

3 Peter Whiteford, *The Miracles of Our Lady from Wynken de Worde's edition*, Middle English Texts, Carl Winter-Universitats Verlag, Heidelberg, 1990, p. 12

4 Charles W. Jones, *The Saint Nicholas Liturgy and its Literary Relationships (Ninth to twelfth centuries)*, Univ. of California Press, Berkeley and Los Angeles, 1963, pp. 3-8.

5 Jacobus de Voragine, *The Golden Legend or Lives of the Saints as englished by William Caxton*, J.M. Dent and Sons, London and N.Y., 1900, pp. 110-13, 117-18.

6 Quoted by John Brand, *Observations on the Popular Antiquities of Great Britain*, revised by Sir Henry Ellis, new ed., 3 vols, Henry H. Bohn, 1848, I, 425. For a recent comment on boy bishops see Nicholas Orme, 'Children and the Church in Medieval England,' *Journal of Ecclesiastical History*, XLV (1994), 581-82.

7 John Brand, *Observations on the Popular Antiquities of Great Britain* (1848 ed.), I, 419.

8 Ibid., I, 420; John Brady, *Clavis Calendria, or a compendious analysis of the Calendar, with ecclesiastical and classical antecedents*, 2 vols, London, 1812, II, 297.

9 E.K. Chambers, *The Medieval Stage*, 2 vols, Clarendon Press, Oxford, 1903, II, pp. 41 ff. One explanation for the origin of the modern Christmas tree is that it comes from the custom of setting up a tree of paradise (decorated with apples and communion wafers) in the dramatic productions of Adam and Eve, celebrated on December 24. Roger E. Reynolds' article on Christmas in *Dictionary of the Middle Ages*, ed. Jospeh R. Stayer, 13 vols, Charles Scribner Sons, N.Y., 1982-89, III, 319.

10 Henry W. Wells, Roger S. Loomis, eds., *Representative Medieval and Tudor Plays*, Sheed and Ward, New York, 1942, pp. 120-30.

11 *The Hymnal 1940 Companion* (3rd rev. ed.) prepared by the Joint Committee on the Revision of the Hymnal of the Protestant Episcopal Church of the USA, Church Pension Fund, N.Y., 1951, p. 210.

12 *The Oxford Book of Carols*, ed. Percy Dearmer, Oxford Univ. Press, London, 1964, carols 3, 56, 81, 88, 90 & 114.

13 William O. Wehrle, *The Macaronic Hymn Tradition in Medieval English tradition*, Catholic Univ. Press, Washington, 1933, p. 68.

14 *Hymns to the Virgin and Christ, the Parliament of Devils and Other Religious Poems*, ed. Frederick J. Furnival, publ. for the Early English Text Society by Kegan, Paul, Trench, Trubner and Co., London, 1867, pp. 4-5.

15 Wehrle, *Macaronic Hymn Tradition*, p. 85. Despite its pagan origins, clerics as well as laymen recognized the boar's head as a yule-time dish. The bishop of Hereford served one in 1289. Ronald Hutton, *The Rise and the Fall of Merry England: the Ritual Year 1400-1700*, Oxford Univ. Press, Oxford and N.Y., 1994, p. 55. The English translation of the Latin in these macaronic selections is by Prof. R.M. Frazer of Tulane University.

CHAPTER IV

1 George Caspar Homans, *English Villagers of the Thirteenth Century*, Russell and Russell, N.Y., 1960, p. 358.

2 Thomas Tusser, *A Hundred Good Points of Husbandry*, with an introduction by Sir Walter Scott, James Tregaskis & Son, 66 Great Russell St, London, 1931, p. 67.

3 John Stow, *Description of London written in the Year 1598 by John Stow*, ed. William J. Thoms, Whittacker & Co. London, 1842, p. 37.

4 Joseph Strutt, *The Sports and Pastimes of the People of England*, London, 1801, pp. 159-61, 339-48.

5 *The Progresses and Public Processions of Queen Elizabeth*, ed. John Nichols, 3 vols, London 1822, I, 131-41 (abridged).

6 *The Christian Prince*, The Malone Society Reprints, 1922, Printed for the Malone Society by Frederick Hall M.A. at the Oxford Univ. Press, July 1923, pp. 106-8, 124-9.

7 *The Progresses, Processions and Magnificent Festivities of King James the First*, ed. John Nichols, 4 vols, London, 1828, I, pp. 480-4 (abridged).

8 *The Works of Ben Jonson, with a Memoir of His Life and Writings*, by Barry Cornwall, Edward Moxon, London, 1838, p. 600.

9 *Poems of George Wither* (Newnes Pocket Classics) George Newnes, Strand, London, Charles Scribners, N.Y., n.d., pp. 217-18.

10 *The Complete Poems of Robert Herrick 1591-1674*, ed. J. Max Patrick, New York Univ. Press, 1963, p. 347.

11 *A Mad World My Masters and other Prose Works by Nicholas Breton*, ed. Ursula Kentish-Wright, 2 vols, Cresset Press, London, 1928, I, 29-31.

12 *The Complete Poems of Robert Herrick 1591-1674*, ed. J. Max Patrick, New York Univ. Press, 1963 p. 482.

13 Hezekiah Woodward, *Christmas Day, The Old Heathens Feasting Day*, London, 1656, preface. The Puritan efforts to suppress Christmas (1643-59) met with varying degrees of resistance: David Cressy, *Bonfires and Bells, National Memory and the Protestant Calendar in Elizabethan and Stuart England*, Univ. of California Press, Berkeley and Los Angeles, 1989, pp. 44-49 and Ronald Hutton, *The Rise and Fall of Merry England: The Ritual Year 1400-1700*, Oxford Univ. Press, Oxford and N.Y., 1994, pp. 206-19.

14 *Diary of Thomas Burton, Member in the Parliaments of Oliver and Richard Cromwell*, ed. John Towhill Rutt, 4 vols, Johnson Reprint Corp., N.Y., London, 1974, I. 229-30

15 John Brand, *Observations on the Popular Antiquities of Great Britain*, revised by Sir Henry Ellis, 3 vols, Henry H. Bohn, London, 1848, I, p. 490

16 Francis M. Misson, *Memoirs et observations faites par un voyageur en Angleterre*, The Hague 1698. Translated into English by J. Ozell, London, 1719, p. 34.

17 'The Diary of Rev. John Thomlinson', *Six North Country Diaries*, Surtees Society, vol. CXVIII (1910), p. 98.

18 *The Yale Edition of Horace Walpole's Correspondence*, 48 vols, Yale University Press, New Haven, 1937-1983, vol. 32, p. 177

19 A.E. Wilson, *King Panto, the Story of Pantomime*, E.P. Dutton, New York, 1935, p. 22

20 Ibid., p. 23

21 Antoinette Taylor, 'An English Christmas Play', *Journal of American Folklore*, vol. 22, no. 86 (Oct., 1909), 389-93.

22 Walter Rose, *Good Neighbours*, Cambridge Univ. Press, 1942, pp. 132-33.

CHAPTER V

1 *English Wycliffite Sermons*, ed. Pamela Gradin, 3 vols, Clarendon Press, Oxford, 1963, 1988, 1990, II, 206-10 (some abridgment, spelling modernized).

2 *The Sermons of John Donne*, ed. with intro. and critical apparatus by Evelyn Simson and George Potter, 10 vols, Univ. of California Press, Berkeley and Los Angeles, 1953, VI, 168-72.

3 *The Poems of John Donne*, ed. Sir H.J.C. Grierson, Oxford Univ. Press, London, 1933, p. xxviii.

4 *The Works of John Taylor, the Water Poet not included in the Folio Volume of 1630*, Burt Franklin, N.Y., 1967, Research of Source Work series 150, Spencer Soc., no. 7, pp. 1-4.

5 Ibid., no. 2, pp. 19-20.

6 *The Hymnal of the Protestant Episcopal Church*, 1940 ed. Church Pension Fund, N.Y., 1940, Hymns nos. 22 and 23.

7 Quoted in John Milton, *Odes, Pastorals, Masques* , eds David Aers, Winifred Maynard, Lorna Sage, John Broadbent, Cambridge Univ. Press, 1975, pp. 33-34

8 Ben Jonson, *Poems*, ed. by Ian Donaldson, Oxford Univ. Press, London, 1975, 128.

9 Quoted in John Milton, *Odes, Pastoral, Masques*, p. 34

10 Ibid., pp. 15-27 (abridged)

11 *The Complete Poetry of Richard Crashaw*, ed. with an introduction and notes by George Walton Williams, Anchor Books, Doubleday & Co. Garden City, N.Y., 1970, pp. 79-81.

12 *The Deer's Cry: A Treasury of Irish Religious Verse*, edited by Patrick Murray, Four Courts Press, Dublin, 1986

13 Ibid.

14 Ibid.

15 *Christmas around the World*, World Books Company, Chicago, pp. 76-79.

16 *The Hymnal of the Protestant Episcopal Church*, 1940 ed., Church Pension Fund, New York, 1940, Hymn no. 317

17 *A Representative Verse of Charles Wesley, selected and edited by Frank Baker*, Epworth Press, London, 1962 pp. 12-13

18 *The Hymnal of the Protestant Episcopal Church*, 1940 ed., Hymn no. 1.

19 *The Hymnal 1940 Companion*, 3rd rev. ed., Church Pension Fund, N.Y., 1951, pp. 32-33.

20 Ibid., pp.31-32.

21 *The Works of George Berkeley D.D., formerly Bishop of Clogher*, ed. Alice Cambell Fraser, 4 vols, Oxford, 1871, IV, 526.

22 *The Works of Alfred Lord Tennyson*, Macmillan, London, 1899, p. 287

23 *The Collected Works of Daniel Gabriel Rosetti*, ed. William O. Rossetti, 2 vols, London, 1901, I, 229-32.

24 Marguerite Wilson, *New Voices: an Introduction to Contemporary Poetry*, The Macmillan Co. New York, 1923, p. 313.

CHAPTER VI

1 University of Georgia Press, Athens, Ga. 1986, p. 13

2 Penne L. Restad, *Christmas in America: A History*, Oxford University Press (New York, 1995) p. 105

3 *The Oxford English Dictionary*, 2nd ed., 20 vols, Oxford, 1989, IX, 795. Thomas Tusser, *Five Hundred Points of Good Husbandry*, J. Tregaskis & Son, London, 1931, p. 65.

4 *The Oxford English Dictionary*, 2nd. ed., IX, 640; *The Lisle Letters*, ed. Muriel St Clare Byrne, 6 vols, Univ. of Chicago Press, 1981, V, 734.

5 John Stow, *Survey of London written in the Year 1598*, ed. William J. Thoms, Whitaker and Co. London, 1842, p. 37.

6 *The Chronicle and Political Papers of King Edward VI*, ed. W.K. Jordan, Cornell Univ. Press, Ithaca, 1966, pp. 102-105.

7 *A Chronicle of England during the Reign of the Tudors from 1485 to 1559* by Charles Wriothesley, Windsor Herald, Royal Hist. Soc., Camden Series, new series, vol. XX (1877) 80. Christ's Hospital was one of the grammar schools founded during Edward VI's reign on former monastic property.

8 *Five Hundred Points of Good Husbandry*, with an introduction by Sir Walter Scott, James Tregaskis & Son, London, 1931, pp. 65, 67, 73

9 *The House and Farm Accounts of the Shuttleworths of Gawthorpe Hall, in the County of Lancashire ... from September 1582 to October 1621*, ed. John Harland, Chetham Society, Manchester, 1856, pp. 48-49, 63, 69, 104, 140, 170.

10 *The Complete Works of Captain John Smith*, Philip L. Barbour, 3 vols, Univ. of North

Carolina Press, Chapel Hill, 1986, I, 245

11 William Bradford, *History of the Plymouth Plantation 1620-1647*, 2 vols, Russell and Russell, New York, 1968, I, 244-46. (copyright Mass. Hist. Soc., 1912, 1960.

12 *Journal of William Shellink's Travels in England 1661-62*, translated from the Dutch by Maurice Exwood, H.L. Lehman, Royal Hist. Soc., Camden Series, 5th series, I, London, 1993, pp. 70-71, 175.

13 *The Diary of Samuel Pepys*, ed. H.B. Wheatley, 10 vols, G. Bell & Sons, London, 1900, VIII, 509-10.

14 Quoted by H.D. Traill *Social History. A Record of the Progress of a People*, 6 vols, Cassell & Co. London, 1895. IV, 523-24.

15 *Lettres de Madame de Sévigné de sa famille et de ses amis*, ed., M. Monmerque, Paris, Librairie de L.Hachette, 1862, IV, 295-300 (abridged).

16 *The Jesuit Relations and Allied Documents*, ed. R.G. Thwaites, 73 vols, Pageant Book Co., New York, 1959, XL, 113-19.

17 16. *Journal of a Voyage to New York* by Jasper Dawkins and Peter Sluyter, Brooklyn, 1867, facsimile, University Microfilms Inc., Ann Arbor, 1966, p. 256.

18 *Memoirs of Sir John Reresby*, ed. Andrew Browning, 2nd. eds Mary K. Geter and W.A. Speck, Royal Hist. Soc., London, 1991, pp. 285-86.

19 Joseph Addison, *The Spectator*, no. 269 (1711).

20 *The Letters of Lisette, Elizabeth Charlotte, Princess Palatine and Duchess of Orleans*, translated by Maria Kroll McCall Publishing Company, N.Y., 1971, p. 145.

21 'Jeux, Fetes, Spectacles' in *La Vie Populaire en France au Moyen Age à nos jours*, Geneva 1965, pp. II, 58-59

22 Johann Wolfgang von Goethe, *The Sorrows of Young Werther*, translated by Victor Lange and Julia Ryan Wellbury, Suhrkamp Publ., New York, 1988, pp. 71-72

23 Sir Walter Besant, *London in the Eighteenth Century*, A. and C. Black, London, 1925, p. 436.

24 *Another Secret Diary of William Byrd of Westover 1739-41*, ed. Maude Woodfin, Dietz Press, Richmond, 1942, pp. 23-24, 122-23.

25 *The Diary of Richard Kay, of Baddingstone near Bury, 1716-51*, Chetham Society, Manchester, 1968, pp. 40, 46, 57-58, 77.

26 *A History of Bethlehem, Pennsylvania 1741-1892*, by Joseph Mortimer Levering, Times Publ. Co., Bethlehem, Pa., 1903, pp. 77-78.

27 *The Autobiography and Correspondence of Mary Granville. Mrs Delany*, ed. Lady Llanover, 6 vols, Irish MSS. Commission, Dublin, 1861-62, II, 408, 629

28 *Peter Kalm's Travels in North America: The English Version of 1770, revised and edited by Adolph Benson*, 2 vols, Dover Publications, New York, 1987, pp. 675-76.

29 *Boswell's London Journal 1762-1763*, introduction and notes by Frederick A. Pottle, McGraw Hill Book Co., N.Y., 1950, pp. 104-07.

30 *The Diary and Autobiography of John Adams*, ed. L.H. Butterfield, 4 vols, Harvard Univ. Press, Cambridge, 1962, vol. I, pp. 273-75.

31 William S. Stryker, *The Battles of Trenton and Princeton*, Boston, 1848, quoted in *Rebels and Redcoats*, eds George F. Sheer and Hugh F. Rankin, Mentor Books, New York, 1959, pp. 240-43.

32 *Gentleman's Magazine* vol. 60 (1790) part 2, p. 1212

33 Clifford Morseley, *News from the English Countryside 1750-1850*, George G. Harrap & Co., London, 1979, p. 155.

34 *The Original Journals of the Lewis and Clark Expedition 1804-06*, ed. Rueben Gold Thwaites, 3 vols, Antiquarian Press Ltd., New York, 1959, III, 290-91

35 Washington Irving, *The Sketchbook of Geoffrey Crayon Gent.*, G.P. Putnam, N.Y., 1860.

36 The celebration of Christmas in English households has been customary since at least the seventeenth century. In 1645, in the *Complaint of Christmas*, John Taylor has Christmas remark, 'in all places I was joyfully received with mirth and merry cheere; ... and all sorts of people in every howse made me heartily welcome.' In twentieth century England Christmas is primarily a family affair. According to polls taken in England in 1969 and 1988, 80% to 90% of those asked expected to spend Christmas with their family, or close relatives. Adam Kuper 'The English Christmas and the Family: Time Out and Alternative Realitites' *Unwrapping Christmas*, p. 157.

37 *Felix Mendelsohn Letters*, ed. G. Selden Goth, Pantheon Books, N.Y., 1945, pp. 104-07.

38 *The Letters of Fanny Calderón de la Barca, with New Materials from the Author's Journals*, edited and annotated by Howard T. Fisher and Marion Hall Fisher, Doubleday, Garden City, N.Y., 1966, pp. 83-84, 90, 364-67.

39 Hamlin Garland, *My First Christmas Tree* first published in *The Ladies' Home Journal*, 1911; reprinted in Edward Wagenknecht ed., *The Fireside Book of Christmas Stories*, Bobbs-Merrill Co., Indianapolis and New York, 1945, pp. 539-43.

40 William Madsen, *Christo-Paganism: A Study of Mexican Religious Syncretism*, Middle American Research Institute, Tulane University, New Orleans, 1957, pp. 167-68.

CHAPTER VII

1 Miller, Daniel, *Unwrapping Christmas*, Oxford University Press (New York, 1993) p. 23

2 Both Ireland and the Southern United States have suffered invasion and defeat, both have experienced economic hardship and civil strife, and both have produced an impressive body of literature. A large selection of Southern literature about Christmas can be found in an anthology published in 1998 entitled *Southern Christmas, Literary Classics of the Holidays*, edited by Judy Long and Thomas Payton and published by Hill Street Press, Athens, Georgia.

3 McCormack, Mike; 'America's First Christmas Card', published on the Celtic Orthodox Christianity webpage. Also see Pyle, Robert L.; 'A Message from the Past', pg. 3; Gallagher, Ida Jane, ' Light Dawns on West Virginia History', p. 7. Fell, Barry; 'Christian Messages in Old Irish Script Deciphered from Rock Carvings in W. Va.', p. 12. *Wonderful West Virginia*, vol. 47, March 1983.

4 Kane, Harnett T., *The Southern Christmas Book, The full story from the earliest times to present*, David McKay Co. New York.

5 'Christmas celebrated in the Quarter since 1717', article by Edith Elliot Long, published in *Vieux Carré COURIER*, December 24, 1965

6 Stephens, William, *A Journal of the Proceedings in Georgia, vol. I*, Ann Arbor, University Microfilms, 1966, p. 363

7 *Twelve Years a Slave, Narrative of Solomon Northup, a Citizen of New York, Kidnapped in Washington City in 1841, and Rescued in 1853, from a cotton plantation near Red River in Louisiana*, Auburn: Derby and Miller; Buffalo: Derby, Orton and Mulligan; London: Sampson Low, Son & Co. (1853), pp. 213-16, 217-18.

8 Strother, David, 'A Winter in the South' published in *Harper's New Monthly Magazine*, no. XCIX, August, 1858, vol. XVII, pp. 293-95.

9 Letter published in the *Crescent Newspaper*, December 26, 1858, courtesy of the Louisiana State Museum, Historical Center.

10 Myers, Robert M. (ed.), *The Children of Pride, A True Story of Georgia and The Civil War*,

Yale University Press, 1972, pp. 825-27, pp. 1236-37. Reprinted with permission.

11 *Christmas in the Confederate White House*, extract from newspaper. Original newspaper clipping available at Jefferson Davis Papers at Rice University (Houston, TX).

12 Griffith, Lucille, Alabama, *A Documentary History to 1900*, 1st edition (1968), revised edition, 1972, pp. 530-31, University of Alabama Press. Reprinted with permission.

13 Published in the *Daily Picayune*, December 25, 1892, p. 21, courtesy of the Louisiana State Museum, Historical Center.

14 From the Collection of the Louisiana State Museum, Historical Center, RG# File 1, St Andrews.

15 Extract from article by Dominic P. Papatola, 'A 90s Nativity' published in *The Times Picayune*, December 24, 1997. Permission granted by The Times Picayune Publishing Corporation. All rights reserved. Reprinted with permission.

CHAPTER VIII

1 The great burial tomb at Newgrange, Co. Meath dates back to *c*.3000 BC. On a single day of the year, December 21st – the winter solstice, the rising sun's rays penetrate the inner most chamber flooding the darkness with a brilliant orange light. This phenomen was discovered by Professor Michael J. O'Kelly in 1969. See O'Kelly, Michael J., *Newgrange. Archaeology, Art and Legend*, Thames & Hudson (London, 1982).

2 Printed in *The Penguin Book of Irish Verse*, second edition, edited by Brendan Kennelly, Penguin Books (London, 1981).

3 Stokes, Whitley; editor and translator, *The Tripartite Life of Patrick with documents relating to that Saint*, Part II (London, 1887) pp. 530-41.

4 From *An Duanaire. An Irish Anthology: 1600-1900: Poems of the Dispossessed*, edited by Sean Ó Tuama, with translations into English verse by Thomas Kinsella (Dolmen Press, Mountrath, 1985).

5 Printed in *An Irish Childhood: An Anthology*, Jeffares, A. Norman and Kamm, Antony, William Collins Sons & Co (London, 1987).

6 'The Irish Way with Words' by David Norris, published in *Destination Ireland*, Insight Travel Library (APA Publications, 1989).

7 Sayers, Peig; *Peig, the Autobiography of Peig Sayers of the Great Blasket Island*, translated into English by Bryan MacMahon, Talbot Press (Dublin, 1974) pp. 73-83.

8 Danaher, Kevin, *Folktales of the Irish Countryside*, Mercier Press (Cork, 1967) 6th edition, 1988, pp. 39-41

9 Kiberd, Declan, 'Irish literature and Irish History' published in *The Oxford Illustrated History of Ireland*, edited by R.F. Foster (Oxford University Press, 1989), p. 294.

10 De Barra, Eibhlís, *Bless 'em All. The Lanes of Cork*, Mercier Press (Cork, 1997) pp. 24-36.

11 Miles, Clement A., *Christmas Customs and Traditions, Their History and Significance*, Dover Publications (New York, 1976).

12 Sayers, Peig, *Peig*, p. 129.

13 Sheridan, John D., *Half in Earnest*, Talbot Press (Dublin, 1948) pp. 39-48.

14 EMI Records, *Give Up Yer Aul' Sins*, Bible Stories from the Children of Dublin's Inner City, introduced by Father Brian D'Arcy CP.

Permissions

Index

Index entries in bold refer to the titles of extracts quoted in this book.